ABA FUNDA

Contract Drafting

POWERFUL PROSE IN TRANSACTIONAL PRACTICE

Lenné Eidson Espenschied

AMERICAN BAR ASSOCIATION
Defending Liberty
Pursuing Justice

Cover design by ABA Publishing.

Library of Congress Cataloging-in-Publication Data

Espenschied, Lenné Eidson.
    Contract drafting : powerful prose in transactional practice / Lenné Eidson Espenschied.
        p. cm.
    Includes bibliographical references and index.
    ISBN-13: 978-1-60442-795-0 (alk. paper)
    ISBN-10: 1-60442-795-7 (alk. paper)
    1. Contracts—United States—Language. 2. Legal composition. I. Title.
    KF807.E84 2010
    808'.06634—dc22

                                                          2010003298

To Erich and Leslie,

my finest compositions

and

To Dennis,

the wind beneath my wings

Table of Contents

Lesson 14: Edit or Review Effectively

Acknowledgements

Writing acknowledgements is a Palsgrafian task akin to applying the concept of proximate cause to determine responsibility under the facts and circumstances. Many people have contributed to my work on this project, and I'd like to thank some of them individually while acknowledging that I might never have finished without the support and encouragement of an entire village of friends and colleagues that would fill the pages of another book to mention by name.

First of all, I'd like to thank my parents for encouraging me to pursue a legal education, and for their constant support and enthusiasm throughout my career. I'd like to thank all the professors who taught me to think like a lawyer, especially Perry Sentell, who taught me what "critical thinking" means.

I'd like to thank Mark Kaufman, Don Kennicott, and Harry Morgan, who taught me most of what I know about practicing law. I'd also like to thank Judy Aust, Allen Buckley, Charles Lee, Judge Susan Kerr Lee, and Phillip Wilkins for encouraging me and supporting my genuine desire to "give back" by seeking to improve the quality of services rendered by my profession.

I'd like to thank the faculty and students at the University of Georgia School of Law who encouraged me with this project. Usha Rodrigues steered me away from the wrong direction, while Camille Watson was ever so generous with her time and advice steering me in the right direction. I'd like to thank my first class, including Dennis Boothe, Brian Christy, Harvey Daniels, III, Esther Hong, Behrouz Kianian, Jennifer Lee, Matthew Mauldin, Mike Melonakos, Brittany Summers, Laura Vest, Matt Weiss, Chris Yarbrough, Gerum Yilma, and especially Robert Swartwood, for encouraging me to write this book. I'd also like to thank my second class of fuzzy guinea pigs, including Candice Barrett, Judson Bryant, Joshua Findlay, Elizabeth Freeman, Sara Gheesling, Jason Howard, Kyllan Lowe, Trent Myers, Jennifer Sudduth, Matthew Woods, and especially Benjamin Caulton, William Lane, Sarah Morang, Christian Morrison, and Major Yevgeny Vindman, whose sharp eyes, edits, and suggestions on the first draft of this book were tremendously helpful in fine tuning this published version.

I'd like to thank the American Bar Association and especially my editor, Erin Nevius, whose experience and insights greatly improved the original manuscript. I'd also like to thank Professor Susan Chesler at Arizona State School of Law for taking the time to review the book and for her insightful comments and suggestions.

Although I'd love to take full credit for writing this book, it's abundantly clear to me that I was blessed with tremendous help from a higher source. Thanks be to God for knitting me together with the passion to write and teach and for inspiring me at times when it seemed the creative well was running dry. Many angels have prayed me through this process, especially Joy Neal and Elise Wilkes, and now it is my hope and prayer that all who read this book will be richly blessed.

Preface

Many great books have been written on the topic of legal drafting in recent years and the reader may wonder why I have chosen to write this one. I'd like to explain the specific objectives I've sought to accomplish in this book and how I believe this book is different.

1. Unity among Scholars. Most drafting books contain very few citations to case law and virtually no citations to the works of other drafting scholars. The lack of references to supporting authority means the recommendations of any author can be, and frequently are, dismissed by the bar as being merely that author's opinion. Consensus has been achieved on most of the techniques presented in this book among those of us who have studied drafting extensively. Because drafters rarely have time to consult multiple treatises to determine whether scholars agree, my first objective is to substantiate unity among drafting scholars with respect to the techniques recommended in this book by incorporating extensive references to the works of others. Another contention among practicing lawyers who continue to ignore recommended drafting practices is that "professors teach and lawyers do," yet this book joins the list of treatises written in the past five years by other authors who have extensive experience in transactional practice. My hope is that when the bar realizes the extent of scholarly authority supporting particular recommendations, it will make a more diligent effort to extinguish bad drafting habits.

2. Basic to Advanced. Several excellent drafting books published recently by other authors are intended to serve as reference materials on style for more experienced lawyers. This book is different because it is intended to serve as a "how to" guide for lawyers new to transactional practice. One broad objective of the book is to explain how the drafting process works: how transactional lawyers work from prior documents to produce effective and complete legal documents that protect the client's interests. The book also features advanced drafting techniques for avoiding ambiguity by making better word choices, drafting sentences well, and eliminating contextual ambiguity. After reading this book, a new drafter should be well equipped to create powerful prose in transactional practice.

3. Accurate Examples. Virtually all of the examples, case studies, and exercises included in this book are extracted from real documents used by national law firms and Fortune 500 companies, which helps to accomplish my objectives of familiarizing readers with the actual language of complex provisions they work with in transactional practice and showing readers how to think critically regarding the language they inherit.

4. Comprehensive Application. A few good drafting books approach the topics of how and why lawyers draft legal documents primarily from the perspective of structuring complicated corporate finance and merger transactions—however, in actual practice, drafting encompasses a much broader array of topics and projects. Since only a tiny fraction of all contracts actually relate to finance and merger transactions, the drafter's role as to "structuring the deal" is largely irrelevant in most drafting projects. The emphasis of this book is drafting *per se* rather than deal-making, and the techniques presented are applicable to all drafting projects whether in real estate; mergers and acquisitions; general corporate practice; business law; lending; corporate finance; or in litigation settlement agreements, waivers, and releases.

5. Practical Orientation. My objective in writing this book is to create a practical guide that is straightforward and straight to the point. While some books are organized around theoretical drafting concepts like "precision" and "concision," this book is organized to emphasize practical techniques: this is the process; do this with words; do this with sentences; do this with context; etc. I practiced transactional law for almost 25 years and based on my experience, this book contains the information new lawyers need to be successful in transactional practice.

6. Use as a Textbook. In writing this book I've come to understand there is a great divide in publishing between "trade books" and "textbooks." This is a trade book because it is designed for use by lawyers in practice. It seems to me, however, that when the objective is to teach transactional skills in a law school classroom, trade books and textbooks should be virtually identical. I have used this material with both audiences and the response has been consistently enthusiastic. An objective of mine in writing this book is to create a realistic resource that can be used to teach drafting skills to law students. Each of the 14 chapters contains about a week's worth of material, with allowances for classroom discussion of graded assignments and special research projects. I've used this book successfully in my advanced drafting course at UGA, and teaching aides for this book including teaching notes, sample documents, drafting assignments, and grading rubrics are available to law school faculty at www.draftingpowerfulprose. com.

Introduction to Legal Drafting

Objective of this Lesson: To introduce the topic of legal drafting and identify characteristics of excellent drafting.

Key Techniques:
- Understand key differences between legal drafting and legal writing.
- Define the characteristics of excellent legal drafting.

Introduction

Legal drafting is one of the most fundamental skills required of transactional lawyers, yet it is perhaps the skill for which lawyers historically have been least prepared. Although legal writing has traditionally been a required course at most law schools, legal drafting has not been widely offered until recently and is seldom required. Even today, legal drafting is taught in most law schools either as a brief segment integrated into a legal writing course or as a survey course where students tackle simple assignments involving drafting a contract, a will, and a statute. This book offers a new, more expansive approach to studying the transactional lawyer's responsibilities as document drafter.

Most practicing lawyers learned what they know about legal drafting from the lawyers who hired them out of law school. Their drafting styles evolved based on what they absorbed as a result of continual exposure to the good, bad, or indifferent works drafted by others. Until recently, few opportunities existed for formal instruction in legal drafting techniques, and practicing lawyers rarely have time to peruse hornbooks on drafting. The lack of formal training in legal drafting for past generations is still evident in the documents new transactional lawyers work with on a daily basis; in many cases, new lawyers simply adapt old documents to their specific needs, perpetuating poor drafting language. Case law and statutes rarely proclaim a "right way" of drafting, which leads many practicing lawyers to conclude, mistakenly, that there is no "wrong way" of doing things, either. The result is that many excellent practicing lawyers have very poor drafting skills, and the standard form documents passed down to new lawyers often need significant revision.

Image Repair

One way the legal profession has earned its unfortunate and largely undeserved bad public image is the pompous, atrocious prose it spouts profusely upon undeserving clients. Most legal documents are still drafted with convoluted sentence structures that clients are unable to decipher. Although lawyers in transactional practice often deal with complicated legal issues, more often than not, the difficulty in understanding legal documents arises from the vocabulary and syntax rather than the substance.[1] Language drafted to impress opposing counsel usually misses the target, because the best measure of a drafter's success *should* be the usefulness of the document to its audience.[2] Like other professions, we have our own jargon that we understand perfectly among ourselves. But because our clients need to understand the documents we draft—and for which we charge generously—we have a special obligation to communicate effectively and clearly beyond the boundaries of our profession.

What is Drafting?

"Drafting" refers to the specific category of legal writing used to create legislation, wills, documents, and agreements that seek to control future events.[3] Drafted documents are intended to set out precisely and unambiguously what a person or entity is expected or has agreed to do in the future. In this respect, drafting differs significantly from legal writing, where the goal is to be persuasive, as well as literary writing, where the goal is to entertain. Because the drafter's goal is to be indisputably clear regarding future events, logic dictates that the style of legal drafting should be significantly different from the style used in legal writing. A lawyer who has not studied legal drafting as a distinct legal skill is not fully prepared for the demands of transactional practice.

What Does a Transactional Lawyer Do?

A transactional lawyer helps clients conduct business. Transactional practice involves representing clients in a wide array of matters related to managing a business or exchanging assets, goods, services, or any kind of property. Transactional lawyers are sometimes called "deal lawyers." A transactional lawyer's duties include advising the client as to how a deal should be structured; identifying legal issues; negotiating legal and, sometimes, business terms; and drafting documents to memorialize the parties' respective rights and duties in the transaction. Transactional practice involves the entire life cycle of a business, from organization of the entity to its ultimate dissolution.

In transactional practice, "drafting" means the process of creating legal documents that implement the client's business deals and objectives.

Exercise:

Based upon the following facts, what types of forms and documents will your client need?

A couple of years ago, Richard and Bobby, two highly intelligent techno-geeks, left the company they had been working for and started their own business in Bobby's garage. They have been developing a new technology for harnessing the power of positive thinking using software imbedded in a micro-chip they call the "Lilypad." They've come into your office today because they are ready to begin marketing their product and have heard that there is a way to limit their personal liability by forming a partnership or some sort of corporate entity they want to call "Tadpole." They have arranged to have their product manufactured at a nearby plant.

The next year, Richard and Bobby realize that their backgrounds as techno-geeks provided them with little sales and marketing experience. They want to hire a sales manager but don't want that person to steal their technology. (In the next year or two, the pair will also realize that they need a CEO and a CFO).

A few years after hiring their sales manager, Tadpole has long outgrown Bobby's garage and Richard and Bobby call you to say they are looking for office/warehouse space. They also are talking with a bank about getting "real" financing. Soon, Tadpole needs outside help from consultants to tweak its technology and design its own plant for manufacturing Lilypads. Tadpole has begun purchasing silicon and other items necessary to manufacture the chips. Five years after initially meeting Richard and Bobby, regional sales are off the charts and Tadpole wants to hire subcontractors to install the Lilypads for customers. Tadpole also wants to figure out a way to sell its product nationally. One of Tadpole's biggest customers has asked for the right to use the underlying technology in another manner.

What types of forms and agreements do you think Tadpole will need?

Current Trends in Drafting

In 1978, President Jimmy Carter issued Executive Order 12044 requiring that a government regulation must be "written in Plain English and understandable to those who must comply with it."[4] In 1998, President Bill Clinton issued a memorandum to the heads of executive departments and agencies reinforcing the requirement for plain language in government writing.[5] Many state legislatures have also passed statutes requiring that consumer contracts be written in plain English.[6] The Securities and Exchange Commission requires that disclosure documents must be written in plain English. Virtually all of today's drafting scholars decree that, to the extent possible, legal documents should be phrased in common, everyday language.[7]

The call for simple language did not begin in modern times. The quest for plain English is actually quite ancient, dating back to the 14th century, when in 1360, the English Parliament enacted the Statute of Pleading, requiring that lawsuits be tried in English. Ironically, the

---

Statute of Pleading was itself written in French, which had been the custom of the gentry as well as the bench and bar since the Norman invasion in 1066. Despite the Statute of Pleading, it took Parliament nearly 400 years to rid itself of French legal customs and some traces still remain in common law today, in words like voir dire, demurrer, affidavit, desist, and residue. These words illustrate one characteristic of legalese: it is surprisingly impervious to change.

Many lawyers do not embrace the objective of drafting legal documents in plain English, as discussed in Lesson 7. The transition towards plain English drafting is sometimes called an "evolution" rather than a "revolution"—some people see it as an inevitable development in the accessibility and relevance of the law, while others see it as a new school of thought and a choice to be made by individual lawyers—but either way, the process seems to have begun to accelerate in recent years. Beware that drafting in plain English is not simple and requires great discipline! Drafting language that is clear, concise, and understandable to the document's audience is a much more difficult endeavor and therefore a higher accomplishment than adhering to the convoluted language which abounds in transactional practice today.

Focus of this Book

The drafting techniques presented in this book are not just about words and sentence structure, although language is key in excellent drafting. The purpose of this book is to equip lawyers new to transactional practice with the skills needed to start and finish drafting projects with excellence and confidence. Our focus is on *understanding* the responsibilities and objectives of drafters and on *implementing* techniques that will help achieve them. Excellent drafting involves:

- understanding of the legal framework of contract drafting;
- planning, designing, and organizing documents;
- choosing the best words to express the concepts addressed in the document;
- drafting precise, clear sentences; and
- understanding how to draft provisions properly to allocate risk among the parties to achieve the results the client intended.

Language is more than a tool for communicating; it is an essential component of the *process* of thinking. Concepts become clarified as we select appropriate language to express them.[8] Thus, where the language is clarified, the substance of a legal document is invariably improved as well.[9]

Ethical Issues in Legal Drafting

Many ethical issues arise for a transactional lawyer in the context of drafting legal documents. For example, how much is "enough" legal advice to a client regarding the risks undertaken in a particular transaction? Should the lawyer attempt to restructure the agreed upon business terms of a transaction if the lawyer believes the terms are disadvantageous to the client? If a lawyer observes that opposing counsel has not provided competent representation to a client with respect to a particular transaction, what is the lawyer's obligation under the Model Rules of Professional Conduct? How should the lawyer handle situations where the client's budget does not permit the scope of representation the lawyer deems necessary to provide the required degree of clarity within a document? Are a lawyer's ethical duties fulfilled if the client does not understand the key provisions of a legal document prepared or reviewed for the client by the lawyer? This text will address each of these ethical issues.

1.1 Understand the differences between legal drafting and legal writing.

Although the objectives of legal writing and legal drafting are completely different, the terms are often used interchangeably, even by text book and hornbook authors. This book distinguishes between "legal writing" and "legal drafting." "Legal drafting" (statutes, wills, and contracts) deals with future behavior, while "legal writing" (pleadings and briefs) typically focuses on historical events. Legal drafting may have a very long shelf life and must anticipate myriad circumstances that may arise as the future unfolds. Statutes may be in effect for hundreds of years, wills may control the transfer of wealth through generations, and contracts often govern relations between parties for decades. By contrast, legal writing is historical in the sense that briefs and pleadings typically describe a specific event that occurred and its known ramifications. The goal of legal writing is to persuade the court that your client's position is favorable, but the briefs and pleadings themselves are quickly forgotten. Briefs and pleadings typically cite, quote, and argue relevant statutes and case law. Contracts occasionally cite statutes but do not quote or argue them, and virtually never reference case law.

Mistakes in legal drafting can be crucial, and each word may have great significance (e.g., "One month" or "30 days?" "No later than" or "within?"). Case law abounds with million dollar matters decided on the basis of nothing more than the placement of a single comma![10] In pleadings, individual words are less important, and amendments can usually be filed to correct errors.

A notable difference between legal drafting and legal writing is that legal drafting may ultimately be subjected to an adversarial reading. Although opposing counsel may disagree with certain words that are used to characterize people or events, or with the arguments presented, opposing counsel is usually not obsessed with tearing apart the meaning of words in a brief or pleadings. In contract litigation, however, the intention of a zealous, highly-trained adversary may very well be to lacerate and dismantle the provisions in dispute. Under the canon of *contra proferentem*, courts construe ambiguities in legal drafting against the drafter who selected the language.[11] This canon provides motivation to ensure that the language in drafted documents is as clear and concise as possible.

The most significant difference between legal drafting and legal writing in a transactional setting may be the intended audience. Briefs and pleadings are generally intended to be read by judges and other lawyers from start to finish. The format of briefs and pleadings, including number of pages, type size, margins, size of paper, etc., is specified by court rules. Contracts are intended to be read and used by lay persons who consult specific provisions sporadically throughout the term of agreement when they need information. The format of most contracts is completely unregulated.

Another significant difference between legal drafting and legal writing is that legal drafting is a collaborative process in at least two major respects. First, lawyers rarely draft documents completely from scratch. Most drafting begins with a "standard form" or excerpted language used in previous agreements. In drafting a new document, the lawyer creates new verbiage, cuts and pastes language from other sources, adds, deletes, and revises until the form fits the current transaction. Specific language in most forms is compiled over time through the edits of many lawyers in a chain of those who have worked with earlier variations and permutations of the forms. The true genealogy of most language in any "standard form," and the purpose for which it was originally intended are seldom, if ever, known. Second, legal drafting is a collaborative process in the sense that during the course of negotiation, all involved parties typically contribute language to be included in the document. The terms of most documents evolve as each party negotiates to edit and refine the language to suit its objectives. Because drafting is a collaborative effort, many documents suffer from poor organization, lack of consistency, misuse or even conflicting use of defined terms, and redundant language.

Because the objectives and purposes of legal writing and legal drafting are so different, lawyers who only study legal writing have not been properly prepared in one of the most fundamental skills required by their trade.

Legal Drafting vs. Legal Writing

• Future behavior	• Historical events
• Must anticipate	• Known effect
• Long shelf life	• Quickly forgotten
• Mistakes very damaging	• Mistakes less important
• May be subject to adversarial reading	• Writing to persuade
• Consulted sporadically	• Read start to finish
• Read by business exec's	• Read by judges and other lawyers
• Format is unregulated	• Format dictated by courts
• Rarely references statutes	• Cites statutes and caselaw
• Collaborative process	• Singular effort

1.2 Understand the Characteristics of Excellent Drafting.

One of the surest ways to arrive at your destination is to have a good idea where you are going and what you hope to achieve. So, before discussing specific drafting techniques, let's begin by defining what "excellence" means in legal drafting. We often recognize excellent drafting when we see it without necessarily being cognizant of what makes it "excellent." Excellent drafting usually is made up of the following five characteristics.

1. Accuracy. The text is substantively accurate. The drafter has selected and arranged the words and provisions so they accurately communicate what the parties intended. Lewis Carroll understood that saying what you mean is not always as easy as it seems, as Alice learned the hard way at a mad tea party in Wonderland:

> *"Then you should say what you mean," the March Hare went on. "I do,"*
> *Alice hastily replied; "at least—at least I mean what I say—that's the same*
> *thing, you know." "Not the same thing a bit!" said the Hatter. "Why, you*
> *might just as well say that 'I see what I eat' is the same thing as 'I eat what I*
> *see'!" "You might just as well say," added the March Hare, "that 'I like what*
> *I get' is the same thing as 'I get what I like'!" "You might just as well say,"*
> *added the Dormouse, which seemed to be talking in its sleep, "that 'I breathe*
> *when I sleep' is the same thing as 'I sleep when I breathe'!"*[12]

In the context of legal drafting, accuracy means that the drafted document reflects what the parties intend, which is rather a different thing than that the parties mean what the documents says. Excellence in drafting means that the document should accurately reflect the entire, substantive agreement of the parties.

2. Clarity. The text is understandable to the reader. The provisions are drafted so their meaning is clear, and capable of only one plausible interpretation—that being the one both parties intended. Clarity is the opposite of ambiguity. Clarity is achieved by structuring sentences properly, choosing words carefully, and ensuring that the terms are internally consistent and complete.

3. Brevity. The text is "long enough and not one word longer."[13] Brevity does not mean that the document is brief, but rather that each word included in the document serves a clear purpose. Brevity also encompasses the goal of expressing each concept only once within a document and avoiding repetitious words, phrases, and provisions. In drafting, brevity means that words and phrases that contribute nothing should be eliminated. Although few lawyers would argue that meaningless words should be included in a legal document, the challenge for drafters is to identify and eliminate *which* words and phrases contribute nothing. Brevity also means that drafters should prefer the shortest words and sentences that successfully convey the intended meaning. "The briefest words and forms of expression, provided they convey the meaning intended, are to be preferred to the longer words and forms of expression."[14]

4. Simplicity. The text is simple to read and comprehend. Simplicity in legal drafting means the concepts are expressed in simple sentences using the simplest possible words. In drafting, "the simplest word, that is the word most commonly understood, should in general be preferred."[15]

5. Tone. The text strikes a balance between being too pompous and too casual. The proper tone for legal drafting is professional, using proper grammar, but avoiding pompous-sounding words that create a barrier between the drafter and the reader.

Exercise 1.2:

Identify which characteristic of excellent drafting is missing from each example.

(Hint: several may apply.)

1. Consultant acknowledges and agrees that the payment of monies hereunder constitutes monies to which Consultant was not previously entitled and, further, that the payment of monies hereunder constitutes fair and adequate consideration for Consultant's execution of this Agreement.

2. In exchange for the promises and/or covenants of Employer contained herein, subject to the provisions of this Agreement, Employee will provide the following to Employee:

3. Company's maximum liability to Service Provider under this GPA (regardless of cause or form of action, whether in contract, tort, or otherwise) shall be limited to the total amount owed Service Provider in payment for Service Provider's fulfillment of its obligations under this Agreement.

Now would define the parties, not "party to the first part"

4. Whereas, the party of the first part has heretofore conveyed unto the party of the second part that certain part, parcel and tract of real property whereupon the premises reside, it behooves the aforementioned party of the first part to bequeath the premises to the party of the second part. *dies, leaves property, something you inherit*

5. The foundation may grant funds to educational institutions and corporations assisting physically impaired individuals. *any institution one that helps physically impaired individuals*

6. Buyer shall remit payment by wire transfer to an account designated by Seller within five days after Closing.

Modify when? Acct designated or w/in 5 days? → ambiguous

1.3 Attend to Appearance.

Regardless of how perfect the language is, if the contract does not have a professional appearance, the audience is going to be suspicious of it. New lawyers may not have all the skills required to draft a complex contract, but they certainly can, and will be expected to, make any contract look "pretty." Appearance includes all of the following:

- Readable typeface and font size;
- Plenty of "white space" on the page;
- Effective numbering system;
- Headings and subheadings;
- Ragged right margin, but above all, consistent margins;[16]
- Tabulations to set off lists;
- Single-spaced text, double-spacing between paragraphs;
- Consistent formatting;
- Correct spelling;
- Correct grammar; and
- Correct cross references.

Case Study

What revisions should be made to correct the appearance of this contract?

MANUFACTURING AGREEEMENT

This Manufacturing Agreement ("Agreement") is entered on this ___ day of June , 2009 between ABC, Inc., a corporation organized and existing under the laws of the State of Georgia, having its principal place of business at 2210 Busy Street, Suite 700, Atlanta, Georgia 30339 ("Buyer"), and Peach State Manufacturing, Inc., a corporation organized and existing under the laws of Georgia, having its principal place of business at 1492 Crowded Parkway, Austell, Georgia ("Manufacturer").

Witnesseth:

WHEREAS, Buyer have designed, owns, and continues to develop for industrial application the specifications for one or more fiberglass vaults (the "Products"); and

WHEREAS, Manufacturer owns and operates manufacturing facilities and is in the business of, among other pursuits, manufacturing products upon the specifications of, for, and on behalf of others; and

WHEREAS, Buyer desires to engage Manufacturer to manufacture its Products upon the terms and conditions of this Agreement.

NOW, THEREFORE, it shall be agreed between the parties as follows:

1. Scope of Agreement. Manufacturer owns and operates a manufacturing facility located at 1492Crowded Parkway. Manufacturer is in the business of manufacturing products designed and owned by others upon their specifications. Buyer have designed, developed and desires to manufacture and sell certain fiberglass vault Products related to backflow testing. Such development efforts are ongoing and remain incomplete as of the date of this Agreement. Upon completion of development, the specifications for Buyer's first Product, Model #___, will be attached to and incorporated into this Agreement as Exhibit A. Pursuant to the terms of this Agreement, Buyer engages Manufacturer, and Manufacturer accept such engagement, too manufacture Buyer's Products upon Buyer's specifications for sale and distribution to Buyer's industrial customers.

2. Purchase Orders and Time of Completion. From time to time during the term of this Agreement, Buyer may submit their Purchase Order for the manufacture of a specified quantity of one or more of its Products. All orders placed by Buyer shall be subject to the terms and conditions of this Agreement and, to the extent that they specify quantities, destinations, and delivery dates, to Buyer's Purchase Orders. Manufacturer shall acknowledge Buyer's Purchase Order within 24 business hours of receipt. No term, condition or provision off this Agreement may be altered, amended, or modified by the terms, conditions, or provisions of any bid, confirmation, invoice, or other business form of Manufacturer unless otherwise specifically agreed in writing signed by both parties containing an express reference to this Paragraph 2 of this Agreement. Timely completion and delivery of the Products is of the essence of this Agreement. In the event that Manufacturer fails to deliver Products by the date specified in the Purchase Order, Buyer may offset against the purchase price a $300.00 penalty for each day that the shipment is late.

3. **PRICE AND PAYMENT.** Buyer shall remit to Manufacturer the per unit price of $_____ for each Model # _____ Product manufactured and delivered in accordance with Buyer's specifications and in accordance with the terms of this Agreement, free from defects, satisfactory to Buyer and free and clear of all liens and claims of any kind. Buyer shall be entitled to deduct from any payment any outstanding penalties for late delivery. Payment shall be made provided that Manufacturer is not then in default under any terms of this Agreement, within thirty (30) days of Buyer's receipt of payment for the Product from the end-user.

4. _Shipment_

   (a.) Destination. Manufacturer shall ship the Products Delivered Duty Paid Atlanta (DDP Destination), via mutually agreed upon carriers.

   (b.) Risk of Loss. Manufacturer shall assume the risk of loss or damage to all Products until delivery to their Destination.

5. **Miscellaneous Provisions**

   a. Relationship of Parties. Nothing contained in this Agreement shall be deemed or construed as creating a joint venture or partnership between Buyer and Manufacturer. Neither party shall have any power or authority to control the activities and operations of the other and their status is, and at all times will continue to be, that of independent contractor with respect to each other. Neither party shall have any power or authority to bind or commit the other.

   b. Governing Laws. This Agreement shall be construed and enforced in accordance with the laws of the State of Georgia, United States of America.

   c. Entire Understanding. This Confidentiality Agreement constitutes the entire understanding of the parties hereto and this Confidentiality Agreement may not be modified or amended except in writing signed by both parties. No person not a party hereto shall have any interest herein or be deemed a third party beneficiary hereof.

NOTES

1. Mark Mathewson, *A Critic of Plain Language Misses the Mark*, 8 SCRIBES J. LEGAL WRITING 147, 149 (2001-2002).

2. Maurice B. Kirk, *Legal Drafting: Curing Unexpressive Language*, 3 TEX. TECH. L. REV. 23, 52 (1971).

3. REED DICKERSON, THE FUNDAMENTALS OF LEGAL DRAFTING, 3 (2d ed. 1986).

4. Exec. Order No. 12044, 43 Fed. Reg. 12661 (1977), at Section 1 (d) (5).

5. The memorandum required that by October 1, 1998, plain language be used in all new documents, other than regulations, that explain how to obtain a benefit or service or how to comply with an administrative requirement. The memorandum further required that by January 1, 1999, plain language be used in all proposed and final rulemakings published in the Federal Register.

6. Almost all states have some form of plain language requirement, although they vary widely from state to state. Some statutes apply only to insurance contracts (See, e.g., Florida Statutes §627.4145), others apply to consumer contracts, generally (See, e.g., Connecticut General Statutes § 42-152 and), and still others apply to contracts involving residential real estate (See, e.g., N.Y. Gen. Oblig. § 5-702). Some states that don't yet have plain language statutes impose similar requirements through regulations. The following states have some form of plain language requirement, but this list may not be exhaustive because the terminology and language requirements vary so widely from state to state: Arizona, Alaska, Arkansas, California, Connecticut, Delaware, Florida, Georgia, Hawaii, Idaho, Indiana, Iowa, Kentucky, Maine, Massachusetts, Minnesota, Montana, Nebraska, Nevada, New Jersey, New Mexico, New York, North Carolina, North Dakota, Ohio, Oklahoma, Oregon, Pennsylvania, South Carolina, South Dakota, Tennessee, Texas, Vermont, Virginia, West Virginia, and Wisconsin. Some statutes reference the Flesch Test of Reading Ease specifically (see section 9.1); others reference language at a fourth or sixth grade reading level.

7. The term "drafting scholars" as used throughout this book references my esteemed colleagues who have written books and articles specifically on the topic of legal drafting as a distinct genre of legal writing, including Bryan A. Garner, Reed Dickerson, Kenneth A. Adams, George W. Kuney, Thomas R. Haggard, David Mellinkoff, Scott Burnham, Richard C. Wydick, Tina Stark, and others cited in this book.

8. DICKERSON, *supra* note 3, at 14.

9. BRYAN A. GARNER, THE ELEMENTS OF LEGAL STYLE, 2 (2002).

10. For example, the October 2006 dispute between Rogers Communications of Toronto, Canada's largest cable television provider, and Bell Aliant, a telephone company in Atlantic Canada, was over the phone company's attempt to cancel a contract governing Rogers' use of telephone poles. The argument turned on a single comma in the 14-page contract but the decision was worth one million Canadian dollars ($888,000). Citing the "rules of punctuation," Canada's telecommunications regulator recently ruled that the comma allowed Bell Aliant to end its five-year agreement with Rogers at any time with notice. The dispute was over this sentence: "This agreement shall be effective from the date it is made and shall continue in force for a period of five (5) years from the date it is made, and thereafter for successive five (5) year terms, unless and until terminated by one year prior notice in writing by either party." The regulator concluded that the second comma meant that the part of the sentence describing the one-year notice for cancellation applied to both the five-year term as well as its renewal. Therefore, the regulator found that the phone company could escape the contract after as little as one year. Telecom Decision 2006-45. Note that the Canadian Radio-television and Telecommunications Commission later determined in August 2007 that there was substantial doubt as to the correctness of the Telecom Decision, and reversed the initial finding. Regardless of the ultimate outcome, the case emphatically demonstrates the importance of accuracy in legal drafting.

11. United States v. Seckinger, 397 U.S. 203, 216, 90 S.Ct. 880, 888 (1970).

12. LEWIS CARROLL, ALICE'S ADVENTURES IN WONDERLAND, excerpt from Chapter 7: A Mad Tea-Party (1865).

13. DICKERSON, *supra* note 3, at 44.

14. J. G. Mackay, *Some General Rules of the Art of Legal Composition,* 32 J. of Juris. 169 (1888), cited in ROBERT N. COOK, *LEGAL DRAFTING* (1951) p. 26-36.

15. *Id.*

16. Research has shown that a jagged right margin is easier to read than a justified right margin. The most important thing, however, is to be sure the margins are handled consistently throughout the document. Inconsistent margins are usually caused when provisions are cut and pasted from other documents.

Drafting in Transactional Practice

Objective of this Lesson: To analyze the current status of drafting in the legal profession and to identify outside factors that influence the drafting process.

Key Techniques:
Explore the status quo of drafting in the legal profession.

- Understand the reasons for the status quo.
- Realize potential costs of deficient drafting.
- Examine how substantive law influences the drafting process.
- Understand how third party contracts affect the drafting process.
- Explore the use of forms versus zero-based drafting.

2.1 Explore the status quo of drafting in the legal profession.

Perhaps Fred Rodell summarized the status quo of legal writing best: "There are two things wrong with almost all legal writing. One is its style. The other is its content."[1] Although Mr. Rodell's comment more than 70 years ago painted all forms of legal writing with the same confrontational brush, his criticism still applies to legal drafting customs today. In fact, most drafting scholars concur that drafted documents are even greater offenders than other legal writings: While lawyers and judges are usually able to decipher the meaning of pleadings and briefs, the work produced by transactional lawyers is virtually incomprehensible to its intended audience, the vast majority of whom do not have law degrees.

Although most lawyers have been trained in law school to write pleadings and briefs, few practicing lawyers have studied legal drafting as a distinct genre of legal writing. The philosophy of legal educators has "traditionally"[2] held that legal writing is an acceptable subject for law students because it teaches them to "think like lawyers," while legal drafting has been considered more of a "trade skill" that should be acquired in actual practice. Until recently, law school graduates were fairly well prepared for litigation practice but had no exposure at all to the separate skill set required for transactional practice. The paradox of the nearly universal educational focus on preparing all law students to litigate is that while SOME lawyers draft pleadings and briefs, virtually ALL lawyers draft contracts! Even practicing lawyers who call themselves "litigators" routinely draft client engagement agreements, settlement agreements, releases, waivers, and their own partnership documents. Settlement agreements are particularly dangerous drafting projects because the parties have already proven themselves to be litigious.

In recent years, law students preparing for transactional practice have petitioned their faculties to offer courses that incorporate transactional skills. Their pleas have gained momentum in recent years, beginning with the revision of Standard 302 of the American Bar Association's Standards for Approval of Law Schools. Since at least 1980, Standard 302 had recommended that law schools should *offer* skills training. In 2005, however, Standard 302 was revised to state that "a law school shall *require*" each student to obtain "substantial instruction" in "professional skills generally regarded as necessary for responsible and effective participation in the legal profession." In 2007, the Carnegie Foundation for the Advancement of Teaching issued its report entitled "Education of Lawyers: Preparation for the Profession of Law," which questioned the "think like a lawyer" model and criticized law schools for failing to provide meaningful training for transactional practice. Most law school faculties have responded—although in some instances, grudgingly—with a smattering of transactional skills-based courses, but these offerings and the faculty who teach them are still often regarded as barely legitimate step-children of more traditional "core" courses and faculty.[3]

A new lawyer with excellent drafting skills may face certain "career imperatives," where senior lawyers may require that certain provisions be drafted in a manner that is inconsistent with current scholarly recommendations. The new lawyer may have to wait until he or she actually controls the drafting process to apply all the skills taught in this text, and even then may encounter contaminating language insisted upon by irrational opposing counsel. The good news is that change is coming rapidly as drafting and transactional skills are offered at more and more law schools. Progressive and conscientious law firms also recognize the need and benefit of formally teaching legal drafting and are using outside resources to provide additional training. If the law firm you work for is concerned enough about your career to require specialized training in legal drafting, the correct response is a resounding "thank you!"

2.2 Understand the reasons for the status quo.

Law students who emerge from law school with some formal training in legal drafting, however slight, enter a profession that does not always recognize these skills. Because legal drafting has not been widely taught, lawyers have taught themselves. Many otherwise exceptionally gifted transactional lawyers have bad drafting habits, and these bad drafting habits have been handed down from one generation of lawyers to the next. Practicing transactional lawyers are largely unaware of the prolific recommendations of drafting scholars and can become quite indignant when informed that they are drafting incorrectly. Most documents new lawyers are given to review and revise contain convoluted language and bad drafting practices handed down from one transaction to the next through untold generations of lawyers.

The greatest barrier to universal improvement of drafted documents is that no definitive source of drafting do's and don'ts currently exists. Although a number of excellent treatises and hornbooks have been presented in recent years by authors like Bryan Garner, Kenneth Adams, and Thomas Haggard, drafting scholars still dispute certain issues among themselves—like where the glossary of defined terms should be located and whether the use of "and/or" automatically creates ambiguity.[4] Lawyers have elevated the ritual of debate into an art form, so even if drafting scholars had settled on a set of drafting rules, absent some compelling reason to adopt them, the legal profession could debate the matter for several generations. And the courts are not confined by either the scholars' or the lawyers' conclusions.

The absence of a definitive source of drafting policy means that transactional lawyers do not have an effective way to measure their drafting proficiency, and clients usually have even less ability to gauge the quality of drafted documents. When contract language ultimately is judicially determined to be ambiguous, the lapse of time between the day the contract was drafted and the day a lawsuit is resolved usually means the offending drafter is protected from accountability through malpractice claims by the statute of limitations. The client's burden of proof is especially steep in a malpractice claim for flawed drafting because in addition to proving the drafting was flawed, the client also has to prove damage: either that the other party to the agreement would have accepted a revised provision if the offending drafter had proffered it, or that the client would not have entered into the transaction in the first place knowing of the flaw. Drafters are almost completely insulated against repercussions from flawed drafting and so have little motivation to improve.

Another barrier to improvement of drafted documents is the time it takes to update standard forms. Lawyers in private transactional practice must bill hours to earn a living, and few clients willingly accept time charges for this type of work. Substantial revision of standard forms might be perceived by some as an admission of incompetence with respect to earlier permutations. Further, in a perverse way, convoluted language provides additional sources of revenue for the lawyers who must attempt to interpret or litigate it.[5]

Finally, practicing lawyers sometimes convince themselves that studying matters of substantive law is a higher calling and more worthy use of time than cultivating drafting skills. These lawyers fail to recognize that it doesn't matter how much you know about the substance if you don't express it properly in the form.

2.3 Realize potential costs of deficient drafting.

While lawyers who draft flawed language are largely insulated against repercussions, their clients are not. An incorrectly drafted provision may cause the client an unintended liability or deprive the client of an anticipated benefit. The client may incur unnecessary legal fees to understand and interpret incomprehensible provisions. Worse, if the document is ambiguous, the parties may dispute its meaning in court at a later date. Litigation is time consuming and expensive, and the client's business relationships may be irretrievably damaged if the parties must resort to litigation to resolve a dispute over the meaning of ambiguous terms.

2.4 Examine how substantive law influences the drafting process.

One of the ways that legal drafting differs from legal writing is that the law is seldom mentioned in drafted documents, whereas in pleadings and briefs, applicable law is analyzed, cited, quoted, discussed, and argued. Contracts do not typically present the law, but a thorough understanding of the applicable law underlying the transaction is essential to ensure that drafted contracts will be enforceable as the parties intended.

Ethical Requirements. A thorough understanding of applicable law is also required according to ethical standards. The Model Rules of Professional Conduct state that "(p)erhaps the most fundamental legal skill consists of determining what kind of legal problems a situation may involve," and "(c)ompetent handling of a drafting project necessarily includes analysis of the factual and legal elements of the problem."[6]

The UCC and other "gap fillers." Drafters need to take the time to research and understand the laws applicable to each transaction. For example, the Uniform Commercial Code provides a general statutory framework for how contracts for the sale of goods will be performed. The parties are free to vary most of the terms of the UCC, but these statutory terms will apply to fill in gaps where terms have been omitted unless the contract is drafted specifically to alter or exclude them. If your client does not want the transaction to be performed according to the UCC, the written contract must either state how the parties DO intend to perform the transaction or state which provisions of the UCC do not apply. Similarly, corporate transactions must comply with the Corporation Code, health care transactions must comply with HIPPA, and so on. Do your homework before drafting or risk unenforceability of contract terms, embarrassment, claims for malpractice, and possibly even ethical censure if the transaction goes sour.

Case law sometimes dictates how certain provisions will be construed. In Georgia, for example, the courts have determined that the phrase "reasonable attorneys fees" means a certain percentage. If the drafter intends that ALL attorneys fees or a greater or lesser percentage than specified by case law should be covered, then the contract must so state.[7]

Required Disclosures. Sometimes, statutes require specific disclosures in writing. Consider the following examples, just to name a few:

Employment and severance agreements—COBRA and other disclosures are required by Federal law to avoid penalties against the employer.

- Corporate documents—minority shareholders rights in mergers and acquisitions are protected by most states' business corporation codes.
- Software licenses—disclosures regarding restrictions on export are required by federal law.
- Government contractors—government trade partners are required to comply, and ensure that their trade partners comply, with federal laws regarding EEOC, debarment and suspension,

lobbying, buy American, no kickbacks, and Executive Order 11246.

- Truth-in-lending—disclosures are required in certain financial transactions.

Enforceability Issues. Drafters should also understand any laws or case precedents applicable to the *enforceability* of specific provisions, like the following:

- Provisions that attempt to terminate the contract if one of the parties files bankruptcy;
- Recitals of consideration in contracts signed under seal;
- Click-wrap licenses;
- Limitations of liability; and
- Arbitration clauses, particularly in certain types of agreements.

Much is written by legal drafting scholars about unnecessary verbiage included in contracts out of habit, but drafters should be aware that most language was inserted into an earlier permutation of every document for some reason. While unnecessary language should certainly be omitted, the drafter should take care to review applicable law to determine whether the reason to include the language still exists, or exists in the present situation, before indiscriminately omitting it.

Each type of contract has its own legal framework, and the drafter who drafts without inquiry and analysis into the legal framework has not fulfilled his or her responsibility to the client. Besides the possibility of claims for malpractice, the careless lawyer may face ethical sanctions as well. Under the Model Rules of Professional Conduct, the penalty for failing to understand the legal framework may be disbarment—which is more than enough reason to take the responsibility seriously!

2.5 Understand how third party contracts affect the drafting process.

In addition to considering the impact of statutes and case law, a drafter must determine whether any third party contracts affect the proposed transaction. Sometimes, one party may have entered into another contract with a third party that impacts the current transaction. For example, if a new employee signed a non-compete agreement with his or her previous employer, your client may not be able to hire the employee without incurring unexpected complications and potential liability. A shareholder's agreement may prevent a shareholder from selling stock or using stock as collateral in a loan agreement. If a borrower has pledged certain assets as collateral, the borrower is probably prevented under the terms of the security agreement from transferring any interest in those assets in another transaction. A pre-emptive rights clause in a company's articles or bylaws may prevent the company from selling additional shares of stock without first offering them to existing shareholders.

It is challenging to know your client's business well enough to know whether the client is a party to any third party contract that affects the proposed transaction. It is even more challenging to know your client's business partner's business. In complex transactions, drafters must perform due diligence reviews of both parties' records to determine whether any third party contracts affect the parties' ability to participate lawfully in the proposed transaction. In smaller matters, the drafter should include a representation and warranty stating, as a minimum, that the business partner is not a party to any agreement that would affect the client's rights in the current transaction.

2.6 Explore the use of forms versus zero-based drafting.

Drafting is a collaborative process in the sense that virtually all drafting begins with a document used in a prior transaction. Lawyers usually find it helpful to develop a portfolio of "standard" forms for transactions that are similar in nature. Be careful that the form you use as your starting template is drafted from the same perspective as the current transaction. For example, if your firm represents the buyer in the current transaction, look for a form from a prior transaction in which your firm also represented the buyer.

Occasionally, a lawyer is engaged to draft a contract where no suitable model form exists. Zero-based drafting for novel transactions is more challenging because the lawyer must anticipate nuances and circumstances that may arise during the term of the transaction and craft language to provide for these legal issues. Even so, language can usually be borrowed from prior documents to simplify the drafting process. For example, in the early 1990's, lawyers were engaged to draft website development agreements for companies that were early pioneers in what became a booming industry. Although no model forms existed at the time, lawyers were able to borrow and adapt language regarding ownership of the intellectual property, confidentiality covenants, payment terms, and boilerplate from software development agreements to fit the current transaction. A decade or so later, these same lawyers borrowed language from software licenses to create internet access services agreements.

Whether drafting from a form or from scratch, every contract should be considered an original composition from beginning to signature. Thinking of each transactional document as unique to its specific deal can help you view every contract with the necessary fresh eyes.

NOTES

1. Fred Rodell, *"Goodbye to Law Reviews,"* 23 Va. L. Rev. 38 (1937) at p. 38.

2. The term "traditionally" is used loosely because historically speaking, lawyers were trained as apprentices until fairly modern times. Over time, the law school concept of teaching law students to "think like a lawyer" may turn out to have been a grand diversion.

3. BRYAN A. GARNER, GARNER ON LANGUAGE AND WRITING, xxvi (2009).

4. SEE KENNETH A. ADAMS, A MANUAL OF STYLE FOR CONTRACT DRAFTING, 132-133 (2004).

5. Mark Mathewson, *A Critic of Plain Language Misses the Mark,* 8 SCRIBES J. LEGAL WRITING 147 (2001-2002).

6. Per Model Rules of Professional Conduct, Rule 1.1, Comments [2] and [5]:

   RULE 1.1 COMPETENCE

   A lawyer shall provide competent representation to a client. Competent representation as used in this Rule means that a lawyer shall not handle a matter which the lawyer knows or should know to be beyond the lawyer's level of competence without associating another lawyer who the original lawyer reasonably believes to be competent to handle the matter in question. Competence requires the legal knowledge, skill, thoroughness and preparation reasonably necessary for the representation.

The maximum penalty for a violation of this Rule is disbarment.

Comments

[2] A lawyer need not necessarily have special training or prior experience to handle legal problems of a type with which the lawyer is unfamiliar. A newly admitted lawyer can be as competent as a practitioner with long experience. Some important legal skills, such as the analysis of precedent, the evaluation of evidence and legal drafting, are required in all legal problems. Perhaps the most fundamental legal skill consists of determining what kind of legal problems a situation may involve, a skill that necessarily transcends any particular specialized knowledge. A lawyer can provide adequate representation in a wholly novel field through necessary study. Competent representation can also be provided through the association of a lawyer of established competence in the field in question.

[5] Competent handling of a particular matter includes inquiry into and analysis of the factual and legal elements of the problem, and use of methods and procedures meeting the standards of competent practitioners. It also includes adequate preparation. The required attention and preparation are determined in part by what is at stake; major litigation and complex transactions ordinarily require more elaborate treatment than matters of lesser consequence.

7. But note that this creates the dilemma of whether the actual fees should still be "reasonable" under the circumstances, which is the reason many lawyers use the phrase "actual attorneys fees reasonably incurred."

Draft to Fit the Transaction

Objective of this Lesson: To explain how a drafter revises a prior document to incorporate the terms of the current transaction.

Key Techniques:
- Understand the audience.
- Eliminate archaic practices.
- Select the contract format.
- Identify the parts of a contract.

3.1 Understand the audience.

The lawyer's responsibility in drafting is first and foremost to the client, who may lack legal sophistication or experience. Yet many lawyers draft to impress opposing counsel, and others draft with a judge and jury in mind. It is true that a contract must be precise enough to withstand the attacks of litigators who will zealously try to twist the words and thwart the intended meaning. But opposing counsel is not paying your fee, and only a tiny percentage of written contracts wind up being interpreted by a judge or jury. Drafting with the primary objective of impressing opposing counsel, judge, or jury usually results in misplaced effort and failure to communicate effectively with the most likely audience of the contract.[1]

A contract's audience consists of a wide variety of people who will read the document for differing, and possibly adversarial, purposes. Before drafting, take a moment to identify the potential users of the written contract and draft with these various users in mind. The drafting style and language you choose should differ depending on the sophistication of the audience.[2] For example, the style you choose in drafting a contract to be used primarily by consumers should differ from the style you would use in drafting a contract for the executive officers of a large corporation. The drafter must also take into account whether the users of the contract are likely to be friendly or hostile to the client's interests.[3]

Although lawyers sometimes pride themselves on creating highly complex language, a contract should be understandable to the people who are going to use it. **"Success" in legal drafting means the degree to which the intended audience is able to understand the document.**[4] The drafter's goal is to ensure that if the audience experiences difficulty in understanding the document, the difficulty arises from the complicated subject matter and not the syntax.[5]

If mere logic is not persuasive enough, Model Rule 1.4 states that lawyers are ethically required to ensure the client is able to make informed decisions, to participate intelligently in the transaction, and to understand all important provisions before signing a contract.[6] The comments to Rule 1.4 state that the lawyer must: 1) provide sufficient information to enable the client to participate intelligently in decisions; and 2) review important provisions with the client before the document is signed.

Exercise 3.1:

You are responsible for drafting a partnership agreement for a technology business that will have five equity partners at inception. More partners may be added at a future date. Each partner may bring one or more employees and a client list to the partnership and will be asked to contribute $100,000 as initial capital. Other financial arrangements for the partnership will be made with a local community bank. The prospective partners have hired a bookkeeper recommended by their outside accounting firm. The partnership agreement will contain typical restrictions on transfer in the event of death, disability, or termination of employment.

How many potential users of this contract can you identify?

3.2 Eliminate archaic practices.

Legal drafting scholars almost unanimously recommend that lawyers should eliminate archaic customs that nevertheless still plague many legal documents.[7] Many documents still contain archaic language such as "witnesseth," "to-wit," and "in witness whereof I have hereunto set my hand and seal." These legal customs may have fulfilled some purpose at the time they arose, but few of us, if any, know now what that purpose was.

Most lawyers believe that the word "witnesseth" is a sort of command, kind of like "listen up!" In actuality, verb forms like "witnesseth" were used only briefly in a small region of England in the Middle Ages.[8] Besides being used in the King James Version of the Christian Bible, these verb forms were also used by famous authors such as John Donne, John Milton, Christopher Marlowe and William Shakespeare to express their poetry more artfully. The word "witnesseth" actually means "witnesses" in the third-person singular verb form, as in "(t)his agreement witnesses that. ..." The word "witnesseth" is seldom used correctly in legal documents, but even if it were, it's both fallen out of colloquial use and never adds anything significant to the document.

Instead of using "witnesseth" with a long string of "whereas" and "now, therefore" recitals, opt for a simpler, more concise "Statement of Purpose" paragraph at the beginning of the document. Most other archaic customs can be eliminated without substitution, such as "know all men by these presents," or "further, affiant sayeth not."

3.3 Select the Contract Format.

Lawyers draft agreements for many different types of transactions. Some transactions are "closings," where once the deal is complete, the parties generally have no ongoing obligations to each other. For example, sales of commercial real estate and mergers are usually structured as closings. When the documents have been signed and filed, the transaction is considered "closed." Other transactions represent "openings," to coin a phrase, because the parties anticipate an ongoing relationship which may be for a specified or unspecified period of time. For example, employment contracts, partnership agreements, software licenses, and distribution agreements are drafted to "open" an ongoing relationship between the parties.

Whether you are drafting for an opening or a closing, the same drafting techniques apply. Although drafting for an opening requires the lawyer to anticipate circumstances and contingencies that may arise over a longer term, a lawyer who drafts closing documents without considering contingencies has failed to provide adequate representation.

Before drafting, the drafter must determine which contract format best suits the particular transaction. The three contract formats used most often in transactional practice are traditional, schedule, and letter.[9] When properly drafted and signed by the parties, each of these contract formats is equally enforceable in most jurisdictions.

A **traditional form contract** is the most common and is the most appropriate format for closings. In a traditional contract, the tone is slightly more formal and the contract components are arranged so the signatures appear on the last page of the text of the agreement, but before schedules and exhibits. (See Appendix A.)

A **schedule agreement** is arranged so the signatures appear on the first page of the agreement. Performance and boilerplate provisions are contained in schedules that are listed and incorporated by reference on the first page of the agreement along with any other schedules and exhibits. Performance and boilerplate provisions are usually included in a schedule called "General Terms and Conditions," or something similar. Other schedules might include specifications for the goods and services, insurance requirements, or terms included in a request for proposal. Caveat: Unless a schedule is listed on the first page and incorporated by reference, it is not considered part of the agreement. A schedule agreement format is most useful as a "standard" form for a series of transactions that are similar in nature.[10] For example, a large utility company might use a schedule format general services agreement to contract with various local contractors to install utility poles from county to county throughout the state. A large corporation might use a schedule format to purchase goods and services from various vendors. (See Appendix B.)

A **letter agreement** is more cordial in nature and is often used in "openings" where the parties anticipate a more personal, ongoing relationship. The terms of the agreement are contained in a letter written from one party to the other. A letter agreement is commonly used in offering employment, as a confidentiality agreement between parties that wish to explore opportunities for a merger, or as a letter of intent, summarizing preliminary discussions for an anticipated transaction. The party sending the letter has already signed it, and a letter agreement must include some mechanism for the other party to indicate acceptance of its terms. This is usually accomplished by including a sentence like this: "If the terms outlined above are acceptable to you, please sign below and return to me." Caveat: Unless the other party signs to indicate acceptance of the terms, no contract has been formed. (See Appendix C.)

3.4 Identify the Parts of a Contract.

Regardless of which contract format is used and how the information is arranged, most contracts consist of the following parts:

1. Name or title of the contract
2. Introduction
3. Statement of Purpose
4. Statement of Agreement
5. Definitions
6. Performance provisions
7. Boilerplate
8. Signatures

1. Name or title of the contract. The name of the contract is usually listed in bold type at the top of the first page. The name should identify the nature of the transaction, such as "Merger Agreement," "Employment Agreement," or "Shareholder's Agreement." Keep the title brief by eliminating extraneous information, such as the names of the parties, but not too brief—"Agreement" reveals nothing and may cause confusion if there are related documents named the same thing.

2. Introduction. The introductory paragraph identifies the parties to the transaction and may include the effective date of the contract. The parties should be referenced by their formal, legal names. For corporations and limited liability companies, this should be the name currently on file with the Secretary of State. The introduction should designate the corporate status of the parties—e.g., "ABC, Inc., a California corporation" means that ABC is a *corporation* incorporated under the laws of the State of California.

Be sure to identify the capacity in which the parties are entering the transaction if there is any doubt. For example, in a stock purchase agreement, the officer who signs on behalf of the Company may also be a party to the contract individually as a selling shareholder. In this case, the company as well as the selling shareholder in individual capacity should be identified as parties in the introduction. The legal capacity in which a person signs a document should be established from the beginning because in some cases, applicable law may depend on whether the party is a corporation, partnership, or an individual. Avoid cluttering up the introduction with extraneous information regarding background, rights and obligations of the parties, or policy. This information should be included in the statement of purpose, performance provisions, or boilerplate instead.

Example:

EMPLOYMENT AGREEMENT

THIS EMPLOYMENT AGREEMENT is made this ___ day of December, 2010, between Quantum Consulting, Inc., a Delaware corporation (the "Company") and _____, a resident of the State of _____ ("Employee").

3. Statement of Purpose. After the introductory paragraph, contracts often begin with a string of "whereas" and "now, therefore" clauses that provide background information with respect to the parties' reasons for entering into the contract. Drafting scholars prefer a simpler "Statement of Purpose," which provides the background information in paragraph form without the archaic clauses. The Statement of Purpose should provide background information but should not include performance terms of the contract. Some courts have held that recitals are not part of the contract because they usually appear before the Statement of Agreement; in other words, before the contract says "the parties agree as follows." The background information could be determinative of what the parties intended when they entered the contract, however, so performance provisions should be construed in light of the background information found in the Statement of Purpose. Ambiguity in the Statement of Purpose could ultimately poison the substantive provisions of the document. For this reason, the Statement of Purpose is as important as every other provision of the contract and must be drafted with care.

Example:

Instead of this:

WITNESSETH:

Whereas, Alpha Services Corporation ("Alpha") is in the business of managing business intelligence and call center operations; and

Whereas, Presto Applicance, Inc. ("Presto") is in the business of designing, manufacturing, and distributing small household appliances; and

Whereas, Presto desires to engage Alpha to provide call center services with respect to warranty claims;

Now, therefore, Alpha and Presto, intending to be legally bound, agree as follows.

Use this:

STATEMENT OF PURPOSE

Alpha Services Corporation ("Alpha") is in the business of managing business intelligence and call center operations. Presto Appliance, Inc. ("Presto") is in the business of designing, manufacturing, and distributing small household appliances. Presto desires to engage Alpha to provide call center services with respect to warranty claims. Alpha and Presto, intending to be legally bound, agree as follows.

4.   Statement of Agreement. Contracts should include a statement confirming that the parties agree to the following terms. The Recital of Consideration or Statement of Agreement is usually included as the last sentence of the Statement of Purpose. Because consideration is a required element of all contracts, some drafters mistakenly conclude that a consideration clause is a required element as well. Under current law in most states, consideration is established when the parties agree to enter into the transaction, so recitals stating that consideration has been exchanged are superfluous in most two-party agreements and should be replaced with a simple statement that "the parties agree as follows." A simple statement that "we agree" or "the parties agree to the following terms" is evidence of a bargain, and hence, consideration, between the parties. In situations where only one party makes promises in the document (e.g., promissory notes and stock option grants), it may be advisable to identify the consideration and have the contract signed under seal if applicable in the governing jurisdiction, but this is not generally necessary in two-party contracts. (See section 13.4.)

Example:

STATEMENT OF PURPOSE

The Company desires to employ Employee and Employee desires to be employed by Company subject to the terms of this Agreement. Intending to be legally bound, the parties agree as follows.

Example:

STATEMENT OF PURPOSE

Debtor and Secured Party entered into an Asset Purchase Agreement dated May _____, 2010 providing for the sale of certain assets owned by Secured Party to Debtor. The unpaid purchase price of the assets is $_____. In consideration of Secured Party's agreement to finance the unpaid purchase price, Debtor promises to pay Secured Party according to the following terms.

5. Definitions. Lawyers define terms in a contract to ensure that the parties interpret the stipulated defined terms with the same meanings. Where five or fewer defined terms are used, the definitions usually appear in the sections where the terms are first used. Where more than five defined terms are used in a contract, most lawyers prefer that the defined terms should appear at the beginning of the document. Other lawyers prefer to put the defined terms at the end of the document or in an attachment to it based on the logic that the defined terms are not as important as the performance provisions of the contract. Recommendations for using defined terms are included in this text at Section 7.3.

---

6. Performance provisions. The performance provisions of the contract describe the promises each party has made to the other. The performance provisions describe who is obligated to do what, when they are obligated to do it, how payment is calculated and made, and what happens if either party fails to perform their obligations under the contract. Performance provisions are unique to each contract and are the terms most heavily negotiated by the parties. Common performance provisions are discussed in Section 4.1.

7. Boilerplate. Boilerplate provisions contain language that can be used in a variety of contracts to have essentially the same meaning. Boilerplate provisions are typically included at the end of the contract under the heading "Miscellaneous Provisions." The term "boilerplate" was coined in the newspaper industry to describe material that was delivered to the newspaper in plate form ready to print without any changes being possible.[11] Although in a legal context, changes can certainly be made to the boilerplate, these provisions are not usually heavily negotiated, and careless drafters have an unfortunate tendency to overlook them. Typical boilerplate provisions are discussed in Section 4.2.

8. Signature Blocks. All parties that have an obligation under the contract must sign it. The signatures ordinarily appear on the last page of a traditional contract but may appear on the first page if a schedule format is used. The enforceability of a contract and other important legal issues can depend on how and whether the contract is appropriately signed, so drafters must pay close attention to the signature blocks, particularly with respect to contracts signed under seal.

The capacity under which each person signs the contract should be indicated. If a person signs on behalf of a corporation and also has individual obligations in the contract, that person's signature should appear in two places. Beware that in most states, only officers of a corporation are authorized to sign on its behalf unless authority has been delegated to someone else by the officers. In most states, members of the Board of Directors are not authorized to sign on behalf of a corporation unless they are also officers. Partners of a partnership are generally authorized to sign on behalf of the partnership unless the partnership agreement provides otherwise. Members of a limited liability company may or may not have authority to sign on behalf of the company, depending upon whether the company is managed by its members or a manager. Authority must be determined by consulting applicable law and the entity's corporate records.

If possible, all signatures should appear on the same page. It may be necessary to insert the phrase "[SIGNATURES ON FOLLOWING PAGE]" at the bottom of the last page of text and move the signature block (beginning with the seal recital, if applicable, i.e., "IN WITNESS WHEREOF, I put my hand and seal" or "Signed, sealed and delivered. ...") to the next page. If the date was not included in the text of the contract, it should appear in the signature block. If the contract is to be notarized, the notary recital, signature, and seal appear last. Make sure that the lines are all the same length, and allow enough space between the lines for signatures.

While many states have abandoned the common law concept of contracts signed "under seal," it can have enormous, unintended consequences in jurisdictions where the concept still applies.[12] In jurisdictions where a seal still carries significance, there is usually no legal distinction between a corporate and a personal seal. A conscientious drafter should understand the ramifications of having a contract signed under seal, particularly when the contract is to be governed and construed under the laws of another jurisdiction. See Section 13.5 for more information on contracts signed under seal.

Signature Block for Contracts Under Seal:

Signed, sealed and delivered as of the 10th day of January, 2009.

ACME:

ACME Widget Corporation [Company, or LLC]*

By: _____

    Paul Jones

Title: _____

[CORPORATE SEAL]

EMPLOYEE:

_____ (SEAL)

Mark P. Smith

Signature Block for Contracts NOT Under Seal:

Effective as of the 10th day of January, 2009.

ACME:

ACME Widget Corporation [Company, or LLC]*

By: _____

    Paul Jones

Title: _____

EMPLOYEE:

_____

Mark P. Smith

* Use formal corporate name as filed with the Secretary of State.

NOTES

1. An exception would be contracts traditionally disfavored by the courts, such as non-competition agreements, which must be proactively drafted to withstand hostile judicial scrutiny.

2. REED DICKERSON, THE FUNDAMENTALS OF LEGAL DRAFTING, 27 (1986); BRYAN A. GARNER, THE ELEMENTS OF LEGAL STYLE, 181 (2d 2002); THOMAS R. HAGGARD AND GEORGE W. KUNEY, LEGAL DRAFTING: PROCESS, TECHNIQUES AND EXERCISES, 130-133 (2d 2007).

3. HAGGARD AND KUNEY, *Id.*, at 131.

4. Maurice B. Kirk, *Legal Drafting: Curing Unexpressive Language*, 3 Tex. Tech. L. Rev. 23, 52 (1971).

5. Mark Mathewson, *A Critic of Plain Language Misses the Mark*, 8 Scribes J. Legal Writing, 147, 149 (2001-2002).

6. **RULE 1.4 COMMUNICATION**

   A lawyer shall explain a matter to the extent reasonably necessary to permit the client to make informed decisions regarding the representation, shall keep the client reasonably informed about the status of matters and shall promptly comply with reasonable requests for information.

   The maximum penalty for a violation of this Rule is a public reprimand.

   Comment

   [1A] **The client should have sufficient information to participate intelligently in decisions concerning the objectives of the representation and the means by which they are to be pursued, to the extent the client is willing and able to do so.** *[Emphasis added]* For example, a lawyer negotiating on behalf of a client should provide the client with facts relevant to the matter, inform the client of communications from another party and take other reasonable steps that permit the client to make a decision regarding a serious offer from another party. A lawyer who receives from opposing counsel an offer of settlement in a civil controversy or a proffered plea bargain in a criminal case should promptly inform the client of its substance unless prior discussions with the client have left it clear that the proposal will be unacceptable. See *Rule 1.2(a): Scope of Representation*. Even when a client delegates authority to the lawyer, the client should be kept advised of the status of the matter.

   [2] Adequacy of communication depends in part on the kind of advice or assistance involved. For example, **in negotiations where there is time to explain a proposal, the lawyer should review all important provisions with the client before proceeding to an agreement.** *[Emphasis added]*

In litigation a lawyer should explain the general strategy and prospects of success and ordinarily should consult the client on tactics that might injure or coerce others. On the other hand, a lawyer ordinarily cannot be expected to describe trial or negotiation strategy in detail. The guiding principle is that the lawyer should fulfill reasonable client expectations for information consistent with the duty to act in the client's best interests, and the client's overall requirements as to the character of representation.

7. KENNETH A. ADAMS, A MANUAL OF STYLE FOR CONTRACT DRAFTING, 14 (2004); RICHARD C. WYDICK, PLAIN ENGLISH FOR LAWYERS, 58-59 (5th 2005); SCOTT J. BURNHAM, DRAFTING AND ANALYZING CONTRACTS, 30, 228, and 223 (3d 2003); LAUREL CURRIE OATES ET AL., THE LEGAL WRITING HANDBOOK, 699 (3d 2002); VEDA R. CHARROW AND MYRA K. ERHARDT, CLEAR & EFFECTIVE LEGAL WRITING, 181 (2001).

8. Robert W. Benson, *The End of Legalese: The Game is Over*, XIII N.Y.U. REV. LAW & SOC. CHANGE 519, 523 (1984-85).

9. Internet terms of use and "click wrap" licenses present an entirely different contract format, but the legal issues involved with these forms of agreement are outside the scope of this book.

10. I have observed in practice that, for whatever reason, a schedule agreement is apparently less intimidating to less sophisticated business partners, because the parties are more likely to sign a schedule agreement without negotiating the terms, perhaps because the signature appears *before* the general terms and conditions rather than after.

11. BRYAN A. GARNER, A DICTIONARY OF MODERN LEGAL USAGE, 112 (2nd Ed. 2001).

12. The seal concept is most common today in jurisdictions along the East Coast of the United States, where the ties to English common law are strongest.

Components of a Contract

Objective of this Lesson: To identify the parts of a contract and introduce common provisions.

Key Techniques:
- Understand the purpose of common performance provisions.
- Examine the potential consequences of common boilerplate provisions.

4.1 Understand the purposes of common performance provisions.

Although every contract is different, certain types of performance provisions appear in most contracts of a similar nature. For example, contracts involving acquisitions and mergers typically include one or two sections called "Representations and Warranties." Contracts for the sale of goods usually include either a limited warranty or disclaimer of warranties, which are similar in some respects to representations and warranties provisions but used to warrant the quality of goods or services. It is also common practice in many different types of transactions to include performance provisions seeking to limit liability,

---

or to transfer liability from one party to the other if something goes wrong when the contract is performed. Some contracts may include liquidated damage provisions. Whether drafting or reviewing contracts, the drafter must understand what these terms mean, and how they can impact a client's rights and obligations. Do not copy these provisions from one document to another without considering their ramifications in the context of the current transaction.

1. Representations and Warranties. Representations and warranties are most common in corporate transactions involving acquisitions, mergers, and similar business combinations, although they may be used in any transaction where one party relies upon statements made by the other in deciding whether to enter the transaction. Although the terms are sometimes used synonymously, "representations" and "warranties" refer to separate legal concepts so the words are not redundant and usually appear together. A representation states a fact as of a particular point in time, while the warranty assures that the fact is true and provides an implied remedy if it isn't.[1] In smaller transactions, all of the representations and warranties of both parties may be grouped into one section. In larger transactions, the representations and warranties of each party are grouped into separate sections.

Representations in corporate transactions usually have to do with a party's having the ability and proper authority to enter in the transaction. For example, in an acquisition, a buyer may rely upon the representation of the seller that a corporation is in good standing with the Secretary of State.[2] The seller may rely upon the representation of the buyer that its financial statements accurately reflect the buyer's ability to pay the purchase price. If a client is asked to make a representation, the drafter needs to investigate with due diligence to ensure that the representation is, in fact, true. A false representation may result in unfavorable remedies, possibly including rescission of the contract, and other unfavorable results, such as lawsuits against the lawyers and accountants involved in the transaction.

Example:

Representations and Warranties of Seller. Seller represents and warrants to Buyer as follows:

   (a) The statements set forth in this Section III are true and correct
         as of the date of Closing.

(b) *Seller owns and has good and marketable title to all of the Assets, and as of the Closing date, the Assets are free and clear of all liens, encumbrances, claims, or rights of others or defects in title of any kind whatsoever.*

(c) *Seller will not default on, breach, or violate any agreement, instrument, or arrangement to which Seller is a party by consummating the transaction contemplated by this Agreement.*

(d) *Seller has the right, power, legal capacity and authority to enter into and perform the obligations under this Agreement, and no approval or consent of any other person is necessary for Seller to enter or perform this Agreement.*

(e) *Seller has no knowledge of any pending litigation, judgment, lien or proceeding relating to the Assets.*

(f) *Seller has not engaged the services of any broker for the sale of the Assets and no broker has brought about this sale.*

(g) *Seller has not assigned, licensed, or in any way granted permission for anyone to use the trade name "XYZ."*

As a practical matter, **the more difficult the representation is to make, the more important it is to make a complete disclosure in order to avoid potential liability.** If a party is unable or unwilling to give a representation required by the other party, it has several choices:

- Refuse to make the representation;
- Give the representation to the best of its knowledge, actual knowledge, or belief;
- Give the representation after disclosing responsive facts, as in "except as disclosed on Schedule 1.3, seller represents that no hazardous materials have been used on the property."

2. Express Warranties, Limited Warranties, and Disclaimers. The common law on warranties evolved primarily with respect to contracts for the sale of goods, but warranties are also used in many other types of contracts. The UCC identifies three primary types of warranties with respect to goods: 1) express warranties; 2) warranties of merchantability; and 3) warranties of fitness for particular purpose. Beware that courts frequently apply UCC warranty concepts beyond contracts for goods. Additionally, the Magnuson-Moss Consumer Warranty Act regulates

---

the manner in which the warranty must be disclosed to the consumer, although it does not dictate what the warranty must cover.

A warranty is the seller's representation about the quality or character of the goods and services. The warranty usually describes what the seller is obligated to do if the goods or services do not conform to specifications. For example, the warranty will state whether the seller is obligated to repair or replace defective goods, or whether the seller must compensate the buyer for damage incurred by the defective goods. In some instances, the warranty may serve as a condition upon the buyer's obligation to pay for the goods.

Express Warranties. Express warranties are very easy to make; in fact, the seller can make an express warranty without even intending to do so. No magic words are required to make an express warranty—in fact, no words at all are required. An express warranty can be based upon:

- a statement of fact made by the seller to the buyer;
- a promise made by the seller to the buyer;
- a description of the goods; or
- a sample or model of the goods provided by seller to buyer.

In order to be construed as an express warranty, the statement of fact must be more than mere "puffing"; it is usually more specific in nature. For example, no express warranty would be made by stating that a vehicle gets "great mileage," but an express warranty can be made if the seller states that the vehicle gets 25 m.p.g.

Warranty of Merchantability. If the seller is a "merchant" with respect to the particular goods sold, the warranty of merchantability may be **implied by law**. The warranty of merchantability means that the goods are of at least average quality within the industry and are fit for the ordinary purpose for which they are used. The goods don't have to be perfect or without defect, but suitable for ordinary tasks. For example, an insect spray that also kills the person who applies it would not be suitable for its intended purpose.

Warranty of Fitness for Particular Purpose. This warranty is implied by law where **the seller knows of the buyer's particular purpose in buying the goods.** The warranty of fitness for particular purpose is applied when 1) the seller knows of the particular purpose; and 2) the buyer is relying upon seller's skill or judgment to select the appropriate goods. The warranty applies when the goods might be fit for their ordinary purpose without being fit for the buyer's specific purpose. For example, the warranty could apply in the case of a seller that sells solvents for cleaning equipment, if, before purchasing, the buyer asks if the product is suitable for cleaning printing presses.

The Limited Warranty Paradox. Paradoxically, most warranties that appear in contracts operate to **deprive** the buyer of rights it might otherwise have under statute or common law. For example, a limited warranty is used to express what the seller agrees to warrant. It virtually always excludes warranties of merchantability and fitness for particular purpose, as well as any express warranties that might have arisen in the transaction under common law. For this reason, according to the Magnuson-Moss Act, disclaimers of warranties must be conspicuous. Type is considered conspicuous if it is larger than other type on the page or of contrasting style or color. This is the reason most warranty disclaimers: 1) are typed in all capital letters; 2) specifically disclaim the warranties of merchantability and fitness for particular purpose; and 3) typically state that the disclaimer applies even if the buyer has mentioned its intended purpose for the goods. Also note that to be effective, a contract with a limited liability clause should include a merger clause to eliminate any express warranties that may have been made outside the contract text.

Exclusion v. Disclaimer. The words "exclusion" and "disclaimer" are sometimes used interchangeably in warranty provisions, but an important legal distinction exists between them. The word "exclusion" or "excluded" used with respect to implied warranties means that those warranties implied by law are denied entry or admission into the agreement. In other words, if implied warranties are "excluded," it means they never were part of the contract. By contrast, if the implied warranties are "disclaimed," those implied warranties were initially part of the contract but have been repudiated or rejected for some reason.

Example (Strongly Favoring Seller):

10. Limited Warranty; Exclusion of Warranties.

10.1 Limited warranty. ABC warrants that it will perform aNY services required under this agreement in a commercially reasonable manner and WILL conform in material respects with the terms of this agreement.

10.2 exclusion of warranties. All implied warranties and conditions of sale including, but not limited to, the implied warranties of merchantability and fitness for a particular purpose are expressly excluded from this agreement.

3. Limitations of Liability. Limitation of liability clauses are often included in contracts to limit one or both parties' liability either under tort law, if damage occurs as a result of negligence, or under contract law, if the contract is breached. The parties may also negotiate a limitation of liability with respect to damage incurred by either party as a result of intellectual property infringement. The point of the clause is to provide a ceiling for any liabilities that may arise, so the parties know when they enter the agreement what their maximum exposure may be. This is particularly important in situations where the fees paid are relatively small compared to the potential liability if something goes wrong.

The limitation of liability can be expressed as a dollar figure or as a sum that is calculable based on information available at the time the liability accrues. The following are typical limitation of liability clauses:

"Vendor's liability for damages to the Customer whether in contract or in tort, including negligence, gross negligence, or willful and wanton conduct, is limited to $50,000.00."

-Or-

"Vendor's liability for damages to the Customer for any cause whatsoever is limited to the sum of fees paid by Customer to Vendor during the two months before the event causing the liability."

[Note that while these two limitation of liability clauses are TYPICAL, they are not ENFORCEABLE in most jurisdictions—see "Tort Claims," below.]

The limitation of liability clause may also specifically exclude all dollar damages and provide an alternative remedy:

"I understand that liability for accurate test materials and adequate administration conditions will be limited to score correction or test retake at no additional fee. I waive rights to all further claims. ..."[3]

Tort Claims. Under the common law, the majority view is that limitations of liability (also called "exculpatory clauses") are valid and binding when a business relieves itself from its own negligence, but not for gross negligence or for willful or wanton conduct. The first two examples of typical limitation of liability clauses shown above are not valid because they include "gross negligence, or willful and wanton conduct" or damages that arise for "any cause whatsoever." Although typical, these limitation of liability clauses are not enforceable in most jurisdictions.

Breach of Contract Claims. Limitations of liability are usually intended to limit one or both parties' liability under contract law for direct or consequential losses that accrue when the contract is breached. Limitations of liability may seek to limit any or all of the following:

"indirect, special, incidental, or consequential damages, including, but not limited to, loss of profits or anticipated profits and loss of data, arising from, or in connection with, the use, delivery, performance or non-performance of any services offered under this agreement."

Limitations of liability for breach of contract claims are enforceable in most jurisdictions unless a party can prove the limitation is unconscionable or commercially unreasonable and that the party did not have the ability to reject the clause in the contract.[4] Judicial tolerance of limitations of liability clauses based on breach of contract claims reflects an underlying laissez-faire attitude: that the parties should be able to manage their business relationships as they desire.[5] Absent a public policy interest, the parties are free to agree to waive numerous and substantial rights, including the right to seek recourse if the other party breaches the contract. In fact, a contracting party may waive ALL recourse if the other party breaches the agreement, so limitations of liability are particularly useful against claims for breach of contract. Because limitations of liability waive substantial rights, could amount to an accord and satisfaction of future claims, and require a meeting of the minds, they should be stated explicitly, prominently, and unambiguously in the agreement. For example: "Vendor's liability for breach of contract or for negligence is limited to $50,000.00."

Limitations of liability are not enforceable if contrary to public policy; however, courts tend to exercise extreme caution in declaring contracts void as against public policy and only do so where there is no doubt of injury to public interests. A contract cannot be said to be contrary to public policy unless the legislature has declared it to be so, unless the contract is entered into for the purpose of doing something immoral or illegal, or unless the consideration of the contract is contrary to good morals or contrary to law. Limitation of liability clauses are sometimes prohibited by statute in certain situations.[6]

4. Indemnification Clauses. The verb "indemnify" means to reimburse someone for a loss suffered because of a third party's claim. Indemnification clauses are included in contracts where one party or both parties agree to absorb any liability or harm that the other party may incur to third parties as a result of entering into the contract. The extent of the liability may be limited or unlimited by the terms of the contract. The purpose of indemnification clauses is **to transfer** the liability from the party that incurs the liability to the party whose act or omission caused the liability. These clauses are particularly useful in situations where one party has a greater ability to control or prevent the liability from arising. For example, in a software license, the party that develops the software is in a far better position than the licensee to ensure that the software does not violate the intellectual property rights of others. But if the licensee intends to use the software to create derivative works, the licensee may be in a better position to ensure that the derivative works do not violate intellectual property rights of others.

Example:

Contractor shall indemnify and defend Company from and against all damages, losses, costs, and expenses (including reasonable attorneys' fees and other costs of litigation) that arise out of or result from any claim that any work produced by Contractor pursuant to this Agreement infringes any copyright or other intellectual property right of any third party. Company shall indemnify and defend Contractor from and against all damages, losses, costs, and expenses (including reasonable attorney's fees and other costs of litigation) that arise out of or result from any claim that any Derivative Works produced by Company pursuant to this Agreement infringe any copyright or other intellectual property right of any third party.

Unlike warranty provisions, which resolve liability between the parties for unsatisfactory performance of the contract, indemnification clauses involve liabilities due to third parties who usually have privity or some relationship with the indemnitee but do not have direct privity with the indemnitor.

Indemnification clauses may be reciprocal or unilateral. A reciprocal indemnification clause essentially states that: "I will be responsible to third parties for injuries I cause, and you will be responsible to them for injuries you cause." In a unilateral indemnification clause, only one party agrees to indemnify the other. Whether you are drafting the contract or reviewing a document prepared by opposing counsel, the indemnification clause should be at the top of your checklist in terms of assessing risk in the transaction. The liability to third parties could be enormous, sometimes even exceeding the fees earned under the contract. As a practical matter, the party with superior bargaining leverage may attempt to strong-arm business partners to create a lop-sided indemnification obligation. Even so, **the indemnification clause is only as effective as the indemnitor's ability to pay any claims.** If the potential liability is disproportionate to the compensation under the contract, it will likely be to both parties' best interests to rely upon insurance instead of indemnification to eliminate risk.

Rather than flip-flop indemnification strategy based on the client's relative bargaining position in each transaction, a lawyer should help the client develop a comprehensive indemnification policy based on the risks inherent in its industry, taking corporate risk management strategies into account. It may be advisable, if not necessary, to have a tiered approach to indemnification, based on specific levels of risk. At times, it may also be advisable to decline transactions where the potential liability under the indemnification clause is too high.

5. Liquidated Damage Clauses. Liquidated damage clauses require one party to make a specific payment to the other if certain events occur during the contract. For example, a contract may provide that if one party terminates for any reason before the specified term expires, a termination fee must be paid. While the courts are reluctant to enforce provisions that are characterized as a penalty, they will enforce liquidated damage clauses in certain instances where it can be shown that:

- the injury caused by breach is difficult or impossible to estimate;
- the stipulated sum is a reasonable preliminary estimate of the probable loss; or
- the parties specifically intended to provide for damages.[7]

Most courts will not enforce a liquidated damage clause that is essentially a penalty or is designed to coerce a party to perform by making non-performance prohibitively and unreasonably expensive. The focus of judicial scrutiny seems to be determining whether the liquidated damage clause is intended to compensate an injured party or to penalize a non-performing party.[8] Liquidated damages clauses will be enforced based on the contract law principle of just compensation but may not be used to reap a windfall.[9]

In most jurisdictions, if the parties do not attempt to estimate potential damages in advance, then any termination fee is considered to be an unenforceable penalty, regardless of whether it is called "liquidated damages" or anything else. Be sure to draft language into the contract that demonstrates explicitly that the parties have attempted to estimate damages. A liquidated damages clause is not enforceable if damages are capable of being calculated—even if the calculation is complex and costly. The clause is only enforceable if the parties are incapable of calculating damages. Note that very little margin for error exists in calculating an estimate that is *reasonable* where damages are *impossible* to calculate. A conscientious drafter will ensure that the client is properly informed that the courts may not enforce even the most skillfully drafted liquidated damages provision.

Although some lawyers and courts blur the distinction between liquidated damage clauses and limitations of liability, these two types of clauses are usually included in contracts for different purposes.[10] A limitation of liability clause is intended to set a cap on the amount of liability a party can incur under the contract for any reason, while the liquidated damage clause is usually intended to address a specific situation.

Example:

"If Client terminates this Agreement less than 36 months from the Production-Ready Date for any reason other than a material breach by ASP, Client shall immediately pay to ASP as liquidated damages and not as a penalty a termination fee equal to the average of the three preceding months' total fees times the number of months remaining under this Agreement. Client acknowledges and agrees that ASP's pricing for this Agreement is based upon a term of no less than 36 months, and this termination fee is a genuine estimate of ASP's damages for Client's early termination of this Agreement. The termination fee is reasonable in light of the harm that will be caused by early termination, the difficulty of proving the extent of monetary loss, and the inconvenience of otherwise obtaining an adequate remedy at law. The termination fee is in addition to and not in lieu of any transaction fees incurred before termination."

6. Term and Termination Provisions. Most contracts contain a section called "Term and Termination," or something similar. The specific provisions included in term and termination sections vary based upon the particulars of the transaction and the parties' negotiations. Term and termination sections can be used: 1) to specify the duration of the contract; 2) to state how the contract can be terminated; and 3) to state what each party's responsibility is following termination. Term and termination provisions can also be used strategically to obtain a better result for your client when the contract is heavily negotiated as explained below.

The first purpose of the termination section is to establish the initial duration, or "term," of the contract. For closing documents, the term is usually relatively short, because the parties want to be able either to close the deal or move on with business as usual. For example, in merger and acquisition documents, the term is ordinarily six months or less, and may be based on whether the deal is consummated by a certain date.

Example:

If the Merger is not consummated pursuant to this Agreement on or before January 31, 2011, this Agreement may be terminated and abandoned by the parties unless their respective Boards of Directors have agreed to an extension of time in which to consummate the Merger.

For opening documents, the term is usually longer. The term of the contract may be open-ended, a definite period of time, or an initial term of a year or so with automatic renewals until terminated by the parties.

Example of open-ended term:

This Agreement is effective when signed by both parties and remains in full force and effect until terminated by either party.

Example of definite term:

The term of this Lease begins on March 6, 2010 and, unless terminated sooner as provided below, the term expires on March 5, 2020.

Example with automatic renewals:

Unless earlier terminated as provided below, this Agreement is effective as of the Effective Date and remains in full force and effect until the first anniversary of the Installation Date. After the initial term, this Agreement will be automatically renewed for successive one year periods (the initial term and all renewal terms are collectively referred to as the "Term"), subject to earlier termination as set forth in Section 9.2 of this Agreement, unless either party notifies the other in writing, on or before 90 days before the end of the then existing Term.

The next purpose of the term and termination section is to state whether, when, and how the agreement can be terminated before it expires. The termination section can be drafted to allow one party or both to terminate the Agreement, either at any time, only after a certain period of time, or only if certain events occur. For example, an executive employment agreement might specify that the employer may only terminate the agreement for "cause." The agreement would then specify what constitutes "cause" for termination. In an employment agreement, "cause" for termination is based on factors negotiated by the parties, from crimes involving "moral turpitude" to failure to meet sales objectives, but the concept of termination for "cause" is also used in other types of agreements. Although it is not as common to prohibit the employee from terminating, some employment agreements include a corresponding "good reason" provision, which states that during the term, the employee can only resign for "good reason."

Example:

This Agreement may be terminated by ABC at any time upon written notice to Consultant. This Agreement may not be terminated by Consultant before the project described in Schedule 1 is completed unless ABC breaches this

Agreement and fails to cure the breach after 30 days written notice from Consultant.

The termination section usually states how notice of termination is given from one party to the other, and, if the agreement is terminated for "cause," whether there is any right to "cure" the problem.

Term and termination sections often include provisions outlining each party's responsibilities upon termination. These responsibilities usually involve how the transaction will be concluded and may address final billing, return of confidential information, and any matters that will continue after termination.

Example:

9.   **Term and Termination.**

9.1   Term of Agreement. Unless earlier terminated as provided in this Section, this Agreement is effective as of the Effective Date and remains in full force and effect until the first anniversary of the Installation Date. After the initial term, this Agreement will automatically renew for successive one year periods (the initial term and all renewal terms are collectively referred to as the "Term"), subject to earlier termination as set forth in Section 9.2 of this Agreement, unless either party notifies the other in writing, on or before 90 days before the end of the then existing Term.

9.2   Termination. ABC may terminate this Agreement without further notice upon: (a) Client's material breach of any term of this Agreement if the breach is not remedied within 15 days from the date of written notice; or (b) immediately if Client makes an assignment for the benefit of creditors or begins any proceeding in bankruptcy, insolvency, or reorganization pursuant to bankruptcy laws, whether the proceeding is voluntary or involuntary.

9.3   Post-Termination Obligations. Upon termination of this Agreement for any reason whatsoever, ABC may immediately disable Client's access to the Software. ABC shall then prepare a final invoice for all fees incurred under Section 4 [payment terms] before the effective date of termination, and Client shall pay the invoice within 15 days of receipt. Within ten days after termination Client shall return to ABC any and all written information or manuals provided to Client by ABC and a certification signed by an officer of the Client stating that all written information or manuals have been returned. Upon termination neither party shall disclose to any third party the terms and conditions of this Agreement or the reason it was terminated.

9.4 *Survival of Terms*. Upon termination or expiration of this Agreement Sections 6.1, 6.2, 7, 8, 9.3, and 10 of this Agreement will continue and survive in full force and effect. *[Note: These sections address issues that might arise after termination of the contract. In the contract this excerpt was taken from, for example, these sections referred to: (6.1) an agreement not to use the business partner's trademarks except as provided in the contract; (6.2) indemnification in the event of intellectual property infringement claims; (7) warranty terms; (8) non-disclosure of proprietary information; (9.3) post-termination obligations; and (10) boilerplate provisions like notices, entire agreement, choice of law and an arbitration clause.]*

In situations where contract terms are heavily negotiated, it is often a good strategy to table discussion of the Term and Termination section until agreement is reached as to the other performance provisions. The Term and Termination section can be used strategically to obtain a better result, especially when the client has been forced to make concessions on other terms. For example, if a commercial lessee negotiates for an expensive build-out, the lessor may negotiate for a longer lease term in order to recoup its initial costs. If a manufacturer is forced to cut its prices to obtain an exclusive contract with a particular buyer, the manufacturer may prefer a shorter term so it will be able to pursue more lucrative opportunities with other potential customers. Conversely, a buyer who negotiates a favorable purchase price may desire to lock-in a longer term.

The client's potential exposure can also be capped by including a buy-out provision in the Term and Termination section, which may provide either party—or both—an "out" if circumstances change or if the transaction doesn't work out for any reason. Celebrities, high profile executives, professional athletes, and coaches often have buy-out provisions which allow the contract to be terminated early upon payment of all or some portion of the remaining compensation due under the contract.

4.2 Understand the consequences of typical boilerplate provisions.

"Boilerplate" is a relatively new term used by lawyers to describe typical housekeeping provisions that can be used in a variety of contracts.[11]

As used by lawyers, boilerplate is not substantive, performance-based language but rather policy regarding how the contract will be interpreted and implemented. In the legal sense, boilerplate is usually a series of miscellaneous provisions collected at the end of the contract that are not usually heavily negotiated by the parties.

To non-lawyers, the term "boilerplate" may mean something slightly different, and drafters must take this distinction into account when communicating with clients. Non-lawyers often think of the performance provisions as being "boilerplate," particularly when they are using a pre-printed standard form. Non-lawyers using pre-printed forms may consider everything printed that does not have to be completed or filled in as boilerplate. For purposes of this lesson, we will consider "boilerplate" from the lawyers' perspective.

Although boilerplate is typically not heavily negotiated by the parties, it is still important to the operation of the contract and must be reviewed carefully. Careless drafters may suffer embarrassing situations where clients, taking more care than the lawyers they pay generously, read through the boilerplate only to find some other client's name mentioned in it. Boilerplate is also edited from time to time to include references to specific related agreements—for example, "This Shareholders' Agreement, the Employment Agreement, and the Confidentiality Agreement represent the entire agreement of the parties"—and if those make their way into a document from a previous contract, it may prove embarrassing if there is no related employment agreement or confidentiality agreement in the current transaction. Conversely, if there is a corresponding Stock Option Agreement that is NOT mentioned in the entire agreement clause, there may also be some red faces (and potential malpractice claims). So even if most of your attention is focused on performance provisions during negotiations, be absolutely certain to review carefully and critically the boilerplate at least once immediately before the contract is signed.

There is no reason that the boilerplate cannot be as well written as the rest of the contract! In order to ensure that boilerplate provisions are used properly, and that the proper provisions are included, drafters must understand the consequences of typical boilerplate provisions and consider whether each provision is applicable to the current transaction. It is handy to have a well-drafted collection of boilerplate terms ready to cut and paste; however, **do not automatically copy a collection of boilerplate provisions into every contract.** Instead, review the boilerplate to ensure it is necessary and applicable to the current transaction. Let's look at the purpose and consequences of some typical boilerplate provisions.

1. Entire Agreement/Integration/Merger Clause. This clause with many names states that the contract as written represents the entire, complete, and final agreement of the parties. Anything spoken or written between the parties before the contract is signed is NOT going to be included unless it appears within the "four corners" of the pages that comprise the actual contract. The clause is valuable because it prevents arguments down the road that something was left out of the document. But, the drafter must take care to ensure that: 1) this really IS the entire agreement of the parties—be sure to list all related documents, if any exist; and 2) all of the terms the client agreed to are, in fact, incorporated into the written form. For example, if certain terms are required in a request for proposal but not included in the agreement signed by the parties, those terms will not be deemed part of the contract. Conscientious drafters can protect against this by incorporating the specific terms or the request for proposal by reference in the entire agreement clause (but take care to avoid contextual ambiguity that could arise if any terms in the request for proposal conflict with the final agreement.)

Example:

15.1   Entire Agreement. This Purchase Agreement and the specifications attached as Exhibit A to the Company's request for proposal dated September 15, 2009 incorporated by reference constitute the entire agreement between the parties and supersede any prior understanding among them. No representations, arrangements, understandings or agreements relating to the subject matter exist among the parties except as expressed in this Purchase Agreement.

2. Severability/Saving Clause. This provision ensures that the rest of the contract is going to be enforceable even if a provision within the contract is determined to be invalid. For example, if a court determines that a restrictive covenant in an employment agreement is invalid, the severability clause ensures that the rest of the agreement is still enforceable. This clause is usually recommended and advantageous, but the drafter should consider whether, for some reason, the client would not want the contract to be enforceable if a certain provision is invalid. If this is the case, the drafter may need to include language that states that the entire contract is UNENFORCEABLE if that specific provision is held invalid. Also, be sure to identify WHO has authority to determine whether a provision is invalid: this is usually a court having jurisdiction but could be a party to the agreement, counsel for a party to the agreement, or an independent arbiter selected by the parties.

Example:

15.8 Severability. If any provision of this Confidentiality Agreement is determined by a court having jurisdiction to be unenforceable to any extent, the rest of that provision and of this Confidentiality Agreement will remain enforceable to the fullest extent permitted by law.

3. Assignment. This provision states whether the contract is assignable by one or both of the parties. The provision may state that the contract may not be assigned at all, that only certain rights may be assigned, that one party may assign but not the other, or that the contract may be assigned only with the prior written consent of the other party. Sometimes, the provision states that the contract may be assigned to an affiliate or subsidiary having approximately equal financial standing, or that it may be assigned to a successor in a change of control transaction. Absent this provision, most contract rights and duties are freely assignable, and your client may wind up doing business with someone they hadn't expected or desired—like a company that is financially unstable, a company with whom the client has previously had an unsatisfactory business relationship, or even a direct competitor! Under common law, however, an assignment only conveys rights unless duties are expressly included. The "successors and assigns" language should be added to impose duties on the assignee under the contract and to obligate the non-assigning party to perform for the assignee.

Example:

15.3 Assignment. The rights and obligations of Contractor are personal and may be performed only by Contractor. Contractor may not assign any rights or obligations under this Agreement to any other Person without the prior written consent of Company. Any purported assignment that does not comply with this provision is void. This Agreement is binding upon and inures to the benefit of the parties and their respective permitted successors and assigns.

4. Governing Law/Choice of Law. This provision specifies what jurisdiction's laws are going to be used to interpret, govern and enforce

---

the contract. The provision often also addresses jurisdiction—where and in what courts any dispute must be litigated. If this provision is not included in a multi-state contract, the conflicts of laws principles in each state will select the governing law. This provision is very important for at least two reasons. First, the vast majority of lawyers practicing in this country are licensed only in one state. This can be problematic when negotiating a contract across state lines. If the contract is to be governed by the laws of a jurisdiction where the drafter is not licensed, then the drafter may not be aware of any idiosyncrasies of that jurisdiction's laws. The client must either retain local counsel licensed in the jurisdiction to review the contract, or accept a degree of risk as to local practices. Second, each party desires "home field advantage" in litigation because it is time consuming and expensive to litigate from a distance, and out of state litigants sometimes perceive bias favoring the home-town party in local courts.

Both parties are going to negotiate hard for the law of their jurisdiction to govern. Unfortunately, there are few compromises, and the party with superior bargaining leverage usually wins. Possible compromises are: 1) leave out the governing law clause, roll the dice and let the courts decide whose law governs based on conflicts of laws principals; 2) to discourage litigation, have the law of one party's jurisdiction control in claims brought by the other party, and vice versa; or 3) pick the law of a neutral site; Delaware is a common corporate haven, particularly if either party is incorporated there, or you can choose a jurisdiction where the subject matter of the transaction has been well defined, such as New York for banking and finance matters. But beware that courts may ignore the choice of law provision, especially if there is no nexus at all to the jurisdiction chosen.

The phrase "without giving effect to its conflicts of law principles" should be added to prevent a *renvoi*, which is a form of circular logic where the laws of each state point to the other.

Example:

15.2 Governing Law. This Merger Agreement must be governed and construed exclusively by its terms and by the laws of the State of Delaware, without giving effect to its conflicts of laws provisions. The parties submit to the jurisdiction of the federal and state courts located within the State of Delaware.

Components of a Contract

5. Notice. This provision gives the ground rules for how any legal notification required under the contract is properly given and received. For example, a warranty provision may state that the buyer has to "notify" the seller within 10 days if the goods are defective, and that the seller has 10 days to correct them. The notice provision specifies:

1) how the buyer can properly give notice—i.e., does notice have to be given by U.S. mail, FedEx, fax, email, or personal delivery?;

2) how the days for giving notice are counted—i.e, is notice deemed to be given on the day the buyer deposits a letter in the mail or when it is delivered into the seller's offices?;

3) how the seller can properly receive notice—i.e., where and in what format is seller entitled to receive notice?; and

4) when the seller is deemed to have received notice—i.e., is notice deemed received when it is deposited in the mail or when it is actually received?

The provision should either include the appropriate addresses for notice for both parties, or reference where this information should be found. Notice provisions almost always come into play at the earliest stages of a dispute, so they must be drafted and followed with care.

Example:

15.14 Notices. (a) Means of Delivering Notice; Effectiveness. A party may give notice or other communications required or permitted to be given under this Operating Agreement in writing, signed by the notifying party. The notice must specify the section of this Operating Agreement pursuant to which it is given. Notice is deemed given on the date of delivery if (i) delivered in person; or (ii) sent by same day or overnight courier service; or (iii) sent by certified or registered United States Mail, return receipt requested, postage and charges prepaid. Notice given to a Member must be sent to the Member at the address of the Member as reflected on the Company's books and records. Notice given to the Company must be sent to the Company at the following address:

_____

_____

_____

Notice is deemed to have been received: (i) on the date of delivery if delivered in person; (ii) on the first business day after the date of delivery

---

if sent by same day or overnight courier service; or (iii) on the third business day after the date of mailing, if sent by certified or registered United States Mail, return receipt requested, postage and charges prepaid. The time period in which a response to notice must be given, or action must be taken with respect to that notice, will begin to run from the date it was received by the addressee. If the addressee rejects or refuses to accept delivery, or if delivery fails as a result of the addressee's changed address for which notice was not given to the Company as provided above, the addressee will be deemed to have received notice on the date delivery was attempted.

(b) **Change of Address.** Each party may change its address for notice, election, and other communications from time to time by notifying the Company of the new address in the manner provided above for giving notice.

(c) **Calculation of Time Periods.** In calculating time periods for notice, when a period of time measured in days, weeks, months, years, or other measurement of time is prescribed for the exercise of any privilege or the discharge of any duty, the first day will not be counted but the last day will be counted.

6. Force Majeure. This provision states what will happen if one of the parties is unable to perform as a result of an act of God, riot, strike, government action, or war—generally, events that cannot be anticipated or controlled when the contract is written. The provision may state that the contract is <u>temporarily</u> suspended, or that it is <u>terminated</u> if the event of force majeure continues for a prescribed period of time. The most common exception negotiated in force majeure clauses is that a party may not suspend the obligation to make timely payments even if a force majeure event occurs.

Example:

15.4 <u>Force Majeure</u>. Neither party is liable for failure to perform (except with respect to payment obligations) solely caused by:

- unavoidable casualty,
- delays in delivery of materials,
- embargoes,
- government orders,
- acts of civil or military authorities,
- acts by common carriers,

- emergency conditions (including weather conditions) incompatible with safety or good quality workmanship, or

- any similar unforeseen event that renders performance commercially implausible.

If an event of Force Majeure occurs, the party injured by the other's inability to perform may elect one of the following remedies: (a) to terminate this Agreement in whole or in part; or (b) to suspend the Agreement, in whole or part, for the duration of the Force Majeure circumstances. The party experiencing the Force Majeure circumstances shall cooperate with and assist the injured party in all reasonable ways to minimize the impact of Force Majeure on the injured party, which may include locating and arranging substitute services if necessary.

7. Amendment/Modification. This provision states that any changes, amendments, or modifications to the written contract must also be in writing. The purpose of this provision is to avoid "he said/she said"-type arguments that the parties have somehow amended the contract orally. Usually, the provision will require the signatures of both parties, or at least the party against whom enforcement is sought, on a writing that explains the changes being made.

Example:

15.13 Amendments. Any amendment to this Operating Agreement must be made in writing and signed by all Members.

8. Waiver/No Waiver. This provision allows one party to overlook a breach by the other party without entirely giving up the right to require strict performance of the breached provision or the entire contract in the future.

Example:

15.6 Waivers. If either party does not seek compensation for breach or insist upon strict performance of any covenant or condition of this Lease Agreement, that party is not prevented from seeking compensation or insisting upon strict performance for a future breach of the same or another provision.

9. Survival. This provision allows certain terms within the contract to continue in force and effect after the contract has been performed or terminated. For example, a contract that provides for the purchase and sale of a large piece of equipment will be completely performed when the equipment has been delivered and installed by the seller and paid for by the buyer. Even though the contract has been performed, the duration of the warranty might be 60 months, which would extend beyond the date of discharge of the contract by performance. The survival clause would state that the warranty terms survive the discharge of the agreement so the warranty could still be enforced by the buyer for the duration of the warranty period. In addition to warranties, it may be desirable that other provisions continue in force and effect for issues that arise after discharge, such as indemnification obligations, confidentiality and restrictive covenants, post-termination obligations, choice of law, and alternative dispute resolution provisions. Before drafting the survival provision, take the time to review the document and consider which provisions should remain in force after discharge. Be sure these are listed in the survival provision.

Example:

Survival of Terms. Upon discharge of this Agreement, Sections 6.1, 6.2, 7, 8, 9.3, and 10 of these General Terms continue and survive in full force and effect.[12]

10. Captions and Headings. Captions and headings should be used liberally in contracts to help the audience identify what information will be found in each section or paragraph. Sometimes, drafters include a boilerplate provision stating that the captions and headings may not be construed as having any meaning.

Example:

15.5 <u>Headings</u>. The headings, titles and captions in this Consulting Agreement are inserted for convenience only and are in no way intended to describe, interpret, define, or limit the scope, extent or intent of this Consulting Agreement or any provision of it.

Besides being illogical, this practice comes under vicious attack from legal drafting scholars, who argue that:

"This should be regarded as an open admission that the drafter is either too lazy to find the proper words to describe a collection of provisions or lacks the linguistic competence to do so."[13]

Ouch! Whether you agree or disagree that captions and headings could or should properly describe a collection of provisions, bear in mind that opposing counsel will gleefully quote this reference if the issue ever comes to fruition. So as not to be considered lazy or lacking,

---

Components of a Contract

drafters should avoid wasting time with this type of provision, and instead, focus on making captions and headings more descriptive.

11. Counterparts. This provision allows each party to sign a separate copy of the signature page, so that all the copies assembled together would contain all of the necessary signatures. The provision is especially useful when the parties are in different locations at closing and desire to sign the document simultaneously, but the provision is unnecessary when the parties are together or the contract otherwise provides that it takes effect when the last party signs.

Example:

15.11 Counterparts. This Operating Agreement may be executed in counterparts, each of which may be deemed an original but all of which constitute one and the same instrument.

Exercise 4.2:

Which of these boilerplate provisions from a limited liability company operating agreement would NOT be appropriate in a software license agreement? What changes would need to be made in the defined terms used?

ARTICLE XV <u>MISCELLANEOUS PROVISIONS</u>

15.1 <u>Entire Agreement</u>. This Operating Agreement constitutes the entire agreement between the parties and supersedes any prior understanding or agreement among them respecting the subject matter included in this Operating Agreement. No representations, arrangements, understandings or agreements relating to the subject matter, oral or written, exist among the parties except as expressed in this Operating Agreement.

15.2 <u>Application of Georgia Law</u>. This Operating Agreement must be governed and construed exclusively by its terms and by the laws of the State of Georgia.

15.3 <u>Execution of Additional Instruments</u>. Each Member must execute in a timely fashion any other instruments deemed necessary by the Company to comply with any applicable laws, rules, or regulations or necessary to effectuate the purposes of the Company and this Operating Agreement.

15.4 <u>Construction</u>. Whenever the singular number is used in this Operating Agreement and when required by the context, the same includes the plural and vice versa, and the masculine gender include the feminine and the neuter genders and vice versa.

15.5 Headings. The headings, titles and captions in this Operating Agreement are inserted for convenience only and are in no way intended to describe, interpret, define, or limit the scope, extent or intent of this Operating Agreement or any provision of it.

15.6 Waivers. If either party fails to seek redress for breach of or to insist upon the strict performance of any covenant or condition of this Operating Agreement, that party is not prevented from seeking redress or insisting upon strict performance for a future breach of the same or another provision.

15.7 Rights and Remedies Cumulative. The rights and remedies provided by this Operating Agreement are cumulative and the use of any one right or remedy by any party does not preclude or waive the right to use any or all other remedies. The rights and remedies provided in this Operating Agreement are given in addition to any other rights the parties may have by law, statute, ordinance or otherwise.

15.8 Severability. If any provision of this Operating Agreement or the application of the provision to any person or circumstance is invalid, illegal or unenforceable to any extent, the remainder of this Operating Agreement and the application of the provision will not be affected and will be enforceable to the fullest extent permitted by law.

15.9 Heirs, Successors and Assigns. Each of the covenants, terms, provisions, and agreements contained in this Operating Agreement are binding upon and inure to the benefit of the parties and, to the extent permitted by this Operating Agreement, their respective heirs, legal representatives, successors and assigns.

15.10 Creditors. None of the provisions of this Operating Agreement are for the benefit of or enforceable by any creditors of the Company.

15.11 Counterparts. This Operating Agreement may be executed in counterparts, each of which may be deemed an original but all of which constitute one and the same instrument.

15.12 Copies. One or more copies of this Operating Agreement may be executed but it is not necessary, in proving that this Operating Agreement exists, to provide more than one original copy.

15.13 Amendments. Any amendment to this Operating Agreement must be made in writing and signed by all Members.

15.14 Notices.

(a) Means of Delivering Notice; Effectiveness. All notices, offers, acceptances and other communications required or permitted to be given to any Member under this Operating Agreement must be in writing signed by the party making the same, must specify the section of this Operating

Agreement pursuant to which it is given, and will be deemed given on the date of delivery if (i) delivered in person; or (ii) sent by same day or overnight courier service; or (iii) sent by certified or registered United States Mail, return receipt requested, postage and charges prepaid, if sent to a Member, at the address of the Member as reflected on the Company's books and records, and if sent to the Company, to:

_____

_____

_____

and such notice will be deemed to have been received (i) on the date of delivery if delivered in person; or (ii) on the first business day after the date of delivery if sent by same day or overnight courier service; or (iii) on the third business day after the date of mailing, if sent by certified or registered United States Mail, return receipt requested, postage and charges prepaid. The time period in which a response to any such notice must be given, or any action taken with respect to it, however, will commence to run from the date of receipt by the addressee. Rejection, failure, or refusal to accept delivery or the inability to deliver because of changed address of which notice was not given will be deemed to constitute receipt of the notice by the addressee.

(b) Change of Address. Each party may change her address for notice, election, and other communication from time to time by notifying the Company of the new address in the manner provided for giving notice in this Agreement.

(c) Calculation of Time Periods. In calculating time periods for notice, when a period of time measured in days, weeks, months, years, or other measurement of time is prescribed for the exercise of any privilege or the discharge of any duty, the first day will not be counted but the last day will be counted.

15.16 Tax Matters Person. John B. Doe, a Member, is designated the "tax matters partner" (within the meaning of Code Section 6231(a)(7) of the Company (the "Tax Matters Person"), as provided in Treasury Regulations pursuant to Code Section 6221 et.seq. If John B. Doe is no longer a Member, then the Tax Matters Person will be another Member designated by the Members by a Majority Vote. The Tax Matters Person will represent the Company (at the expense of the Company) in connection with all examinations of the affairs of the Company by any foreign, federal, state, or local tax authorities, including any resulting administrative and judicial proceedings relating to the determination of items of income, deduction, allocation and credit of the Company and the Members, and to expend funds of the Company for associated professional services and costs. All

Tax Decisions will be made by the holders of a Majority in Interest in their sole discretion.

15.17 Arbitration. Any dispute, controversy or claim arising out of or in connection with, or relating to, this Operating Agreement or any breach or alleged breach hereof will, upon the request of any party involved, be submitted to, and settled by, arbitration in the City of Atlanta, State of Georgia, pursuant to the commercial arbitration rules then in effect of the American Arbitration Association (or at any time or at any other place or under any other form of arbitration mutually acceptable to the parties so involved). Any award rendered will be final and conclusive upon the parties and a judgment thereon may be entered in the highest court of the forum, state or federal, having jurisdiction. The expenses of the arbitration will be borne equally by the parties to the arbitration, but each party must pay for and bear the cost of its own experts, evidence and counsel's fees. Even so, any award may, in the discretion of the arbitrator(s), include the cost of a party's counsel if the arbitrator expressly determines that the party against whom such award is entered has caused the dispute, controversy or claim to be submitted to arbitration in bad faith.

15.18. Determination of Matters Not Provided for in this Operating Agreement. The Members will decide any questions arising with respect to the Company and this Operating Agreement that are not specifically or expressly provided for in this Operating Agreement.

15.19 No Action for Partition. No Member has any right to maintain any action for partition with respect to the Property of the Company.

NOTES

1. CHARLES M. FOX, WORKING WITH CONTRACTS: WHAT LAW SCHOOL DOESN'T TEACH YOU, 9 (2002).

2. Note that while a representation regarding good standing may seem like an insignificant formality, it actually has great significance and should be carefully verified by both parties to the transaction. If a corporation is not in good standing, the Secretary of State will not accept any filings on its behalf, which means the documents effecting the acquisition cannot be filed and the transaction cannot be formally completed.

3. This particular provision was at issue in Harris v. National Evaluation System, Inc., 719 F. Supp. 1081 (N.D. Ga. 1989); Affirmed, 900 F. 2d 266 (1990).

4. Some jurisdictions, however, treat a limitation of liability clause as a liquidated damage provision. See e.g., Connecticut: Mattegat v. Klopfenstein, 717 A. 2d 276 (1998), and Ohio: Samson Sales, Inc. v.

Honeywell, Inc., 465 N.E.2d 392 (1984). See discussion of liquidated damage provisions in this Section.

5. WILLISTON ON CONTRACTS, § 65.10.

6. For example, in Georgia, limitation of liability clauses are not permitted in contracts for construction or repair, or in leases involving a landlord-tenant relationship with regard to a dwelling. Country Club Apartments v. Scott, 246 Ga. 443; 271 S.E. 2d 841 (1980).

7. Note that several jurisdictions consider the intention of the parties to be irrelevant, and for opposite reasons. Some jurisdictions apply a 2-prong test (by simply omitting the 3rd prong shown above) and will ENFORCE the clause regardless of the parties' intentions, while other jurisdictions will NOT ENFORCE the clause regardless of the parties' intentions. See WILLISTON ON CONTRACTS, §65.1 et seq.

8. Restatement (2d) of Contracts, § 356 Comment (a).

9. JKC Holding Co., LLC v. Washington Sports Ventures, 264 F. 3d 459 (4th Cir. 2001), applying New York law.

10. See Nahra v. Honeywell, Inc., 892 F. Supp 962 (N.D. Ohio 1995), discussing the distinctions between these types of clauses and noting the tendency of lawyers and judges to blur them.

11. Bryan Garner indicates that the phrase was first coined in the legal sense in 1956. SEE BRYAN A. GARNER, A DICTIONARY OF MODERN LEGAL USAGE, 112 (2nd Ed. 2001).

12. See the sample termination provision on page 53 for an explanation of which sections are referenced in the survival clause.

13. THOMAS R. HAGGARD AND GEORGE KUNEY, LEGAL DRAFTING: PROCESS, TECHNIQUES, AND EXERCISES, 235 (3d 2007).

5

Understand the Transaction

Objective of this Lesson: To explain what it means, and why it is necessary, to have a complete understanding of the transaction.

Key Techniques:
- Have a complete understanding of the proposed transaction.
- Gather data effectively.
- Divide, classify, and arrange information.
- Organize documents logically.

5.1 Have a complete understanding of the proposed transaction.

As simple as it sounds, having a complete understanding of the subject matter of the proposed transaction will ultimately save more time than all other drafting techniques put together. Too often, lawyers begin drafting the document without having a clue what the client intends to accomplish or how the transaction relates to the client's long-term objectives. A lawyer who completely understands the transaction will save hours needlessly incurred "spinning wheels" or "chasing rabbits" and in revising documents that failed to capture the essence of the parties' agreement. In fact, one of the most frequent complaints clients have about the lawyers that represent them is that written documents often do not bear any resemblance to the parties' agreement.

The preparation stage of legal drafting includes gathering and analyzing information; perceiving the relationship of one circumstance to another; evaluating the relative importance and priority of the information in terms of the client's goals; and last, but not least, planning to present the information logically.[1] Preparation involves sifting through the trees to find the proverbial forest, which in turn reveals the proper focus of the document. One legal drafting scholar noted that: "Only when you yourself clearly see what is central or significant can you get your reader to focus on these points, instead of dispersing his attention over a mass of details in which nothing stands out."[2] In other words, muddled understanding almost always yields muddled language.

Before you begin drafting, invest time to understand the particulars of the transaction. Interview the client to be sure you understand all the facts. Research applicable law to understand potential legal issues presented. Learn industry customs, jargon, and usage applicable to the transaction. Review documents from similar previous transactions to gain insight as to what provisions should be included. Understand how the current transaction fits into the client's long-term plans.

The objective of being well-informed is not just a theoretical platitude; it is required of lawyers under the Model Rules. The comment to Rule 1.1 addresses thoroughness and preparation, and states that:

> "Competent handling of a particular matter **includes inquiry into and analysis of the factual and legal elements of the problem**, and use of methods and procedures meeting the standards of competent practitioners. It also includes **adequate preparation**. The required attention and preparation are determined in part by what is at stake; major litigation and complex transactions ordinarily require more elaborate treatment than matters of lesser consequence."

Lawyers who draft legal documents without being fully informed of the client's objectives and circumstances have not fulfilled their responsibility to their clients under the Model Rules of Professional Conduct. The maximum penalty for a violation of Rule 1.1 is disbarment—reason enough to take the responsibility seriously.

Ethics Discussion Questions

1. In a complex transaction, how much is "enough" legal advice regarding the risks the client is undertaking in a particular transaction? What is a matter of "lesser consequence," and is this determined from the lawyer's perspective or the client's? Is the discussion over at the point the informed client is willing to accept the risk?

2. Should you [always? sometimes? never?] attempt to restructure the business terms of a transaction if you believe the terms are disadvantageous to the client?

3. If your client has agreed in principle to the business terms of a transaction, but the other party's lawyer refuses to accept the agreed upon terms, what is your duty to your client, and how do you perform it?

4. If you observe that opposing counsel has not fulfilled the requirements of Rule 1.1—Competence, what is your obligation to the Bar under Rule 8.3?

Model Rules Applicable to this Lesson

RULE 1.1 COMPETENCE

A lawyer shall provide competent representation to a client. Competent representation as used in this Rule means that a lawyer shall not handle a matter which the lawyer knows or should know to be beyond the lawyer's level of competence without associating another lawyer who the original lawyer reasonably believes to be competent to handle the matter in question. Competence requires the legal knowledge, skill, thoroughness and preparation reasonably necessary for the representation.

The maximum penalty for a violation of this Rule is disbarment.

Comments

Legal Knowledge and Skill

[1A] The purpose of these rules is not to give rise to a cause of action nor to create a presumption that a legal duty has been breached. These Rules are designed to provide guidance to lawyers and to provide a structure for regulating conduct through disciplinary agencies. They are not designed to be a basis for civil liability.

[1B] In determining whether a lawyer employs the requisite knowledge and skill in a particular matter, relevant factors include the relative complexity and specialized nature of the matter, the lawyer's general experience, the lawyer's training and experience in the field in question, the preparation and study the lawyer is able to give the matter and whether it is feasible to refer the matter to, or associate or consult with, a lawyer of established competence in the field in question. In many instances, the required proficiency is that of a general practitioner. Expertise in a particular field of law may be required in some circumstances.

[2] A lawyer need not necessarily have special training or prior experience to handle legal problems of a type with which the lawyer is unfamiliar. A newly admitted lawyer can be as competent as a practitioner with long experience. Some important legal skills, such as the analysis of precedent, the evaluation of evidence and legal drafting, are required in all legal problems. Perhaps the most fundamental legal skill consists of determining what kind of legal problems a situation may involve, a skill that necessarily transcends any particular specialized knowledge. A lawyer can provide adequate representation in a wholly novel field through necessary study. Competent representation can also be provided through the association of a lawyer of established competence in the field in question.

[3] In an emergency a lawyer may give advice or assistance in a matter in which the lawyer does not have the skill ordinarily required where referral to or consultation or association with another lawyer would be impractical. Even in an emergency, however, assistance should be limited to that reasonably necessary in the circumstances, for ill-considered action under emergency conditions can jeopardize the client's interest.

[4] A lawyer may accept representation where the requisite level of competence can be achieved by reasonable preparation. This applies as well to a lawyer who is appointed as counsel for an unrepresented person subject to *Rule 6.2: Accepting Appointments.*

Thoroughness and Preparation

[5] Competent handling of a particular matter includes inquiry into and analysis of the factual and legal elements of the problem, and use of methods and procedures meeting the standards of competent practitioners. It also includes adequate preparation. The required attention and preparation are determined in part by what is at stake; major litigation and complex

transactions ordinarily require more elaborate treatment than matters of lesser consequence.

Maintaining Competence

[6] To maintain the requisite knowledge and skill, a lawyer should engage in continuing study and education.

RULE 8.3 REPORTING PROFESSIONAL MISCONDUCT

(a) A lawyer having knowledge that another lawyer has committed a violation of the Model Rules of Professional Conduct that raises a substantial question as to that lawyer's honesty, trustworthiness or fitness as a lawyer in other respects, should inform the appropriate professional authority.

(b) A lawyer having knowledge that a judge has committed a violation of applicable rules of judicial conduct that raises a substantial question as to the judge's fitness for office should inform the appropriate authority.

There is no disciplinary penalty for a violation of this Rule.

Comment

[1] Self-regulation of the legal profession requires that members of the profession initiate disciplinary investigations when they know of a violation of the Model Rules of Professional Conduct. Lawyers have a similar obligation with respect to judicial misconduct. An apparently isolated violation may indicate a pattern of misconduct that only a disciplinary investigation can uncover. Reporting a violation is especially important where the victim is unlikely to discover the offense.

5.2 Gather Data Effectively.

Before lawyers can intelligently draft contracts, they must know all the facts concerning the proposed transaction. Unfortunately, clients seldom have a clear understanding of how to structure the transaction they are contemplating, or even what information is relevant to it. The client usually has a vague idea in mind but has not thought about the particulars as to how the transaction will actually be implemented. For example, a client that sells pet products may request that you draw up a contract so Ms. Jones, who lives in Alaska, can sell dog houses there, but the client likely will not have considered whether Ms. Jones should be hired as an employee, an independent contractor, a sales representative, a value-added reseller, or a distributor. The lawyer must gather the necessary information to help the client structure the deal, while ensuring that the arrangement complies with applicable labor and tax laws.

Often, in fact, clients have little patience with the legal issues surrounding what they invariably believe will be a simple deal where nothing can go wrong. It is usually up to the drafter to identify and elicit the information necessary to document the transaction successfully.

Whether your "client" is the senior partner giving an assignment, a fellow employee of a corporate law department, or a client in the traditional sense, the best way to gather information is with a personal conversation. The personal conversation can take place by telephone or in a face-to-face interview. Although lawyers usually have impressive offices and conference rooms, if you are working with a "client" in the traditional sense you will gather far more information by meeting at the client's place of business. It is much easier to understand the client's business when you actually see it, and a better understanding will help you create better language to protect and advance the client's interests. As the representation evolves and you begin to grasp the inner workings of their business, interviews can be conducted by telephone or even email but it is still a good idea to meet at the client's offices from time to time to cultivate the relationship and observe any changes that might open opportunities to provide additional legal services.

The drafter should start the interview with the basic journalistic questions—who, what, when, where, how, and why—to elicit the information in a logical manner. Some form books provide checklists, but conscientious drafters usually want to use them merely as a jumping-off point to develop their own checklists to prompt questions and to structure the initial interview.

WHO:

- Parties, names and addresses, including formal legal names of business entities according to Secretary of State records
- General historical information—has the client previously done business with this person or entity? Was the relationship satisfactory?

- Who is authorized to transact business for each party? Who has legal authority to negotiate, sign, and bind?
- Is there anything significant or unique about the business partner—for example, is this the ONLY supplier of a key ingredient or software?
- Are both parties "merchants" for purposes of UCC transactions?
- Do the parties have legal capacity to contract?
- Is either party bound by a previous agreement that would preclude full performance of the contemplated transaction?
- Who will own any intellectual property involved in the transaction, particularly after termination?

WHAT:

- What is the subject matter of the transaction—the assets, goods, or services to be acquired?
- What is each party required to perform, and what is the measure of satisfactory performance?
- What does the client assume WILL happen? What does the client assume WILL NOT happen?
- What risks does the client anticipate?
- What is the financial basis of the transaction? What fees and expenses are involved?
- What should happen if the contract is breached?
- What are the client's concerns about the proposed transaction?

WHEN:

- When is the contract to be performed? Is the time of performance essential to the contract?
- When will possession, title and delivery take place?
- What is the duration of the contract? What happens when the contract is terminated?
- When is payment to be made?

WHERE:
- Where will the contract be performed?
- Where are deliveries made?
- Is the contract location specific?

HOW:
- How are the goals of this transaction going to be achieved?
- What are the different steps or milestones for delivery?
- What are the mechanics of getting from the concept to the implementation of the transaction?

WHY:
- Why is the client interested in this transaction?
- How does this transaction fit into the client's long range plans?
- Is this transaction complete of itself or part of a larger series?

Exercise 5.2:

What are some questions you would include in a checklist for:
1. A commercial lease agreement?
2. A partnership agreement?

5.3 Divide, Classify, Arrange.

After the drafter has a good understanding of the legal framework for the proposed transaction and has gathered the facts, the next step is to divide, classify, and arrange the information in a logical manner. Excellent drafting begins with the audience in mind. Contracts are not intended to be read from start to finish, but rather to be consulted from time to time as information is needed. The art of legal drafting involves arranging the information within the contract in a way that is most useful to the audience.

1. Divide. First, the drafter must identify a logical manner for dividing the information based upon who is going to use the contract and how. Division involves creating a logical scheme for the location of each piece of information within the contract. Division schemes differ from contract to contract, based on what is most important to the parties in each transaction. The division scheme as a whole: 1) should encompass all the parts; 2) should be logically consistent; and 3) should be mutually exclusive, so a particular provision can go only in one place. For example, the provisions of an operating agreement might rationally be divided into sections addressing rights of members, economic interest holders, and managers. But a division scheme based on members, women, and people who are over 65 would violate all three rules of division schemes.

2. Classify. Classification involves determining to which division each provision belongs. To facilitate the audience's use of the contract, similar provisions should be grouped together where the user would most likely expect to find them. If the drafter has divided the topics properly, classification is easy. For this reason, if you are having trouble classifying information, it may be that your division scheme is inadequate. If the information could logically appear in more than one division, pick one and cross reference to the other if necessary.

3. Arrange. The last step is to arrange the substantive provisions logically within the contract. Generally, substantive provisions should be arranged in order of importance, but in certain circumstances another arrangement may be preferable. For example, if a contract is going to be performed in stages, it may be preferable to arrange the substantive provisions chronologically.

Exercise 5.3A: Merger Agreement

Divide, classify, and arrange the following provisions in a Merger Agreement.

1. This Agreement constitutes the entire agreement of the parties.

2. Financial information related to the Merger will be prepared according to generally accepted accounting principles.

3. At the effective time, each share of Acquired Co. will be converted into the right to receive one share of Surviving Co. Common Stock.

4. On or before the Closing Date, the parties shall cause Articles of Merger to be filed with the Secretary of State.

5. "BCC" means the New York Business Corporation Code.

6. At the effective time, each outstanding option or warrant to acquire Acquired Co. Common Stock will entitle the holder to receive the same number of shares of Surviving Co. Common Stock that the holder would have been entitled to receive of Acquired Co. Common Stock.

7. Within two business days after this Agreement is approved by Acquired Co. shareholders, Acquired Co. shall send a notice relating to dissenter's rights to its shareholders.

8. "Acquired Co." means Acquired Corporation, a Texas corporation having offices at 123 Maple Lane, Dallas, Texas 75080.

9. Surviving Co. is a corporation duly organized, validly existing, and in good standing under the laws of the State of New York.

10. Acquired Co. warrants that there are no strikes, work stoppages, grievances, or other material controversies pending or threatened against it.

11. This Agreement may be amended by action of the Boards of Directors of the parties. Any amendment must be in writing, signed by both parties.

12. This Agreement may be executed in one or more counterparts.

13. This Agreement may be terminated if the shareholders of Acquired Co. do not approve and adopt the Plan of Merger.

14. The Shareholders of Acquired Co. shall indemnify and defend Surviving Co. and its officers, directors, and employees.

15. This Agreement may be terminated by Surviving Co. if any of the conditions contained in Section X have not been satisfied in all material respects on or before the Closing Date.

16. Acquiring Co. represents and warrants that it has not employed a broker or incurred any liability for brokerage fees, commissions, or finder's fees in connection with this transaction.

17. "Effective Time" means the time on the closing date when the Merger takes effect, which is 5:00 p.m., eastern standard time.

18. Surviving Co. represents and warrants that the execution, delivery, and performance of this Agreement have been duly authorized by all necessary corporate actions.

19. The closing of the Merger will take place at the offices of Buckley & Banish, 525 Times Square, New York, New York 10036.

20. If this Agreement is terminated, it will become void and have no further effect without any liability on the part of any party.

21. This Agreement will be governed and construed according to the laws of the State of New York.

22. No party may assign its rights or obligations under this Agreement without the prior written consent of the other party.

Understand the Transaction

23. "Code" means the Internal Revenue Code of 1981.

24. Acquiring Co.'s shareholders are not obligated to indemnify Surviving Co. unless the aggregate damages exceed $75,000. *Acquired*

Exercise 5.3B: Services Agreement

Create classifications and articles and see where its best

Divide, classify, and arrange the following provisions in a Services Agreement.

25. Supplier shall not assign any right or obligation under this Agreement. *Boilerplate*

26. Supplier shall comply at its own expense with all applicable federal, state, and local laws. *Supplier's obligations*

27. Supplier shall perform the services according to the terms of this Agreement.

28. No licenses under any patents, copyrights, trademarks or other intellectual property rights are granted by Company to Supplier under this Agreement.

29. Supplier represents and warrants that the Services will be performed diligently in a first class, professional manner.

30. Supplier retains ownership of any intangible work or work products developed or produced before entering this Agreement. *IP*

31. This Agreement constitutes the entire agreement of the parties. *Boilerplate*

32. Supplier shall establish and maintain safeguards to protect customer data. *Suppliers obligations*

33. Supplier hereby assigns to Company all rights, title, and interests in and to all work developed or produced under this Agreement.

34. Supplier grants Company a non-exclusive, royalty-free license to use pre-existing works and any derivative works.

35. No specifications, drawings, models, samples, or information furnished by Supplier to Company may be deemed confidential or proprietary.

36. Supplier will submit invoices promptly upon completion of the work.

37. This Agreement will be governed by the laws of the State of California.

38. If a dispute arises out of or related to this Agreement, the parties will attempt to resolve the dispute through mediation.

39. Supplier shall maintain Worker's Compensation insurance during the term of this Agreement.

40. Supplier may not disclose the terms of this Agreement to any third party without the prior written consent of Company.

41. Supplier warrants that any goods furnished by Supplier pursuant to this Agreement will be merchantable, free from defects in design, fit for Company's particular purpose, and perform according to specifications.

42. Company may terminate this Agreement at any time by written notice to Supplier.

43. Invoices are payable 45 days after receipt.

44. Obligations of the parties, which, by their nature, would continue beyond termination, cancellation, or expiration of this Agreement will survive termination.

45. Supplier warrants that the Services will not infringe the proprietary rights of any third party.

46. Supplier warrants that it has the right, power, and authority to assign title to the work product.

47. Supplier is an independent contractor, and nothing contained in this Agreement may be deemed to create an agency relationship between Supplier and Company.

48. Supplier will bear all travel-related expenses it incurs in performing the Services.

49. All notices required under this Agreement must be given in writing and delivered by hand or by facsimile.

5.4 Organize Documents Logically.

Lawyers put the terms of a transaction in writing to memorialize the promises, rights and obligations the parties agreed to at a certain point in time. The written document primarily serves as a reference material that can be consulted from time to time as questions arise. When the parties consult the document, they rarely intend to read it from start to finish; rather, they consult specific provisions to find the information sought at the time. A well-drafted document should be arranged logically to assist the readers in finding the needed information.[3]

Most experienced transactional lawyers understand the types of provisions that should be included in a written contract. But lawyers often fail to have a clear plan for organizing topics and ideas within the document, and this problem is exacerbated as language is added from various sources. A successful drafter must understand how to organize and group ideas.

To the greatest extent possible, group all related ideas in a document together. Organize the ideas in sections from the most important to the least. Next, organize the terms within each section in logical order from the most important to the least. [4] Absent a compelling reason to arrange it otherwise, general information should precede specific; "what" should precede "how"; more frequently used provisions should appear before less; permanent provisions should appear before temporary, and provisions involving current operations should appear before future operations. Order events chronologically. Housekeeping items such as an arbitration clause and typical "boilerplate" provisions should appear last.[5]

Sometimes, careful editing will reveal that an entire section is out of order. For example, a shareholders' agreement ordinarily should not begin with a section called "Removal of the CEO," and a merger agreement should not begin with a reciprocal indemnification provision. Other times, a single sentence may be out of order, like when a stray entire agreement provision is included in the introductory paragraph of the contract. Eventually, thinking it has been omitted, someone in the drafting chain will add another entire agreement provision in the boilerplate section, resulting in contextual ambiguity as to which should control.

A term may be applicable to more than one topic within the document. For example, if a transaction provides for a termination fee, the drafter could logically include this information in both the compensation and payment section and the termination section of the document. Avoid drafting the same information into multiple sections to eliminate contextual ambiguity caused by internal inconsistency that can occur if one section is revised but not the other. Group all of the relevant information in the same section, and cross-reference as necessary to direct the reader where to find the information. Even so, strive to minimize cross-references within a document because cross-references can be distracting and confusing to readers.[6]

After the topics have been arranged in a logical order, implement a simple numbering system that is easy to follow. Avoid confusing decimal-based numbering systems, as in "1.1.1.1.2." Use no more than one decimal. Use subparts only if there are at least two corresponding concepts. Use headings and hanging indents to reveal the structure clearly, like this:

1. Concept

    1.1   Section

        (A)   Paragraph

            (1)   Subparagraph

            (2)   Subparagraph

        (B)   Paragraph

    1.2   Section

2. Concept

CASE STUDY 5.4

Do you notice any organizational problems in this excerpt from a Joint Venture Agreement between a technology company and a German investor?

ARTICLE 4 ALLOCATIONS, DISTRIBUTIONS AND OTHER FISCAL MATTERS

4.1 AUDITORS. The firm of Coopers & Lybrand is hereby designated as the initial Auditors for the JVC; Auditors shall not be changed without the approval of the Sagent Visiting Director.

4.2 INFORMATION AND ACCESS. The JVC shall keep its accounting and Tax records on Sagent's fiscal year (calendar year) basis and shall provide Sagent with financial statements (to include a balance sheet, income statement, and statement of cash flows) no less frequently than within 21 days after the end of each calendar quarter. JVC shall also provide Sagent with a personnel roster at such time, listing each employee and significant consultant of the JVC by name, position held and salary. Sagent shall have the right at any time to inspect JVC's books records and facilities and to talk with the officers, Members of the Advisory Board, employees and consultants of the JVC.

4.3 LIMITATION ON LIABILITY. In the event of termination by either party in accordance with any of the provisions of this Agreement, neither party shall be liable to the other, because of such termination for compensation, reimbursement or investments, leases or commitments in connection with the business or goodwill of Sagent or JVC. Termination shall not, however, relieve either party of obligations incurred prior to the termination.

4.4 Regardless of whether any remedy fails of its essential purpose, in no event will either party be liable to the other party for incidental, indirect, special or consequential damages, notwithstanding being aware of the possibility of such damages. Neither party's liability for any damages or claims shall exceed US $500,000 or DM 900,000 whichever amount is lower.

Comments: *Article 4 is entitled "Allocations, Distributions and Other Fiscal Matters." Anyone who uses this agreement will expect to find information about allocations and distributions here, but that information is absent in this provision. While designation of auditors (§ 4.1) and access to financial information (§ 4.2) may be properly classified as "other fiscal matters," this information should appear after allocations and distributions, given the order of importance and the heading. Section 4.3 calls itself "Limitation on Liability," but this is really a termination provision. The drafter apparently could not think of a heading for Section 4.4, which is actually a limitation on liability provision, since that heading had been previously used.*

NOTES

1. HENRY WEIBOFEN, LEGAL WRITING STYLE, 255 (1961).
2. *Id.,* at 256.
3. THOMAS R. HAGGARD AND GEORGE W. KUNEY, LEGAL DRAFTING: PROCESS, TECHNIQUES, AND EXERCISES, 189 (2d 2007).
4. *Id.*
5. REED DICKERSON, THE FUNDAMENTALS OF LEGAL DRAFTING, 90 (1986).
6. *Id.,* at 92.

6

Avoid Ambiguity

Objective of this Lesson: To define the three types of ambiguity and identify common sources of each in legal drafting.

Key Techniques:
- Strive for clarity; avoid ambiguity.
- Consider canons of construction.

6.1 Strive for Clarity; Avoid Ambiguity

Defining "Clarity," "Ambiguity," and "Vagueness." Let's begin our discussion of clarity and ambiguity by considering what these terms mean. For our purposes, "clarity" in legal drafting means that the terms of the document are understandable to the reader. A lawyer's interest in clarity is neither a frivolous pursuit nor a rhetorical exercise in semantics. Clarity is a primary goal of good legal drafting.

The antonym of clarity is "ambiguity." "Ambiguity" means that two or more different interpretations of a word or phrase are equally appropriate.[1] While lawyers sometimes claim that they intend to allow ambiguity in documents, they usually mean to allow vagueness. "Ambiguity" is not the same as "vagueness," which refers to the degree to which language is uncertain when applied to the facts.[2] Words like "reasonable," "due diligence," "best efforts," and "materially" may

---

be vague with respect to how they apply to the facts of a particular transaction, but these terms are not ambiguous. While vagueness may at times be desirable in drafting legal documents, ambiguity is always bad.

What Happens When Courts Encounter Ambiguity in Transactional Documents? In most jurisdictions, interpreting contract language is a three-step process. The **trial court** must first decide whether the contract language is ambiguous, which is a question of law. If the language is determined to be ambiguous, the **trial court** must then apply the applicable canons of construction. (See Section 6.2.) If the court is unable to resolve the ambiguity after applying the canons of construction, the jury must determine what the parties intended, but appellate courts are reluctant to accede this much power to a jury, so most cases are decided one way or the other at the appellate level.

In interpreting contracts, the court's fundamental goal is to find and give effect to the true intent of the contracting parties. Where the contract terms are clear and unambiguous, the parties' intent is to be determined from the plain meaning of the words. If the parties' intended meaning is clear, and it violates no rule of law, it will be enforced.

Who Knew What, and When? The manner of construing the ambiguous provision varies depending upon "who" knew "what." If, at formation, the parties interpreted the ambiguous term differently, three possible scenarios emerge:

- Each party interpreted the term differently, but neither was aware of the other's interpretation;
- Each party interpreted the term differently and one party (but not the other) was aware of the other party's interpretation; or
- Each party interpreted the term differently and both parties were aware of the other party's interpretation.

In the second scenario, where the parties attach different meanings to a contract term and one party is aware of the second party's meaning, or has good reason to know of it, but the converse is not true, a contract is formed and interpreted according to the second party's meaning.[3] This approach reflects the policy that one party is at fault for attaching a meaning that did not match the other party's meaning when the first party knew of the discrepancy at formation.

The problem is much more severe in the first and third scenarios, where the parties have attached different meanings and either both parties knew it or neither knew it. Both of these scenarios reflect a lack of mutual assent, and either no contract has been formed, or if the parties have agreed on other terms, a contract has been formed MINUS the disputed term. This is the worst-case scenario in terms of legal drafting, the transactional lawyer's ultimate nightmare.

Because the effect of a lack of mutual assent is so much more severe, the courts appear reluctant to so hold. Oliver Wendell Holmes explained it like this:

> **"In the case of contracts, to begin with them, it is obvious that they express the wishes not of one person but of two, and those two adversaries.** If it turns out that one meant one thing and the other another, speaking generally, the only choice possible for the legislator is either to hold both parties to the judge's interpretation of the words ..., or to allow the contract to be avoided because there has been no meeting of minds. The latter course not only would greatly enhance the difficulty of enforcing contracts against losing parties, but would run against a plain principle of justice. **For each party to a contract has notice that the other will understand his words according to the usage of the normal speaker of English under the circumstances, and therefore cannot complain if his words are taken in that sense."[4]** (emphasis added)

Although courts are reluctant to find that ambiguity exists to the point that there has been no mutual assent, it has happened. For example, Cox Broadcasting entered into an agreement with the NCAA for programming rights to certain college football games.[5] Even as the contract was signed, the parties disagreed as to whether the contract precluded the NCAA from permitting WTBS to broadcast a supplemental series of NCAA games. At the time of signing, both parties knew of the other's intended meaning. Because each party knew of the other's interpretation, the court held there was no mutual assent with respect to precluding WTBS' broadcasts, and refused to grant the injunction requested by Cox. This case highlights the drafter's responsibility to ensure that any disputed language is clarified before the contract is signed. It also highlights the litigator's responsibility to ascertain at the earliest stages of the dispute what both parties believed the provision meant when they signed the contract, because this information might significantly influence litigation strategy.

Types of Ambiguity. Drafters must be aware of the types of drafting errors that cause ambiguity and adopt deliberate, proactive methods to avoid those errors. Ambiguity can be semantic, syntactic, or contextual, meaning that ambiguity can arise in interpreting:

- a specific word;
- a phrase or sentence; or
- paragraphs or sections of a single document or overlapping provisions in multiple related documents.

Semantic Ambiguity.

Some words are ambiguous because they have multiple meanings. For example, does the word "residence" mean "abode" or "domicile?" Does the word "burglary" necessarily entail entering premises without authorization at night? Does the word "contract" refer to the terms of the agreement between the parties or the written instrument memorializing the transaction? Ambiguity that has to do with the meaning of a particular word can often be resolved by defining the term in the document.

Some words are patently ambiguous, meaning that every one knows or should know that they have different meanings. Other words are latently ambiguous, meaning that the ambiguity is only obvious when information outside the document is introduced. The most famous example of latent ambiguity is the famous old English case studied by most first year law students, Raffles v. Wichehaus,[6] involving delivery of goods via a ship called "Peerless." The latent ambiguity arose when the parties discovered that there were two ships called "Peerless" in the same harbor. Because neither party had reason to know of the other party's meaning, there was no mutual assent, and the court held that no contract had been formed.

Corbin on Contracts notes that seldom in a litigated case do the words of a contract convey one identical meaning to both parties, and it is even less likely that the words would convey the same identical meaning to both parties AND a third party or trier of fact.[7] Oliver

---

Wendell Holmes observed that, "(i)t is not true in practice (and I know of no reason why theory should disagree with the facts) a given word or even a collocation of words has one meaning and no other. A word generally has several meanings, even in a dictionary."[8] The problem is further complicated because the meanings of words tend to shift over time.[9]

Usually, the context is helpful in determining which of many different possible interpretations is intended. But this is not always the case. Some words are more inherently imprecise than others. For example:

> "ABC may not license the software to any other company **located** in the Territory."

Does the word "located" in this sentence mean:

- organized under the laws of the States included within the Territory?
- having any size or kind of office in the Territory?
- headquartered within the Territory?
- who sells or distributes in the Territory?

Each of these phrases is more specific than, and therefore preferable to, the ambiguous word "located."

Sometimes, less obviously ambiguous words have been considered to be ambiguous. For example, when is a chicken not a chicken? When is a wife not a wife? When is a dollar not a dollar? A chicken is not a chicken when one party (the buyer) means a "young chicken, suitable for broiling and frying" and the other party (the seller) believes that the term "chicken" includes "older chickens, best suited for stewing."[10] A wife is apparently not a wife if the insured is co-habitating with another woman when he purchases a life insurance policy.[11] And a dollar is not a dollar when the extrinsic evidence reveals that both parties meant a *confederate dollar* instead of a U.S. greenback.[12]

Strangely, some words in the English language have equal, opposite meanings. For example, "sanction" can mean either to approve or to penalize. The word "doctor" can refer to either an M.D. or a Ph.D., as well as a dentist, chiropractor, or veterinarian. The word "associate" can mean either a person having equal or nearly equal status or a person who is granted only partial status or privileges. The word "leased" can simultaneously refer to the lessor's grant of property rights and the lessee's receipt of them. The word "demise" may refer to a death or to a specific transfer of property. The word "children" is notoriously tricky in estate planning because of uncertainty as to whether the word is intended to include adopted children, step children, spouses of children, grandchildren, family members raised as children, etc. The word "residence" is equally deceptive in tax law because it can refer to a house, a second home, or domicile.

These cases may give the impression that lawyers need a crystal ball to determine whether a particular word will be considered ambiguous under the circumstances. In any event, these cases illustrate the need for each drafter to review every word in the contract from the perspective of a reader in bad faith.

Semantic ambiguity may arise because an otherwise un-ambiguous word is misused or used inconsistently. Although "elegant variation," the practice of using different words to entertain the reader, has its merits in other forms of writing, lawyers should carefully avoid it in legal drafting. The risk in using more than one word per meaning is that using different wording may create a presumption that a difference in meaning is intended. In interpreting contracts, the courts must endeavor to give each word meaning and may strain to find distinctions between words where none were intended. Conversely, using the same word to have many different meanings will confuse the reader as to which meaning applies to any given usage. Ambiguity that results from inconsistent usage is always avoidable. (See Section 8.1.)

Syntactic Ambiguity.

Syntactic ambiguity usually is a result of the order in which words are arranged in a sentence and can often easily be eliminated by shortening average sentence length. It can arise in something as small as the careless placement of a comma.[13] Syntactic ambiguity often involves one or more of the following errors[14] (although this list is by no means exhaustive):

1) poorly organized sentences;
2) squinting modifiers;
3) dangling or misplaced modifiers;
4) uncertain pronoun reference;

5) misplaced prepositional phrases; and

6) ambiguous conjunctions.

Squinting modifiers usually appear in the middle of a sentence or phrase. They are called "squinting modifiers" because they could be intended to modify the words before or after them. In the ph rase "charitable organizations or institutions performing educational functions," does "charitable" modify "organizations" and "institutions?"[15] Do the charitable organizations have to perform educational functions? Avoid this type of ambiguity by repeating the modifier before each word it is intended to modify or by using tabulations to show whether a modifier modifies all of the items in a list or only some of them.

In the phrase "all inventory, including but not limited to agricultural chemicals, fertilizers, and fertilizer materials sold to Debtor by the Creditor," does the phrase "sold to Debtor" apply to:

- fertilizer materials?

- agricultural chemicals, fertilizers and fertilizer materials?

- all inventory?

Based on the facts rather than the drafting, the court concluded that "sold to Debtor" applied to all inventory. The litigation could have been avoided, however, if the drafter had drafted more carefully.[16]

Dangling modifiers modify other words or phrases that do not appear in the sentence. Proofread carefully to ensure that the sentence identifies the party or item modified by each modifying word or phrase. Dangling modifiers usually appear in sentences written in passive voice. For example: "Reasoning that the evidence supported an alternative conclusion, the motion was denied." In this sentence, the motion is not doing the reasoning; the court is, but "the court" does not appear in the sentence. If this sentence is rewritten in active voice, the dangling modifier disappears: "Reasoning that the evidence supported an alternative conclusion, the court denied the motion."

Syntactic ambiguity can also result from careless use of **pronouns**, when it is uncertain to what or whom the pronoun refers. For example: "The Beneficiary and the Trustee disagree as to whether she is entitled to payment." Does "she" refer to the beneficiary or the trustee? Beware of other pronouns such as "they," "them," and "that."

Prepositional phrases can cause ambiguity, particularly if they are separated from the word they modify. To avoid ambiguity, keep prepositional phrases next to the word they modify, and limit use of multiple, successive prepositional clauses within a sentence.

> **"Excluded Information"** means any data or information that would otherwise be Confidential Information or a Trade Secret: ...

> (2) that has been independently developed and disclosed **to** the public so as to have become generally known **by** parties, **without** a breach **of** any obligation **of** confidentiality **by** any such person running directly or indirectly **to** the Company **other than** the Employee or the Company;"

> *[Note: the prepositional phrase "other than the Employee or the Company" has been separated from its object, "parties," by multiple, successive prepositional phrases, causing ambiguity as to what "other than" was intended to modify.]*

Conjunctions like "and" and "or" seem innocuous enough, but even these simple words often create ambiguity. Both words can be interpreted to mean "both" or "either." For example, in this sentence: "Retired and disabled people may apply for assistance," does a person have to be retired AND disabled to qualify for assistance, or may people who are retired and people who are disabled qualify?

Similarly, the "or" in the following sentence could signal exclusive or cumulative remedies: "If borrower fails to make a payment when due, lender may sell the collateral or assess a late fee of 5% against the past due amount." Naturally, the borrower is going to argue that the lender must choose; the lender will argue the "or" is inclusive and it may elect both remedies. Syntactic ambiguity exists because the sentence could be interpreted either way. To resolve ambiguity resulting from conjunctions, add explanatory words like "lender may *either*," "lender may exercise *one or more* of the following options," "all of the following," "together," or "people who are *both* A & B," or add "or both" as a separate option among the options listed.

A Special Word About "Only." The word "only" is a notorious troublemaker as a source of syntactic ambiguity. Placement of the

---

Avoid Ambiguity

word can change the entire meaning of a sentence. Consider how the placement of the word "only" changes the meaning of this sentence:

Only beneficiary claims that she is entitled to payment.

Beneficiary only claims that she is entitled to payment.

Beneficiary claims that only she is entitled to payment.

Beneficiary claims that she only is entitled to payment.

Beneficiary claims that she is entitled only to payment.

To avoid ambiguity, the word "only" should appear immediately before the word it is intended to modify. Beware of similar problems with nearly, simply, hardly, merely, exactly, and almost.

Contextual Ambiguity.

Contextual ambiguity usually arises from omissions or inconsistencies. If important information is omitted, the reader must supply and interpret the missing pieces, and when different readers make differing assumptions regarding the missing information, ambiguity arises. For example, a will might provide that certain property is to be distributed according to a list attached. If the list is omitted, the will could be ambiguous if the parties dispute what items of property are distributed to whom. Contextual ambiguity can also arise among related documents or parts of a document when one provision contradicts another, making it unclear which is intended to prevail. Contextual ambiguity is always avoidable. (See Lesson 12.)

Other Ways to Avoid Ambiguity. In essence, all of the techniques described in this book are methods of avoiding ambiguity.

Consider how each of these techniques attacks various sources of ambiguity:

Have a complete understanding of the proposed transaction in order to explain it clearly.

Organize the document to keep related provisions together and reduce the likelihood of contextual ambiguity that can result from inconsistent terms.

Eliminate archaic customs that are sources of confusion.

Choose language that is easy to understand.

Avoid words that are inherently imprecise.

Use words consistently throughout the document.

Eliminate unnecessary words and phrases, as they create environments where ambiguity can arise.

Use "that" and "which" correctly to identify whether the information contained in the phrase is fundamental or supplementary.

Shorten sentence length and avoid convoluted sentence structures.

Draft in active voice to identify the party that is required to act.

Avoid interruptive phrases.

Draft in parallel structure and use tabulations to clarify what it is that a modifier is modifying.

Keep overlapping provisions in related documents consistent.

Don't rely on Canons of Construction to eliminate ambiguity (for more on the Canons, see section 6.2).

Edit effectively.

Ethical Considerations in Achieving the Correct Balance Between Clarity and Vagueness. Because legal drafting seeks to direct future behavior, absolute clarity is not attainable. All circumstances that could possibly affect the outcome cannot be anticipated or addressed in a simple form, or even a 1,000-page document, and few clients can or would choose to absorb the expense associated with drafting to that level. Hence, drafters do not seek *absolute* clarity, but rather the level of clarity that satisfies the client's goals and objectives and that will satisfy the courts in an adversarial situation. Some uncertainties will have to be resolved by those who administer the document.

The preamble to the Model Rules of Professional Conduct states that, "[a]s advisor, a lawyer provides a client with an informed understanding of the client's legal rights and obligations and explains their practical implications." The comment to Rule 1.4 states that the lawyer must provide sufficient information to enable the client to participate intelligently in decisions concerning the objectives of the representation. Rule 1.2 requires a lawyer to abide by the client's decisions concerning the objectives of the representation. The question of how much clarity is desired versus how much vagueness is tolerable in a particular document depends on a fully informed client's preferences, not the lawyer's. At the same time, the Rules of Professional Conduct do not permit the lawyer to limit the scope of representation to the extent that Rule 1.1—Competence is violated. The lawyer must balance these requirements based on the facts and circumstances of each matter.

Exercise 6.1:

Underline the ambiguous language in the following sentences. (Sample answers found in Appendix A.)

1. These pages summarize the attached Franchise Agreement, the details of which will control in the event of any conflict. *Can be either of these*

2. Company may merge with, acquire, or start other businesses, which sell similar or dissimilar, competitive, or non-competitive products and services anywhere and Company may take all reasonable steps attendant to such business combinations without incurring any liability to Distributor.

3. Taxpayers who file their returns promptly receive their refunds. *either filing promptly or receiving funds promptly*

4. When distributions are made frequently no compensation is paid to the partners. *(comma needed) fix it after frequently can apply to either clause*

5. Lessee shall use the common areas only for recreation. *difficult word, can change meaning depending on where put it*

6. Shares are sold to the public only by the parent corporation.

7. Being ignorant of the law, the judge ruled that he should receive a lighter sentence. *unclear who is ignorant of the law*

8. Licensor's termination fee is included in the provisions of the first amendment to the License Agreement that was entered into on August 4. *what was entered into on 8/4*

9. Fees and expenses, which must not exceed $250, must be invoiced within 30 days.

10. Any action required or permitted to be taken at a shareholders' meeting may be taken without a meeting if all the shareholders entitled to vote on such action, or the appropriate percentage of shareholders necessary to approve the action at a meeting of the shareholders at which all shareholders entitled to vote were present and voted, sign one or more written consents.

Ethics Discussion Questions

1. How should the lawyer handle situations where the client's budget does not permit the scope of representation the lawyer deems necessary to avoid violating Rule 1.1—Competence?

2. A client insists on condensing a document to two pages, regular type, but the lawyer knows all of the issues cannot be covered adequately in this space. What should the lawyer do?

Model Rules Applicable to this Lesson:

RULE 1.2 SCOPE OF REPRESENTATION

(a) A lawyer shall abide by a client's decisions concerning the objectives of representation, subject to paragraphs (c), (d) and (e), and shall consult with the client as to the means by which they are to be pursued. A lawyer shall abide by a client's decision whether to accept an offer of settlement of a matter. In a criminal case, the lawyer shall abide by the client's decision, after consultation with the lawyer, as to a plea to be entered, whether to waive jury trial and whether the client will testify.

(b) A lawyer's representation of a client, including representation by appointment, does not constitute an endorsement of the client's political, economic, social or moral views or activities.

(c) A lawyer may limit the objectives of the representation if the client consents after consultation.

(d) A lawyer shall not counsel a client to engage in conduct that the lawyer knows is criminal or fraudulent, nor knowingly assist a client in such conduct, but a lawyer may discuss the legal consequences of any proposed course of conduct with a client and may counsel or assist a client to make a good faith effort to determine the validity, scope, meaning or application of the law.

(e) When a lawyer knows that a client expects assistance not permitted by the rules of professional conduct or other law, the lawyer shall consult with the client regarding the relevant limitations on the lawyer's conduct.

The maximum penalty for a violation of this Rule is disbarment.

Comment

Scope of Representation

[1] Both lawyer and client have authority and responsibility in the objectives and means of representation. The client has ultimate authority to determine the purposes to be served by legal representation, within the limits imposed by law and the lawyer's professional obligations.

Avoid Ambiguity

Within those limits, a client also has a right to consult with the lawyer about the means to be used in pursuing those objectives. At the same time, a lawyer is not required to pursue objectives or employ means simply because a client may wish that the lawyer do so. A clear distinction between objectives and means sometimes cannot be drawn, and in many cases the client-lawyer relationship partakes of a joint undertaking. In questions of means, the lawyer should assume responsibility for technical and legal tactical issues, but should defer to the client regarding such questions as the expense to be incurred and concern for third persons who might be adversely affected.

[2] In a case in which the client appears to be suffering mental disability, the lawyer's duty to abide by the client's decisions is to be guided by reference to *Rule 1.14: Client under a Disability.*

Independence from Client's Views or Activities

[3] Legal representation should not be denied to people who are unable to afford legal services, or whose cause is controversial or the subject of popular disapproval. By the same token, representing a client does not constitute approval of the client's views or activities.

Services Limited in Objectives or Means

[4] **The objectives or scope of services provided by a lawyer may be limited by agreement with the client or by the terms under which the lawyer's services are made available to the client. For example, a retainer may be for a specifically defined purpose.** Representation provided through a legal aid agency may be subject to limitations on the types of cases the agency handles. When a lawyer has been retained by an insurer to represent an insured, the representation may be limited to matters covered by the insurance policy. The terms upon which representation is undertaken may exclude specific objectives or means. Such limitations may include objectives or means that the lawyer regards as repugnant or imprudent.

[5] **An agreement concerning the scope of representation must accord with the Rules of Professional Conduct and other law. Thus, the client may not be asked to agree to representation so limited in scope as to violate *Rule 1.1: Competence*,** or to surrender the right to terminate the lawyer's services or the right to settle litigation that the lawyer might wish to continue. The agreement should be in writing.

Criminal, Fraudulent and Prohibited Transactions

[omitted]

RULE 1.4 COMMUNICATION

A lawyer shall explain a matter to the extent reasonably necessary to permit the client to make informed decisions regarding the representation, shall keep the client reasonably informed about the status of matters and shall promptly comply with reasonable requests for information.

The maximum penalty for a violation of this Rule is a public reprimand.

Comment

[1A] **The client should have sufficient information to participate intelligently in decisions concerning the objectives of the representation and the means by which they are to be pursued, to the extent the client is willing and able to do so.** *[Emphasis added]* For example, a lawyer negotiating on behalf of a client should provide the client with facts relevant to the matter, inform the client of communications from another party and take other reasonable steps that permit the client to make a decision regarding a serious offer from another party. A lawyer who receives from opposing counsel an offer of settlement in a civil controversy or a proffered plea bargain in a criminal case should promptly inform the client of its substance unless prior discussions with the client have left it clear that the proposal will be unacceptable. See *Rule 1.2(a): Scope of Representation*. Even when a client delegates authority to the lawyer, the client should be kept advised of the status of the matter.

[1B] The timeliness of a lawyer's communication must be judged by all of the controlling factors. "Prompt" communication with the client does not equate to "instant" communication with the client and is sufficient if reasonable under the relevant circumstances.

[2] Adequacy of communication depends in part on the kind of advice or assistance involved. For example, **in negotiations where there is time to explain a proposal, the lawyer should review all important provisions with the client before proceeding to an agreement.** *[Emphasis added]* In litigation a lawyer should explain the general strategy and prospects of success and ordinarily should consult the client on tactics that might injure or coerce others. On the other hand, a lawyer ordinarily cannot be expected to describe trial or negotiation strategy in detail. The guiding principle is that the lawyer should fulfill reasonable client expectations for information consistent with the duty to act in the client's best interests, and the client's overall requirements as to the character of representation.

Avoid Ambiguity

Rule 1.5 Fees

(a) A lawyer's fee shall be reasonable. The factors to be considered in determining the reasonableness of a fee include the following:

    (1) the time and labor required, the novelty and difficulty of the questions involved, and the skill requisite to perform the legal service properly;

    (2) the likelihood that the acceptance of the particular employment will preclude other employment by the lawyer;

    (3) the fee customarily charged in the locality for similar legal services;

    (4) the amount involved and the results obtained;

    (5) the time limitations imposed by the client or by the circumstances;

    (6) the nature and length of the professional relationship with the client;

    (7) the experience, reputation, and ability of the lawyer or lawyers performing the services; and

    (8) whether the fee is fixed or contingent.

(b) When the lawyer has not regularly represented the client, the basis or rate of the fee shall be communicated to the client, preferably in writing, before or within a reasonable time after commencing the representation.

(c) (1) A fee may be contingent on the outcome of the matter for which the service is rendered, except in a matter in which a contingent fee is prohibited by paragraph (d) or other law. A contingent fee agreement shall be in writing and shall state the method by which the fee is to be determined, including the percentage or percentages that shall accrue to the lawyer in the event of settlement, trial or appeal, litigation and other expenses to be deducted from the recovery, and whether such expenses are to be deducted before or after the contingent fee is calculated.

    (2) Upon conclusion of a contingent fee matter, the lawyer shall provide the client with a written statement stating the following:

        (i) the outcome of the matter; and,

        (ii) if there is a recovery, showing the:

            (A) remittance to the client;

            (B) the method of its determination;

            (C) the amount of the attorney fee; and

(D) if the attorney's fee is divided with another lawyer who is not a partner in or an associate of the lawyer's firm or law office, the amount of fee received by each and the manner in which the division is determined.

(d) A lawyer shall not enter into an arrangement for, charge, or collect:

(1) any fee in a domestic relations matter, the payment or amount of which is contingent upon the securing of a divorce or upon the amount of alimony or support, or property settlement in lieu thereof; or

(2) a contingent fee for representing a defendant in a criminal case.

(e) A division of a fee between lawyers who are not in the same firm may be made only if:

(1) the division is in proportion to the services performed by each lawyer or, by written agreement with the client, each lawyer assumes joint responsibility for the representation;

(2) the client is advised of the share that each lawyer is to receive and does not object to the participation of all the lawyers involved; and

(3) the total fee is reasonable.

The maximum penalty for a violation of this Rule is a public reprimand.

Comment

[3] An agreement may not be made, the terms of which might induce the lawyer improperly to curtail services for the client or perform them in a way contrary to the client's interest. For example, a lawyer should not enter into an agreement whereby services are to be provided only up to a stated amount when it is foreseeable that more extensive services probably will be required, unless the situation is adequately explained to the client. *[Emphasis added]* Otherwise, the client might have to bargain for further assistance in the midst of a proceeding or transaction. However, it is proper to define the extent of services in light of the client's ability to pay. A lawyer should not exploit a fee arrangement based primarily on hourly charges by using wasteful procedures.

6.2 Consider Canons of Construction

Be Aware of Canons but not Consumed by Them. Canons of Construction (sometimes called Canons of Interpretation or Rules of Construction) are traditional rules and principles that explain how written legal instruments are to be interpreted. The courts use the Canons to help them interpret ambiguous language in transactional documents. Some of the Canons tend to restrict language, while other Canons may broaden it. Most Canons of Construction have evolved through case law, although the Canons have been codified in some states.[17]

Several problems arise if lawyers attempt to use the Canons of Construction to streamline the legal drafting process. First, as a group, the Canons tend to be contradictory, and for every viable Canon, an equal and opposite rule of construction can be found.[18] The process of ascertaining meaning requires balancing many factors, no one of which is always conclusive. In construing language, the courts usually presume, unless circumstances indicate otherwise, that the drafter:

- used words in their normal sense;
- meant what was said;
- did not intend a contradiction; and
- intended to produce a reasonable result.

Courts typically do not apply a Canon of Construction if the result is to rebut one or more of these basic presumptions—meaning, for instance, that if the evidence shows that one of the parties clearly did not mean what the language said, the Court would not seek to interpret the language by referring to a Canon.

It is lazy and poor drafting practice to rely upon Canons of Construction in preparing legal documents because, by definition, these are the principles the courts apply when the drafter has *failed* in the quest to draft language that is clear and understandable. The lawyer who relies upon the Canons of Construction and the courts to interpret provisions is shirking responsibility and creating an inferior work product.[19]

Another problem in relying upon the Canons of Construction in drafting documents is that each legal document tends to be unique, so knowing what the court has said about specific language in a specific case is largely irrelevant to the extent that it is based on the facts and circumstances underlying the case. Rather than focusing on a court's holding in a particular case, the lawyer's objective in drafting is to determine "what particular words and phrases generally mean as a result of established usage,"[20] and this may or may not be reflected in the court's holding or in the application of a particular Canon of Construction under the circumstances.

Some Canons have evolved as a result of established usage, and while it is important to be aware of them, do not rely on them in lieu of striving to create language that does not require judicial interpretation.

Noscitur a Sociis.

Sometimes called "the mother's rule," this Canon translates into "the thing is known by its companions." *Noscitur a sociis* means that the meaning of questionable words is determined by the words that accompany them. For example, in the phrase "Crown Victoria, Camry, Accord, and Impala," the word "impala" would be construed as referencing an automobile rather than an animal because of the meaning of the accompanying words.

Ejusdem Generis.

This Canon translates into "of the same class, kind, or nature." It is similar to *noscitur a sociis*, but there is a subtle difference in that *ejusdem generis* is applied to situations where general language follows the list of items in the class. *Ejusdem generis* means that where general words follow a list of things, the general words are not construed to their widest possible extent but are interpreted as applying only to things of the same general kind or class as the other items in the list. "Common sense and experience teach that when a group of related things are specifically enumerated, the mind is focused upon that class of things, and that the addition of general terms is purposed to avoid inadvertent omission and to include like things of the same class."[21]

Ejusdem generis tells the courts how to interpret general phrases like "any other person," and "other kinds of vegetation," as shown in the examples below, but even when applying *ejusdem generis*, uncertainty abounds.

Example: Does "any sheriff, constable, peace officer, state road officer, or any other person charged with the duty of enforcement of the criminal laws of this state" include prosecuting lawyers?[22]

Example: Does "pines, firs, spruce, or other kinds of vegetation" include trees generally? Or is it limited to a certain type of tree—pine or conifer?[23]

Note that in this example, the drafter's attempt to name every possibility has resulted in ambiguity. The drafter would have been much better off to commit to a single word as recommended in Lesson 10.1 and eliminate the string of words from which the ambiguity arose.

Expressio Unius Est Exclusio Alterius.

This Canon translates roughly into "the enumeration of particular things excludes the idea of something else not mentioned."[24] For example, if certain people are mentioned as beneficiaries under a will, it may be inferred that others, not mentioned, are intended to be excluded. This Canon is of limited utility because the courts do not apply it consistently. In the will situation, for example, failure to mention someone who would otherwise naturally be an heir has in some instances been grounds to invalidate the will. The Canon is also of limited utility in that the expression of virtually anything excludes something.

Example: The sky is blue.

This does not mean that nothing else is blue even though nothing else is mentioned; nor does it mean that the sky can be no other color than blue, although no other colors are mentioned.

In some cases, the language may include items that are expressly mentioned as examples, although the list is not intended to be exhaustive. Lawyers often use the phrase "including, but not limited to" to avoid application of *noscitur a sociis, ejusdem generis,* and *expressio unius,* but this practice is only marginally successful and courts may apply these Canons to restrict the language even where this phrase appears.

Contra Proferentem.

This Canon translates roughly as "against the offerer." Used in interpreting legal documents, *contra proferentem* means that an ambiguous phrase or provision will be construed against the person who selected the language. The courts are reluctant to apply this

---

Canon when other rules or maxims of construction come into play and the evidence reveals that the parties intended a different result. For example, the "golden rule" prohibits an interpretation causing a ludicrous or unfair result. The court may choose to apply the golden rule, and ignore *contra proferentem*.

Reddendo Singula Singulis.

This Canon translates roughly into "by referring each to each." *Reddendo singula singulis* means that each item in a series of items refers to its corresponding item in a matched series. This Canon is so universally applied in modern American legal usage that few would question it.

> **Example:** My children, Stacy, Macy, and Casey, are 7, 9, and 13.

Applying *reddendo singula singulis*, from this sentence you may safely infer that Stacy is 7, Macy is 9, and Casey is 13, without the necessity of including the word "respectively" at the end of the sentence.

In Pari Materia.

This Canon means that in construing a provision of a contract, to the extent possible, all provisions relating to the same subject or having the same general purpose should be read in connection with it.

> For example, in a recent case,[25] the Second Circuit Court of Appeals was required to interpret a possible discrepancy in the following provisions of a contract:
>
> "15. All disputes concerning or arising out of this Agreement shall be referred to arbitration to the International Chamber of Commerce, New York, New York, in accordance with the rules and procedures of International Arbitration. This Agreement and the rights and obligations of the parties shall be construed in accordance with and governed by the laws of New York.
>
> 16. This Agreement shall be deemed to have been executed and delivered in New York, New York, and shall be interpreted and construed in accordance with the laws of New York, U.S.A."

The appellees argued that the choice of law provision in Section 16 required that New York laws regarding arbitration procedure should control, despite the reference in Section 15 to the rules and procedures of the ICC with respect to International Arbitration. The court rejected this argument, however, on the basis of *in pari materia*, stating that it was obliged to give full meaning and effect to all contract provisions, and that an interpretation of a contract that has the effect of rendering at least one clause superfluous or meaningless is not preferred and will be avoided if possible. In other words, in interpreting the broad choice of law language in Section 16, the court was required to take into account the intent of the parties expressed in Section 15, which meant that the rules of the ICC, rather than New York law, governed the arbitration procedure. Adopting the appellees' position would have rendered the clause in Section 15 "in accordance with the rules and procedures of International Arbitration" meaningless.

NOTES

1. REED DICKERSON, THE FUNDAMENTALS OF LEGAL DRAFTING, 33 (1986).

2. *Id.*, at 39.

3. CORBIN on Contracts, Volume 5, § 24.5 at p. 18.

4. Oliver Wendell Holmes, *The Theory of Legal Interpretations*, 12 Harv. L. Rev. 417, 419 (1898).

5. Cox Broadcasting Corp., v. National Collegiate Athletic Ass'n, 250 Ga. 391, 297 S.E. 2d 733 (1982).

6. 2 Hurl. & C. 906, 159 Eng. Rep. 375 (Ex. 1864).

7. Corbin, *supra* note 3, at p. 30-31.

8. Holmes, *supra* note 4, at p. 417.

9. "A word is not a crystal, transparent and unchanged; it is the skin of a living thought and may vary greatly in color and content according to the circumstances and the time in which it is used." Towne v. Eisner, 245 U.S. 418, 425 (1918).

10. FRIGALIMENT IMPORTING CO. V. B.N.S. INT'L SALES CORP., 190 F. Supp 116 (S.D.N.Y. 1960). Regulations of the U.S. Department of Agriculture at 7 C.F.R. §70.301 recited the various classes of chickens as being broiler or fryer, roaster, capon, stag, hen or stewing chicken or fowl, and cock or old rooster.

11. In re Soper's Estate, 196 Minn. 60, 264 N.W. 427 (1935).

12. Thorington v. Smith, 75 U.S. 1, 19 L.Ed. 361 (1868). In Magnetic Resonance Plus, Inc. v. Imaging Systems International, 273 Ga. 525 (2001), the court was called upon to determine whether the words "**prevailing party**" were ambiguous in clause requiring the non-prevailing party to pay attorney's fees. The trial court initially awarded attorney's fees but was reversed because the underlying damages award was based on lost profits, and another contractual provision shielded both parties from awards of lost

profits or special damages. Upon appeal, the "prevailing party" argued that it was still entitled to attorney's fees because it had prevailed despite the lack of monetary damages. The attorney ingeniously argued that ambiguity must exist since two courts construed the language differently. The Georgia Supreme Court disagreed, however, stating that "a contract is not ambiguous, even though difficult to construe, unless and until an application of the pertinent rules of interpretation leaves it really uncertain as to which of two or more possible meanings represents the true intention of the parties." In Greer v. IDS Life Insurance Company, 149 Ga. App. 61 (1979), the court was called upon to determine whether the word "occupation" was ambiguous where an accidental death benefit in a life insurance policy excluded coverage for poison or gas taken accidentally or voluntarily, except in the course of his **occupation.** In this case, a nightclub singer was poisoned by a defective furnace in a friend's home after performing in an out of town night club. He did not die while performing, but he died as a result of pursuing his occupation. The court declined to construe the policy language so strictly as to afford coverage only when the death occurred in the course of **employment**, stating that if the insurance company desired coverage to be more restrictive, it should have drafted accordingly.

13. *In re* Estate of Thompson, 164 NW2d 141, 147-148 (Iowa 1969). Also see Rogers Communications v. Bell Aliant, Telecom Decision 2006-45, a dispute heard by the Canadian Radio-television and Telecommunications Commission.

14. Kermit L. Dunahoo, Note, *Avoiding Inadvertent Syntactic Ambiguity in Legal Draftsmanship*, 20 Drake L. Rev., 137 (1970).

15. DICKERSON, *supra* note 1, at 110-113.

16. Similarly, in Traveler's Insurance Company v. Blakely, 255 Ga. 699 (1986), the court was called upon to construe the phrase "physicians or surgeon's services for surgical procedures and other medical care and treatment." The question presented was whether "other medical care and treatment" had to be performed by a physician or surgeon to be covered under the insurance policy. The trial court determined that this language was ambiguous and turned it over to a jury, who awarded coverage to the insured for massage treatments. On appeal, the court upheld the trial court and noted that "In construing an insurance policy, the test is not what the insurer intended its words to mean, but what a reasonable person in the position of the insured would understand them to mean. The policy should be read as a layman would read it and not as it might by analyzed by an insurance expert or an attorney."

17. For example, California Statutes, § 1303 includes the following rules of construction:

(d) A course of performance or course of dealing between the parties or usage of trade in the vocation or trade in which they are engaged or of which they are or should be aware is relevant in ascertaining the meaning of the parties' agreement, may give particular meaning to specific terms of the agreement, and may supplement or qualify the terms of the agreement. A usage of trade applicable in the place in which part of the performance under the agreement is to occur may be so utilized as to that part of the performance.

(e) Except as otherwise provided in subdivision (f), the express terms of an agreement and any applicable course of performance, course of dealing, or usage of trade must be construed whenever reasonable as consistent with each other. If such a construction is unreasonable: (1) express terms prevail over course of performance, course of dealing, and usage of trade; (2) course of performance prevails over course of dealing and usage of trade; (3) course of dealing prevails over usage of trade.

(f) Subject to Section 2209, a course of performance is relevant to show a waiver or modification of any term inconsistent with the course of performance.

(g) Evidence of a relevant usage of trade offered by one party is not admissible unless that party has given the other party notice that the court finds sufficient to prevent unfair surprise to the other party.

18. For a discussion of arguments and counterarguments with respect to applying Canons of Construction, SEE Karl Llewellyn, *Remarks on the Theory of Appellate Decision and the Rules or Canons About How Statutes Are to Be Construed*, 3 VAND. L. REV. 395, 401-06 (1950).

19. DICKERSON, *supra* note 1, at 47.

20. *Id.*, at 48

21. Heathman v. Giles, 13 Utah 368, 370, 374 P.2d 839, 840 (1962). Note that this case is an example of where the court in its holding is discussing generally established usage, rather than explaining the basis for a novel construction.

22. *Id.*, at 839. "It seems so plain that it is unnecessary to dwell on the matter that the defendants as prosecuting attorneys, although "charged with the duty of enforcement of criminal laws," are officers of such a significantly different character that they are not within the class for whom the protections of this statute was intended."

23. DICKERSON, *supra* note 1, at 49.

24. SCOTT J. BURNHAM, DRAFTING AND ANALYZING CONTRACTS 93 (3d 2003); DAVID MELLINKOFF, LEGAL WRITING: SENSE AND NONSENSE 19 (1982); Bloemer v. Turner, 281 Ky. 832, 137 S.W. 2d 387 (1939).

25. Shaw Group Inc. v. Triplefine Intern. Corp., 322 F. 3d 115 (2nd Cir. 2003).

Focus on Word Selection

> **Objective of this Lesson:** To demonstrate how semantic ambiguity can be caused, and avoided, by word choices.
>
> **Key Techniques:**
> - Choose plain language.
> - Avoid certain words in drafting.
> - Use defined terms correctly.
> - Use "that" or "which" correctly.

7.1 Choose Plain Language.

Is Plain Language At Odds With Professionalism? Simplicity is one of the characteristics of excellent legal drafting identified in Lesson 1. Although virtually all of today's legal drafting scholars recommend that lawyers should draft legal documents in plain, conversational English, few drafting techniques spark as much controversy. Despite statutory requirements that consumer contracts must be written in plain English, some lawyers argue against drafting in simple language. Let's consider some of the arguments against plain English drafting.

- **It is not possible to draft in plain English because the ideas that have to be expressed are complex.** This argument may have merit in limited circumstances, but for the most part, the complexity of language in legal documents is caused by the sentence structure rather than the ideas expressed. Complexity that is caused by the subject matter may not be avoidable, but complexity caused by syntax is.

- **Legal drafting involves terms of art for which no suitable substitutes exist.** This argument may be valid for certain legal words like merchantable, unconscionable, proximate cause, and venue, but the instances for which no plain language alternative exists are few enough to allow room for substantial improvement in the rest of the document. If terms of art are unavoidable, the drafter can still aid the reader by including an explanation of the meaning of these terms.

- **Clients demand and expect forms filled with archaic jargon.** No clients have yet been spotted *demanding* forms filled with archaic jargon and nearly incomprehensible sentence structures. It is true to some extent that clients have come *to expect* this from our profession. Many clients and non-lawyers are surprised to learn that legal documents are not required to be written in indecipherable legal lingo in order to be enforceable. The measure of a drafter's success lies in the utility of the written document to the client. Your client will be pleasantly surprised to receive a document that is clearly written, although the client may need to be reassured that documents written in plain English are, in fact, enforceable.

- **Drafting in plain English would necessitate more time explaining documents to clients.** This surprising argument seems contradictory: That lawyers would spend more time explaining *simpler* language? Yet, some lawyers have noticed that when clients understand *most* of the language in a contract or a will, they are more likely to question the provisions they don't understand. Consider the ethical requirements under Model Rule 1.4, which in Comment 2 advises that "in negotiations where there is time to explain a proposal, the lawyer should review all important provisions with the client before proceeding to an agreement." Surely less time would ultimately be incurred to explain simpler provisions than incomprehensible ones.

- **Drafting in plain English would make it harder to charge what documents are worth.** Apparently, the point of this argument is that if the client can easily read and understand the document, he or she may wonder why it costs so much to prepare it. Proponents of this argument apparently suppose that it is easier to draft in plain English than typical "lawyer language." Most lawyers rapidly discover it is a much more difficult endeavor, at least initially, to craft language that is clear, concise, and understandable to non-lawyers. Even so, as lawyers become more proficient applying these drafting techniques, they begin to save time and produce a significantly improved work product. Most informed clients will appreciate the effort and may even be willing to pay more for a document they can read and understand than one they can't. Rule 1.5 of the Model Rules of Professional Conduct states that one factor for determining the reasonableness of a fee is the skill requisite to perform the legal service properly. If plain-English drafting is a higher intellectual achievement, upon mastery of the techniques presented in this book, you should be able to *raise* your billing rates!

- **Willful obscurity is a desirable objective and a means of catching opposing counsel off guard.** This reasoning is the most dangerous of all the objections to plain English drafting. The lawyer who drafts provisions that are purposefully obscure is calculating that a court will interpret the language to mean what he or she intends but is not willing to make clear, and the consequences of miscalculating can be severe. For example, a lawyer might stuff definitions with clauses that change the direction of the provisions in which the defined term is used, hoping the opposing lawyer does not catch the misdirection. What happens if one provision is revised but not the other? Or if the form is used in a subsequent transaction by another lawyer who is unaware of the original obscurity? Willful obscurity almost always results in ambiguity, which is never desirable.

- **The meaning of language that has been litigated is fixed and sure.** The thrust of this argument is that legal drafters should maintain archaic jargon and customs because the courts have "blessed them" in prior cases. Two problems exist with this logic. First, language that has been litigated by definition is subject to two or more interpretations. Second, each transaction is unique, and the interpretation of each document depends on the facts and circumstances particular to it. So the court's holding with regard to specific language in a particular case is irrelevant except to the extent the holding reveals what particular words mean as a result of established usage.[2]

How to Draft in Plain English. The drafting techniques described in this book will help you draft language that is easier to read and understand, regardless of which side of the fence you land on with respect to the debate for or against drafting in plain English. If you are convinced that plain English drafting is a worthy objective, the first step is to eliminate words and phrases used only by lawyers. Choose simple words instead of more difficult ones. Avoid phrases like "on the ground that," "notwithstanding the foregoing," and "in the event that" and replace them with everyday English equivalents, like "because," "even so," and "if."[3] Here are more examples:

Instead of this:	Use this:
• a large number of	many
• along the lines of	like
• at the time at which	when
• by means of	by
• pursuant to the provisions of	under
• at this point in time	now
• notwithstanding the fact that	even though, although
• prior to	before
• subsequent to	after
• until such time as	until
• by reason of the fact that	because
• give rise to	cause
• due to the fact that	because
• with the result that	so that
• in consideration of the agreements herein contained, the parties hereto agree	we agree, the parties agree

- at the time   when
- during such time as   while
- for the purpose of   to
- institute   begin
- effectuate   carry out
- cease   stop
- accorded   given

Exercise 7.1:

Suggest a plain language alternative to each word or phrase.

attains the age of 21

for the duration of *during*

in the event that *if*

sufficient number of *enough*

excessive number of *too many*

under the provisions of

for the reason that *b/c*

forthwith

commence

contiguous to

is authorized to

Ethics Discussion Question

1. Given Rule 1.4, is the lawyer's duty fulfilled if the client does not understand the provisions of a written legal document he or she must sign? Is there any difference in the lawyer's responsibility with respect to documents prepared versus those that are reviewed?

7.2 Avoid These Words in Legal Drafting.

Ambiguous Words: And/or, provisos, and herein. Some commonly used words are considered inherently ambiguous and should not be used in drafting legal documents.

And/or: The Janus-faced Monstrosity. The origin of the hybrid "and/or" is uncertain although it has been involved in litigation since 1854.

The phrase is consistently condemned by courts yet many lawyers persist in using it.[4] It is inherently imprecise because the reader is unable to determine whether all items in a list are required (and), or whether any one of them is sufficient (or). Replace this taboo phrase with "or both" as in "1 or 2 or both."

Of the imprecise words discussed in this section, legal drafting scholars and judges rail most viciously against the use of "and/or," yet use of it seems to be proliferating in current practice! The six English appellate judges who first construed "and/or" came up with six different interpretations.[5] Since both "and" and "or" can be ambiguous, combining them into one term multiplies the problem exponentially. Either the transactional lawyers who use it are unaware of the wrath it engenders among scholars and judges, or they don't care. Beware! The careless drafter's foible with respect to "and/or" is the ambitious litigator's delight. Judges repeatedly express extreme displeasure over the use of "and/or":

- "We are confronted with the task of first construing "and/or," that befuddling, nameless thing, that Janus-faced verbal monstrosity, neither word nor phrase, the child of a brain of someone too lazy or too dull to express his precise meaning, or too dull to know what he did mean, now commonly used by lawyers in drafting legal documents, through carelessness or ignorance or as a cunning device to conceal rather than express meaning with a view to furthering the interests of their clients.[6]"

- "(t)he abominable invention, "and/or", is as devoid of meaning as it is incapable of classification by the rules of grammar and syntax."[7]

- "(t)hat linguistic abomination. …"[8]

- "In the matter of the use of the alternative, conjunctive phrase 'and/or,' … we take our position with that distinguished company of lawyers who have condemned its use. It is one of those inexcusable barbarisms which was sired by indolence and damned by indifference, and has no more place in legal terminology than the vernacular of Uncle Remus has in Holy Writ."[9]

- "… [we] deplore the use in contracts and statutes of that hybrid, contradictory combination, frequently as bewildering, mystifying, and perplexing as Poe's raven—or was it fiend? on the 'night's Plutonian shore.'"[10]

- "I confess I do not know what is meant by the use of the phrase 'and/or.' There is no reason why a statute, contract or legal document of any kind cannot be stated in plain English. The use of the symbol 'and/or' has been condemned by some courts and should be condemned by every court."[11]

Legal drafting scholars are just as adamant against the use of and/or:

- "The high failure rate of legal papers that depend on and/or for anything of importance should have long since eliminated it from the legal vocabulary. Yet it persists, and is widely used in legal and ordinary writings. For the writer in a hurry, for the writer content to let others solve the problems created by the writer, and/or is such a short, quick and easy way out. It has a special currency in academia, where the lure of the scientific ... gulls some into confusing the compact form of and/or with the precision of a lopsided fraction. ... If the lawyers did invent and/or, they owe it to the common language to atone, by now eliminating and/or from the legal vocabulary, and hope that the common language will follow. It is still confusing readers and costing litigants money. Anything and/or can do, ordinary English can do better."[12]

- "And/or, though undeniably clumsy, does have a specific meaning (x and/or y means x or y or both), but though the phrase saves a few words, it lends itself ... as much to ambiguity as to brevity. ... It cannot intelligibly be used to fix the occurrence of past events."[13]

- "The dwindling remnant of drafters who still defend the use of *and/or* contend that it is a concise way of saying *A or B or both*. Certainly, that is one way that it can be construed. But since there are also other ways it can be construed, the phrase remains fatally ambiguous despite their protestations."[14]

- "A device for the encouragement of mental laziness."[15]

- "The only conclusion that can be derived from the foregoing is that the field in which the term "and/or" can properly be used is a very narrow one and that even in that field the intent and meaning is left for determination, and may thus be misunderstood, or subject to an adverse or even a wrong interpretation. In view of all this uncertainty and hostility, the only safe rule to follow is not to use the expression in any legal writing, document or proceeding, under any circumstances."[16]

Surely, that's enough said on "and/or" for transactional lawyers and litigators alike!

Provided, that; provided, however: Archaic Leftovers. Provisos are consistently condemned by most legal drafting scholars as being both inherently imprecise and *prima facie* evidence of poor drafting, yet experienced lawyers carelessly continue to use them.[17]

Provisos apparently originated in England during the middle ages and were first criticized on record by Lord Coke five centuries ago. Provisos apparently derive from the latin "provistum est," which translates in English as "it is provided that."[18] Provisos were first used to introduce separate sections of statutes, which at least makes sense grammatically, because it makes sense to begin a statutory provision with "it is provided that." The correct interpretation of a proviso within a statute remains unclear, however, as evidenced by the cases construing them. For example, in 1888, the U.S. Supreme Court noted that a proviso is ordinarily used in a statute to limit the scope of the provision, but that provisos in statutes can also be interpreted as an exception, an additional requirement, a "but" or an "and."[19]

What a proviso means in a contract is unclear; hence, the inherent ambiguity in using them. Drafters use provisos to accomplish many different things, so courts are forced to interpret them on a case-by-case basis. Because provisos in contracts have been interpreted so many different ways, a drafter cannot be sure that a court would interpret a proviso as the drafter intended, or even that opposing counsel interprets it in the same way. Provisos have been held to create:

- **a condition:** The prevailing judicial view seems to be that a proviso is generally used in a contract to introduce a clause that states a condition.[20] If a "safe" use of provisos existed, this would be it.[21]

- **a duty:** Some courts have held that a proviso always implies a condition *unless* subsequent words change it to be a covenant.[22]

- **a limitation:** Provisos in contracts are sometimes interpreted to limit the scope of the preceding phrase or sentence.[23]

- **an exception:** Provisos are sometimes interpreted to carve an exception to the scope of the preceding phrase or sentence.[24]
- **an additional requirement:** Provisos are sometimes interpreted to add new requirements to the scope of the preceding phrase or sentence.[25]

Another problem with provisos is that they sometimes appear in tandem as counsel for each party seeks to alter the scope of the original provision. These inserts would best be stated as separate sentences.

Example:

(b) All reasonable fees of the Shareholder Agent and all reasonable costs, attorney's fees, and expenses incurred by the Shareholder Agent in connection with the performance of its duties hereunder shall be paid out of the Representative Escrow Fund, upon presentation by the Shareholder Agent to the Escrow Agent of an accounting of such fees, costs and expenses, which accounting is subject to Parent's reasonable agreement, provided, however, that no such claim for fees, costs and expenses shall be paid until the later of the Expiration Date or the end of the last Pending Claim Extensions, if any, to terminate; and provided, further, that in the event the Escrow Agent has received Officer's Certificate(s) from Indemnified Parties with respect to Losses that exceed the Escrow Amount, the Escrow Agent shall, subject to the provisions of Section 7.3(e) hereof, deliver to Parent out of the Representative Escrow Fund, as promptly as practicable, cash held in the Representative Escrow Fund in an amount equal to such Losses; provided, however that if such Losses are greater than the amount of cash in the Representative Escrow Fund then the Escrow Agent shall deliver to Parent the entire cash amount in the Representative Escrow Fund; and, provided, further, that, in the case of Pending Claim Extensions, on the Expiration Date the Escrow Agent shall distribute to the Escrow Contributors (and in the case of Vested Assumed Options, such options shall be released from the provisions of Section 7.3(c)) the portion of the Representative Escrow Fund that is not necessary (as determined in the preceding proviso) to satisfy such unsatisfied claims.

Provisos continue to be used simply because most transactional lawyers have never heard they should not be. Yet, provisos are almost universally condemned in books and articles on legal drafting:

- "If you look at the literature on legal drafting—and by that I mean modern legal drafting, and by that I mean post-1842 books and articles on legal drafting—you'd come away with the idea that no self-respecting drafter would ever be caught using the phrase *provided that.* You'd gather that everyone knows that provisos are horrible, horrible form. Embarrassing blemishes."[26]

- "[T]he words *provided that* are a reliable signal that the draft is not going well."[27]

- "What is left defies grammatical analysis. Provisos produce single sentences that are often hundreds of words long. Knowledgeable drafters have railed against them for years. Apart from being a grammatical abomination, "provided that" is ambiguous because it can be used variously to introduce exceptions, qualifications, conditions, and even new substantive provisions."[28]

- "[U]sing *provided that* is an imprecise way to signal the relationship between two adjoined contract provisions. A more precise alternative is always available...."[29]

Despite the nearly universal condemnation of provisos from drafting scholars, the courts grumble relatively mildly about provisos as compared to their vicious rantings with respect to the use of "and/or." The courts appear to be more than willing to interpret provisos on a case-by-case basis for lawyers who are willing to abdicate the very responsibility for which they've been engaged.

Until a court finds, as a matter of law, that provisos used in legal documents signify conditions (or some other operation), the issue remains unsettled and ripe for further review. When the issue comes up for judicial review again, scholarly authority will likely be considered. If the weight of scholarly authority on the deficiencies of provisos has been unconvincing thus far, consider this: Under the canon *contra proferentem*, the language of a contract will be construed against the drafting party. If a proviso you have written comes into litigation, opposing counsel will be able to cite countless drafting authorities who concur that the language you drafted is deficient. Those cavalier souls who continue to brandish provisos in light of overwhelming scholarly recommendations against them had best be sure their malpractice premiums have been paid.

Even if provisos were "officially" condoned, their use in legal drafting violates most, if not all, characteristics of excellent drafting (Section 1.2) and many other drafting techniques recommended in this text:

- Eliminate archaic practices (Section 3.2)
- Strive for clarity; avoid ambiguity (Section 6.1)
- Choose plain language (Section 7.1)
- Use words consistently (Section 8.1)
- Choose the correct language for the intended consequence (Section 8.3)
- Shorten average sentence length (Section 9.1)
- Structure sentences logically (Section 9.4).
- Avoid intrusive phrases and clauses (Section 10.2)

The only safe use of provisos in contracts is none. Avoid provisos by using:

- "if," to signal a condition;
- "shall" to create a duty;
- "but,"[30] to signal a limitation
- "except," to signal an exception; and
- "and" or "also," to signal additional requirements.

Example:

Before: The matter shall be settled by arbitration conducted by one arbitrator with experience in the area of corporate transactions involving technology companies. Parent and Agent shall mutually agree upon an arbitrator (which shall be independent), <u>provided</u>, that if Parent and Agent cannot agree upon an arbitrator within ten (10) business days then such arbitrator shall be determined in accordance with the JAMS rules.

Better: The matter will be settled by arbitration conducted by one arbitrator with experience in the area of corporate transactions involving technology companies. Parent and Agent will select an independent arbitrator. If Parent and Agent cannot agree upon an arbitrator within ten business days, the arbitrator will be determined according to JAMS rules.

Herein: This word is inherently ambiguous because it could mean "in this phrase," "in this sentence," "in this subsection," "in this section," or "in this document."[31] Each of these phrases is more specific, and therefore, preferable to herein. "Therein" is equally problematic and resolved the same way.

Other words to avoid in drafting. Some words are not inherently ambiguous but should nevertheless be avoided in legal documents.

Legalese.

The phrase "legalese" usually connotes words and phrases used only by lawyers. Lesson 1 identified proper tone as a characteristic of excellent legal drafting. Chronic use of legalese impairs the tone of the document. Avoid legalese in legal drafting because stuffy, pompous language creates a barrier between the drafter and the reader. Save this language for communications with judges and other lawyers, but opt for modern, plain language in drafting contracts for use by non-lawyers. Technical terms can be used where necessary, but drafters should avoid legal jargon and phraseology that serves no real purpose. Here are some words and phrases to avoid in contracts:

- *legalese not used in normal conversation*—Compound words that begin with here-, there-, and where-, such as hereinabove, heretofore, thereabout, thereunto, wheresoever, whereupon, and so on should not be used in contracts except as a last resort to avoid unwieldy phrasing.[32] For example, "The first payment is due on October 1 and installments will be due on the first day of each month thereafter for 35 consecutive months." Use of the word "thereafter" in this example is less cumbersome than other ways of describing the months that follow October 1, but with a little effort a better alternative to legalese can usually be found in most instances. Also avoid words like aforementioned, behoove, forthwith, henceforth, thence, hitherto, whence, within-named, and so on, which legal drafting scholars call "gobbledygook."[33]

- *such, said, and same*—Standup comedy routines and diatribes roasting lawyers are filled with these words. Take the hint! Replace these offending words with "the," "this," "that," or "these."[34]

- *foreign phrases*—Foreign Phrases such as *a fortiori, ad hoc, arguendo, caveat emptor, de facto, et al, ex post facto, id, in personam, inter alia, non sequitur, res gestae, res judicata, supra,* and so on should not be used in contracts.[35] Non-lawyers are unfamiliar with these phrases.

7.3 Use Defined Terms Correctly.

*"There's glory for you!" "I don't know what you mean by 'glory,'" Alice said. Humpty Dumpty smiled contemptuously. "Of course you don't—till I tell you. I meant 'there's a nice knock-down argument for you!" "But 'glory' doesn't mean a 'nice knock-down argument," Alice objected. "When I use a word," Humpty Dumpty said, in a rather scornful tone, "it means just what I choose it to mean—neither more nor less." "The question is," said Alice, "whether you can make words mean so many different things." "The question is," Humpty Dumpty said, "which is to be master—that's all." ....
"Impenetrability! That's what I say!" "Would you tell me, please," said Alice, "what that means?" "Now you talk like a reasonable child," said Humpty Dumpty, looking very much pleased. "I meant by 'impenetrability' that we've had enough of that subject, and it would be just as well if you'd mention what you mean to do next, as I suppose you don't mean to stop here all the rest of your life." "That's a great deal to make one word mean," Alice said in a thoughtful tone. "When I make a word do a lot of work like that," said Humpty Dumpty, "I always pay it extra." "Oh!" said Alice. She was too much puzzled to make any other remark.[36]*

At one time or another, almost all of us who work with contracts have felt exactly like Alice. Unfortunately, many drafters have also thought like Humpty Dumpty! Lawyers use defined terms as a sort of shorthand way to refer to an entity or concept to minimize repetition. For example, instead of writing International Business Machines Corporation every time the company is referred to in the text, the drafter may use as a short hand reference the defined terms "IBM," "Company," "Corporation," or another suitable label depending on the context, such as "Employer," or "Purchaser." The definition might look like this:

> "This Agreement is between International Business Machines Corporation, a Delaware corporation ("IBM") and Meritage Partners, LLC, a Georgia limited liability company ("Meritage")."

Defined terms help the parties resolve semantic ambiguity where a word or phrase could have more than one possible meaning. For example, does "IBM" refer to the parent holding company or a specific subsidiary for U.S. operations? Defined terms are also used to expand or limit the scope of the item or concept being identified. Does "IBM"

---

include subsidiaries, affiliates, and successor corporations? Does the term include IBM's officers, directors, and shareholders? These questions can be resolved by properly defining the term. The operative word in the preceding sentence is … properly! An ambiguously drafted definition can poison every provision in the contract in which the term appears.

Some definitions appear in the middle of a sentence, some definitions are set off as a separate sentence, and other times the drafter may elect to create an entire glossary. If the definition appears in the middle of a sentence, the first issue is where to place the parenthetical and what information should be included in it. Generally, the parenthetical should be placed after the information that identifies the term:

E.g., The Internal Revenue Code of 1981 (the "Code") is determinative.

Not: The Internal Revenue Code (the "Code") of 1981 is determinative.

Not: The Internal Revenue Code of 1981 is determinative (the "Code.")

If the definition is set off as a separate sentence or included in a glossary, use "means" if the definition is intended to be complete, or "includes," if the definition is NOT intended to be complete.[37] Do not use "means and includes," because that infers that the meaning is both complete and incomplete, which causes ambiguity as to which interpretation was intended.[38] Do not clutter definitions with useless extra words, like "shall mean," "shall have the following meaning," "has the following meaning," or "shall mean and refer to."

E.g., "ERISA" means the Employee Retirement Income Security Act of 1974, as amended.

Defined terms are handy tools in drafting, but all sorts of problems arise when they are not used correctly. Although drafting scholars recommend that defined terms should be used sparingly and carefully,[39] drafters sometimes use them excessively and incorrectly. First of all, lawyers can get so carried away defining things that they create definitions for terms that are not even used within the document! The opposite also occurs, and often, lawyers use capitalized terms in a document as if they were defined terms, but no corresponding definition appears. Often, as a result of copying verbiage from other sources and poor editing, lawyers inadvertently include definitions for the same word or phrase in multiple sections with conflicting, inconsistent meanings, resulting in contextual ambiguity. Many lawyers "stuff" definitions with substantive provisions that should be included in the text of the document.[40] Lawyers often compile a glossary of defined terms, but the glossary does not include all of the defined terms used in the document. Careful editing will eliminate most of these problems.

When and How to Use a Glossary. Unless the document contains more than five defined terms, the definitions should appear in the text where the term is first used. Drafting scholars differ as to whether the glossary should be at the end or beginning of the document when there are more than five defined terms.[41] The argument for putting the glossary at the end of the document is based on organizing topics within the document in order of importance.

This writer's preference is to put the glossary at the beginning of the document so the reader knows where it is and that it is there and can glance at the defined terms before reading the text to which they relate. An experienced transactional lawyer knows where many hazards are likely to be lurking, either with the definitions *per se*, or within the provisions that include them, and will appreciate the opportunity to scan those definitions before reading the provisions in which they are used. Even so, location of the glossary is strictly a matter of personal preference, and neither alternative is necessarily "right" or "wrong." Until the legal profession reaches consensus on the issue of where the glossary should be located, consider it a matter of professional courtesy and a bargaining chip to acquiesce to an opposing counsel's stringent preference.

Some drafting scholars recommend that if a word is used in only one section, the word should be defined in that section. This may work well in theory, or in shorter contracts that have only a handful of defined terms, but usually spells disaster in more sophisticated documents with many defined terms. Because drafting is a collaborative process, often using language cut and pasted from various sources, an extraordinarily high percentage of contracts contain words defined multiple times with different meanings, resulting in contextual ambiguity as to which definition controls.[42] For this reason, if a document is long enough to warrant a glossary, ALL defined terms should be defined there.

Defined terms should match their intuitive meanings. Using defined terms to have counter-intuitive meanings may create a trap for the reader and the drafter as well, because our minds automatically infer reasonable meanings and reject absurdness, even when fully and explicitly informed.[43]

Tips on using defined terms:

- Proofread carefully to ensure that defined terms are used, are used correctly and consistently, and that all terms used as defined terms are, in fact, defined.

- When using a list or glossary, make sure it contains all defined terms used in the text.

- If using a list or glossary, define the terms there; do not state that the term "has the meaning given in Section 10.14 of this Agreement."

- Make sure that the part of speech in the definition matches the defined term—when the defined term is a noun, the definition should describe a noun, not a verb.

- Unless a word is used at least three times in a document, it is usually a waste of ink to create a defined term for it, except to simplify an unusually complicated provision.[44]

- Do not use defined terms where the meaning is obvious—for example, Congor Corporation ("Congor"),[45] or first transfer notice ("First Transfer Notice.")

- Avoid using defined terms for ordinary legal words that do not need definition, such as "litigation," unless a specific alternative meaning is intended.

- Avoid using defined terms differentiated only by a couple of letters, such as "Employer" and "Employee."

- Avoid Alice in Wonderland-type definitions, such as "black" means "white," and stick to intuitive meanings.[46]

- Do not put substantive provisions in definitions.[47]

- Cut the clutter—use "means" as opposed to "shall mean," "shall have the following meaning," "shall mean and refer to," "is when," or "is where."

Case Study 7.3

Observe the chronic and unnecessary overuse of defined terms in these excerpts from a joint venture agreement.

7.5 INDEMNIFICATION PROCEDURES.

(a) Any **Indemnified Person** making a claim for indemnification pursuant to Section 7.2, 7.3 or 7.4 above (an **"Indemnified Party"**) must give the party from whom indemnification is sought (an "Indemnifying Party") notice of such claim (in a manner consistent with Section 10.1 hereof) describing such claim with reasonable particularity and the nature and amount of the Loss to the extent that the nature and amount of such Loss is known at such time (an "Indemnification Claim Notice") promptly after the Indemnified Party receives any written notice of any action, lawsuit, proceeding, investigation or other claim (a "Proceeding") against or involving the Indemnified Party by a Governmental Authority or other third party or otherwise discovers the liability, obligations or facts giving rise to such claim for indemnification; provided that the failure to notify or delay in notifying an Indemnifying Party will not relieve the Indemnifying Party of its obligations pursuant to Section 7.2, 7.3 or 7.4, as applicable, except to the extent that (and only to the extent that) such failure shall have (i) caused or materially increased the Indemnifying Party's liability, (ii) resulted in the forfeiture by the Indemnifying Party of substantial rights and defenses or (iii) otherwise materially prejudiced the Indemnifying Party.

(b) The Indemnifying Party shall have 30 days from the date the Indemnification Claim Notice is deemed given pursuant to Section 10.1 hereof (the "Notice Period") to notify the Indemnified Party (i) whether or not the Indemnifying Party disputes the liability of the Indemnifying Party to the Indemnified Party with respect to such claim or demand and (ii) whether or not it desires to defend the Indemnified Party against such claim or demand.

•••

11.1.45 "INDEMNIFICATION CLAIM NOTICE" shall have the meaning set forth in Section 7.5(a).

11.1.46 "**INDEMNIFIED PARTIES**" shall have the meaning set forth in Section 7.5(a).

11.1.47 "INDEMNIFYING PARTY" shall have the meaning set forth in Section 7.5(a).

Comments: The complexity of this provision is caused by over use and poor use of defined terms. The drafter has created two definitions for the same term: Indemnified Party is circularly defined as an Indemnified Person. The glossary lists Indemnified Parties (plural) but does not include Indemnified Person. Query whether any definition is needed of a person seeking indemnification under the agreement? What else could an indemnified party/parties/person be? The definition of Indemnifying Party is equally unnecessary in this provision. Next, the drafter burdens the provision with other unnecessary definitions: Indemnification Claim Notice, Proceeding, and Notice Period. The need for these definitions could exist if, for example, a contract provided for multiple Notices or Notice Periods, but this contract did not. The definition of "Proceeding" is superfluous because it is not used as the provision continues to refer to "such claim" and "such claim and demand." This provision would be vastly simplified, and therefore, improved, if the defined terms were defined in the glossary instead of merely referenced there.

7.4 Use "That" or "Which" Correctly.

Many highly skilled legal drafters do not know the distinction between the correct use of "that" or "which," and there are certainly more pressing errors to correct in legal drafting. According to the more persnickety grammar experts, "that" is restrictive while "which" is not.[48] A "that" phrase tells a necessary piece of information about its antecedent. For example, "the copier that is down the hall is jammed." In this case, the "that" phrase tells us *which* copier, presumably among multiple copiers, is jammed. If the information in the clause defines the antecedent, use "that."

A "which" phrase provides useful, but not grammatically necessary, information about its antecedent. For example, "the copier, which is down the hall, is jammed." In this case, there is apparently only one copier, and the "which" phrase tells where it is located. If you can remove the phrase beginning with "which" from the sentence without changing the meaning of the sentence or the sentence structure, you have probably used "which" correctly. If not, you should have used "that."

It is, admittedly, a subtle difference; here are some rules of thumb.

First, if the phrase needs a comma, you should probably use "which." In fact, when you use "which" you will most likely need a pair of commas, unless the phrase comes at the end of a sentence.

Second, if you can tell which thing is being discussed without the "which" or "that" clause, use "which"; if not, use "that."

Finally, if all else fails, use whichever word sounds right, but put a comma before "which" and do not put a comma before "that."

Exercise 7.4:

Write "C" beside the sentences in which the word "that" or "which" is used correctly. Edit incorrect sentences.

1. The world is full of obvious things which nobody by any chance ever observes.

2. We have developed a plan for operating a business, which sells printed business products and services.

3. The Company may elect to purchase the Membership Interest or Economic Interest which is the subject of the proposed Transfer for the same price and on the same terms and conditions as described in the Transfer notice.

4. A Member may not voluntarily withdraw or take any other voluntary action which directly causes a withdrawal event.

5. "Reserves" means funds set aside or amounts allocated during any fiscal period to reserves which will be maintained in amounts deemed sufficient or necessary by the holders of a Majority in Interest to meet the needs of the business of the Company.

6. Any and all printed, written, or electronic material that Distributor obtains, produces, or prepares in performing services under this Agreement will be and remain the exclusive property of Owner, subject to paragraph 9.3 (c) of this Agreement.

7. The Members will decide any questions arising with respect to the Company and this Operating Agreement, which are not specifically or expressly provided for in this Operating Agreement.

NOTES

1. Mark Mathewson, *A Critic of Plain Language Misses the Mark*, 8 SCRIBES J. LEGAL WRITING 147, 149 (2001-2002). Mathewson also notes that "(e)ven other lawyers deserve relatively simple, clear, plain prose."

2. SCOTT J. BURNHAM, DRAFTING AND ANALYZING CONTRACTS, 217 (3d 2003); REED DICKERSON, THE FUNDAMENTALS OF LEGAL DRAFTING, 48 (1986); DAVID MELLINKOFF, LEGAL WRITING: SENSE AND NONSENSE, 8 (1982).

3. BRYAN A. GARNER, THE REDBOOK: A MANUAL ON LEGAL STYLE, 157-164 (2002); TINA L. STARK, DRAFTING CONTRACTS: HOW AND WHY LAWYERS DO WHAT THEY DO, 201-206 (2007); KENNETH A. ADAMS, A MANUAL OF STYLE FOR CONTRACT DRAFTING, 208 (2004); RICHARD C. WYDICK, PLAIN ENGLISH FOR LAWYERS, 11 (5th 2005); HENRY WEIHOFEN, LEGAL WRITING STYLE, 57-60 (1961); MELLINKOFF, *supra* note 2, at 105.

4. BRYAN A. GARNER, GARNER ON LANGUAGE AND WRITING, 180-181 (2009); ADAMS, *supra* note 3, at 129-130; Thomas Haggard, *The Ambiguous And and Or*, 8 SCRIBES J. LEGAL WRITING 169-171 (2001-2002); BURNHAM, *supra* note 2, at 97; Editorial, "And/Or," 18 A.B.A. Journal 456 (1932); Dwight D. McCarty, *That Hybrid "and/or,"* 39 Mich. State B.J. 9, 17 (May 1960).

5. In the first and second recorded cases interpreting "and/or," Cuthbert v. Cumming, 156 Eng. Rep. 668 (Ex. D. 1855), *aff'd*, 156 Engl. Rep. 889 (Ex. Ch. 1855), and Stanton v. Richardson, 45 L.J.O.B. (H.L. 1875), six English judges interpreted "and/or" in the phrase "full and complete cargo of sugar, molasses and/or other lawful produce" a total of six different ways: 1) A and B and C, or A and B, or C only; 2) A and B and C, or A and B; 3) just A and B; 4) A or B or C; 5) A, or A and B, or A and C, and 6) any combination of A or B or C. SEE: Kermit L. Dunahoo, Note, *Avoiding Inadvertent Syntactic Ambiguity in Legal Draftsmanship*, 20 Drake L. Rev., 137, 150 (1970).

6. Employers' Mut. Liability. Ins. Co v. Tollefsen, 263 N.W. 376, 377 (Wis. 1935).

7. American General. Ins. Co. v. Webster, 118 S.W. 2d 1082, 1084 (Tex. Civ. App 1938).

8. Commercial Standard Ins. Co. v. Davis, 68 F.2d 108, 109 (5th Cir. 1933).

9. Cochrane v. Florida East Coast Ry. Co., 107 Fla. 431; 145 So. 217 (1932).

10. Davison v. Woolworth Company, 186 Ga. 663, 665; 198 S.E. 738, 740 (1938).

11. Adler v. Douglas, 339 Mo. 187, 189, 95 S.W. 2d 1179, 1180 (1936). The best case scenario for judicial review of "and/or" seems to be the position taken by the Louisiana Supreme Court: "In other words such an expression in

a contract amounts to a direction to those charged with construing the contract to give it such interpretation as will best accord with the equity of the situation, and for that purpose to use either "and" or "or" and be held down to neither." State v. Dudley, 159 La. 872, 878, 106 So. 364, 365 (1925). However, the Adler Court noted that "the use of this symbol arises in part from a doubt as to which of the two words should be used. Is it any solution of this doubt to leave the question to be solved by construction at a later time?"

12. MELLINKOFF, *supra* note 2, at 55-56.

13. BRYAN A. GARNER, A DICTIONARY OF MODERN LEGAL USAGE, 56 (2d 1995). SEE also Burnham, *supra* note 2, at 97: "The possible combinations are so boggling that it is difficult to tell what was intended." "In addition to the strong possibility of creating confusion, use of *and/or* may incur the wrath of the reader or judge. The bottom line on *and/or*? Its use is usually sloppy and careless. When you must clarify a several *and* or an inclusive *or*, spell it out. *Don't use and/or.*" *Id.*

14. THOMAS R. HAGGARD AND GEORGE W. KUNEY, LEGAL DRAFTING IN A NUTSHELL, 255 (3d 2007). I believe that Haggard's optimism that the "remnant of drafters" who use "and/or" is "dwindling" is unwarranted. In the past few years of my practice, I have seen usage of this incorrigible expression expand exponentially. Similarly, Michele Asprey believes that most lawyers know they shouldn't use provisos, although I have found the exact opposite to be true. MICHELE ASPREY, PLAIN LANGUAGE FOR LAWYERS, 132 (3d 2003). When informed that provisos are unacceptable by judges and scholars, most lawyers respond first with shock, then with rage and personal insults! SEE GARNER, GARNER ON LANGUAGE, *supra* note 4, at xxix.

15. Editorial, "And/Or," 18 A.B.A. Journal 456 (1932).

16. Dwight D. McCarty, That Hybrid "and/or," 39 Mich. State B.J. 9, 17 (May 1960).

17. BRYAN A. GARNER, ELEMENTS OF LEGAL STYLE, 51-52 (2d 2002); GARNER, GARNER ON LANGUAGE, *supra* note 4, xxviii, 181; DICKERSON, *supra* note 2, at 128-129; MELLINKOFF, *supra* note 2, at 178; ADAMS, *supra* note 3, at 164; STARK, *supra* note 3, at 250.

18. THOMAS R. HAGGARD AND GEORGE W. KUNEY, LEGAL DRAFTING: PROCESS, TECHNIQUES AND EXERCISES, 213 (2d 2007).

19. Ga. Banking Co. v. Smith, 128 U.S. 174, 181 (1888). "The difficulty attending the construction of the clause following this one arises from the doubt attached to the meaning of the term 'provided.' The general purpose of a proviso, as is well known, is to <u>except</u> the clause covered by it from the general provisions of a statute, or from some provisions of it, or to qualify the operation of the statute in some particular. But it is often used in other senses. It is a common practice in legislative proceedings, on the consideration of bills, for parties desirous of securing amendments to them

to precede their proposed amendments with the term 'provided,' so as to declare that, notwithstanding existing provisions, the one thus expressed is to prevail; thus having no greater signification than would be attached to the conjunction '<u>but</u>' or '<u>and</u>' in the same place, and simply serving to separate or distinguish the different paragraphs or sentences. Several illustrations are given by counsel of the use of the term in this sense, showing, in such cases, where an amendment has been made, though the provision following often has no relation to what precedes it." *Id.*, at 181 (emphasis added).

20. Black's Law Dictionary defines a "condition" as a "future and uncertain event on which the existence or extent of an obligation or liability depends." In other words, a condition is something that must happen before a duty arises.

21. See, e.g., Western Publishing Co., Inc. v. Mindgames, Inc. 995 F. Supp 949, 954-955 (E.D. Wis. 1998); aff'd, 218 F. 3d 652 (7th Cir. 2000): "Although Paragraph 2 of the licensing agreement could have been better drafted, it is unambiguous. It states that the licensing agreement will automatically continue until January 31, 1994, if two conditions are met… Paragraph 2 thus set up requirements that have a recognized name in contract law: conditions precedent." "This language also creates a condition. It imposes no duty on the licensee to pay a renewal fee." Does this mean that provisos are not ambiguous? No, because the decision was based solely upon the facts and circumstances of this case.

22. See, e.g., Marsh v. Marsh, 949 S.W. 2d 734, 744 (Tex. App. 1997): "While no particular words are necessary to create a condition, such terms as "if," "provided that," "on condition that," or some other phrase that conditions performance, usually connote an intent for a condition rather than a promise. In the absence of such a limiting clause, whether a contractual provision is a condition, rather than a promise, must be gathered from the contract as a whole and from the intent of the parties. Because of their harshness in operation, conditions are not favorites of the law, and courts are inclined to construe the provisions in a contract as covenants rather than as conditions."

23. See e.g., In Re Explorer Pipeline, 781 A. 2d 705, 719 (Delaware, 2001): "A proviso, as introduced here by the word "provided," acts as a limitation on the language that describes the scope of the provision and is read in reference to the specific scope of the language defining the provision's application."

24. Note that Charles Fox breaks ranks with most other drafting scholars who condemn EVERY use of provisos by stating that the only acceptable use of a proviso is to carve an exception that trumps the concept that immediately preceded it. CHARLES M. FOX, WORKING WITH CONTRACTS: WHAT LAW SCHOOL DOESN'T TEACH YOU, 95-96 (2002). This position is supported in some cases interpreting provisos but inconsistent with others cited in this section. *See* Burgwyn v. Whitfield, 81 N.C. 261, 263 (N.C. 1879)

(provided means "unless"); and Millard v. McFadden, 57 N.Y.S. 2d 594, 596 (N.Y. 1945) (provided is a limitation or exception).

25. *See e.g.*, Obsen v. Grosshans, 71 N.W. 2d 90, 97 (Neb. 1955) (provided means "and" or "but").

26. GARNER, GARNER ON LANGUAGE *supra* note 4, at xxviii.

27. GARNER DICTIONARY, *supra* note 13, at 710.

28. HAGGARD/KUNEY PROCESS, *supra* note 18, at 213.

29. ADAMS, *supra* note 3, at 164.

30. To the chagrin of some, it is currently considered grammatically proper to begin sentences with And and But. In fact, many great literary writers and jurists have so done for centuries. SEE GARNER, GARNER ON LANGUAGE *supra* note 4, at 63-87 for examples from the writings of Jonathan Swift, Geoffrey Chaucer, William Shakespeare, James Madison, Benjamin Franklin, Percy Bysshe Shelley, Albert Einstein, Oliver Wendell Holmes, and others.

31. *Id.*, at 122; GARNER DICTIONARY, *supra* note 13, at 402; MELLINKOFF, *supra* note 2, at 172.

32. HOWARD DARMSTADTER, HEREOF, THEREOF, AND EVERYWHEREOF: A CONTRARIAN GUIDE TO LEGAL DRAFTING, 5 (2008); BURNHAM, *supra* note 2 at p. 291; DICKERSON, *supra* note 2, at 207; GARNER REDBOOK, *supra* note 3, at 161; MELLINKOFF, *supra* note 2 at 3, 134; STARK, *supra* note 3, at 202. I enjoy using here-, there-, and where- words as much as any other lawyer even though virtually all legal drafting scholars recommend against the use of *such* words in contracts! *Said* scholars also recommend against using words like such and said, except in communications intended solely for other lawyers! Thankfully, *there* is an acceptable outlet for these bad habits and expressions (and others such as using "there" as the subject of a sentence) in legal books and journals!

33. WEIHOFEN, *supra* note 3, at 62; DICKERSON, *supra* note 2, at 156; GARNER REDBOOK, *supra* note 3, at p. 162; LAUREL CURRIE OATES ET AL., THE LEGAL WRITING HANDBOOK, 700 (3d 2002).

34. *Id.*, at 704; DICKERSON, *supra* note 2, at 217; BURNHAM, *supra* note 2, at p. 283; MELLINKOFF, *supra* note 2, at p. 3.

35. MELLINKOFF, *supra* note 2 at p. 5, 193-194; OATES ET AL., *supra* note 33, at 701.

36. LEWIS CARROLL, THROUGH THE LOOKING-GLASS AND WHAT ALICE FOUND THERE, ch. VI (1871).

37. DICKERSON, *supra* note 2, at 147; Thomas Haggard, *Definitions*, 8 SCRIBES J. LEGAL WRITING 165 (2001-2002).

38. *Id.*

39. DICKERSON, *supra* note 2, at 148. Most lawyers are surprised to learn that legal drafting scholars recommend that defined terms should be used sparingly, if at all. GARNER, GARNER ON LANGUAGE, *supra* note 4, at 185-186.

40. DICKERSON, *supra* note 2, at 151.

41. SEE GARNER, GARNER ON LANGUAGE, *supra* note 4, at 189; ADAMS, *supra* note 3, at 81. BUT SEE STARK, *supra* note 3, at 76; HAGGARD/ KUNEY NUTSHELL, *supra* note 14, at 376; and BURNHAM, *supra* note 2, at 226.

42. I would conservatively estimate that at least 80 percent of the contracts I reviewed during my practice, spanning over two decades, contained words defined multiple times with multiple different meanings. Reed Dickerson also mused that drafters are prone to this error, and the problem has gotten worse with the advent of personal computing. DICKERSON, *supra* note 2, at 137. Although I agree with Mr. Adams that the legal profession can learn certain new tricks (SEE Note 10 at Section 8.2), this issue is more complicated. While the analysis of whether "shall" is used correctly, for example, is based on its usage in a single sentence, the question of whether a defined term has been used consistently involves analysis of the entire document. I am convinced, given the collaborative nature of the drafting process where lawyers for both parties participate in crafting the language, the only foolproof method to avoid inadvertent duplication in a lengthy document is to group ALL defined terms in a single section. When the defined terms appear alphabetically, side by side, duplication becomes obvious.

43. DICKERSON, *supra* note 2, at 140-144.

44. For example, it is nearly impossible to draft a simple restrictive covenant without using definitions for terms like "competing business," "business of employer," "the territory," and "employee's duties," even though these terms may be used only once. See Case Study 10.2, in which key defined terms are added though they are used only once to simplify a complicated provision.

45. Note that use of a defined term would be entirely appropriate if "Congor" is intended to include successors, assigns, subsidiaries, or affiliates of Congor Corporation, but the definition must so state.

46. DICKERSON, *supra* note 2, at 140-144.

47. DICKERSON, *supra* note 2, at 151.

48. DARMSTADTER, *supra* note 32, at 13.

8

Use Words Consistently

> **Objective of this Lesson:** To explain what it means to use words inconsistently and demonstrate how semantic ambiguity can be avoided by consistent word usage.
>
> **Key Techniques:**
> - Use words consistently.
> - Use the word "shall" consistently.
> - Choose the correct language for the intended consequence.

8.1 Use Words Consistently.

Consistent use of terminology is one of the simplest tools for improving legal drafting and avoiding semantic ambiguity.[1] Within any legal document there should be one word per meaning and one meaning per word. This means lawyers must use every recurring word or term consistently throughout the document.

In journalistic and literary writing, authors sometimes strive to make their prose more interesting by intentionally varying the language. The English language facilitates variation by supplying many words having similar or overlapping meanings. For example, a journalist might use any of the following words and phrases in a newspaper article to mean "postpone": wait, put off, suspend, defer, reschedule, delay, shelve, put on the back burner, or table. In periodicals or literature, a lawyer might alternatively be referred to as the attorney, legal representative, trial lawyer, defense lawyer, or counsel.

Although elegant variation has its merits in other applications, lawyers should carefully avoid it in legal drafting.[2] For one thing, elegant variation is a source of confusion and ambiguity. Does a reference to "the vehicle" in one section mean the same thing as "the automobile" in another? The risk in using more than one word per meaning is that using different wording will create a presumption that a difference in meaning is intended. Conversely, using the same word to have many different meanings will confuse as to which meaning applies to any given usage. Further, in interpreting contracts, the courts must endeavor to give each word meaning and may strain to find distinctions between words where none were intended.

As Kenneth A. Adams so eloquently stated, "(v)ariety is the bane of drafting: it befuddles readers and quickens the blood of sharp-eyed litigators."[3] The principle of eschewing variety in legal drafting is nothing new. Writing on the topic of elegant variation more than 100 years ago, J. G. McKay recommended:

> "4. As to the choice of words, words should be preferred which have one meaning only.

> "5. The same word should always be used throughout the same writing in one and the same meaning. Although there may be exceptions to rule 4, to this rule, there is no exception. A change of meaning must always produce ambiguity. Language is not so poor that it should ever be necessary, or even convenient, to employ the same word to express different things in the same legal composition."[4]

Few lawyers would dispute these principles, but drafters sometimes fail to understand their application in legal documents. Consider this example:

"If any **particular provision** herein is construed to be in conflict with the *provisions* of the Delaware Act, the Delaware Act will control and such **invalid or unenforceable provision** will not affect or invalidate the other provisions hereof, and this Agreement must be construed in all respects as if **such conflicting provision** were omitted."

Note that this relatively simple sentence contains three words per meaning and three meanings per word. The drafter has "elegantly" referenced the offending provision three different ways: the particular provision, the invalid or unenforceable provision, and such conflicting provision. Besides that, the word "provision" itself has been used to mean three different things: the offending provision, provisions of the Delaware Act, and the other, presumably unoffending provisions of the Agreement.

A poorly drafted contract for the purchase and sale of a fleet of cars may alternately refer to **the fleet, the vehicles, the cars, the automobiles, the lot, the Fords, the Taurus's, the batch, the equipment, the pool, etc.** This elegant variation creates ambiguity in a contract. The problem is more obvious when the words appear in proximity, as in this paragraph, but much less obvious when the variations are dispersed throughout a 20-or 30-page contract.

The concept of using words consistently goes beyond the words used to identify the goods or the parties to the transaction. For example, if the terms within the contract **identify, indicate, specify, set forth, describe, provide, contain, include, list, designate, state, AND express,** ambiguity also results from these alternate word choices. "Unless you have a reason, a distinction to be made, a deliberate and different shade of meaning in mind, don't hop from one to another for the sake of variation—or through inadvertence. ... If the context is the same, in the same writing, pick one word and stay with it. Otherwise, someone might come to the conclusion that the variation was intended to convey a different meaning, or at least COULD convey a different meaning. Indicates could be weaker than specifies."[5] Indeed, one court concluded a different operation of the word "including" was signaled when the words "including but not limited to" were used in one provision and the words "including... but not including" were used in another.[6]

Carefully consider the use of terms like "best efforts," "reasonable efforts," and "commercially reasonable efforts." If you intend to create varying standards, different words should be used, but if you intend to impose the same standard, the words must be used consistently throughout the document.

Carefree and inconsiderate drafters sometimes give alternate defined terms for the same concept, as in **"(hereinafter referred to as the "Corporation," the "Company," or ABC)."** This usually happens when the drafter notices that the terminology in language inserted from various sources differs from the terminology used in the primary document, and the drafter either doesn't have or doesn't take the time to fix the variations. These alternates give the drafter "freedom to slip freely from name to label without warning, leaving the reader with the burden of identification, and destroying whatever claim to precision or clarity the label was to achieve."[8] To be sure, a reference that identifies the variations is better than nothing, but if time allows, choose one appellation and stick with it.

8.2 Use the Word "Shall" Consistently.

Although this Lesson is really just an extension of the concept addressed in Lesson 8.1, misuse of the word "shall" is so pervasive in legal drafting today it warrants its own discussion. Words that impose a duty or obligation must be used consistently within the document.

"Shall" is chronically misused in legal drafting to mean many different things interchangeably, often within the same paragraph, by even the most experienced lawyers.[9] The word is used just as often in an attempt to create or negate rights, create or negate privileges, and to create conditions as it is used to create duties. New drafters should beware: The word "shall" is misused in template documents far more often than it is used correctly, and it is incumbent upon enlightened drafters to correct misuses by understanding that the language used to create duties, rights, privileges, and conditions, or to negate them, should logically be different.[10]

Even in otherwise well-written documents, it is not uncommon to find the word "shall" used as often as 20 times per page of text, with a rate of misuse as high as 90 percent. If the word "shall" is used when "may" is meant, the word could be construed to mean "may" when a duty is intended. In almost any legal document, the word "shall" can be found:

- to impose a duty on the subject of the sentence;
- to impose a duty on an unnamed party, such as "notice shall be given," or "Defective products shall be examined";
- to mean "may," as in "shall be entitled to assign";
- to mean a conditional duty, as in "changes to the proposed specifications shall be submitted" (no *duty* exists in this example unless changes are submitted);
- to be used as a modal verb, such as "notice shall have been given when…"; and
- to express an entitlement, as in "Licensor shall be reimbursed for expenses."

Note that defective products do not have a duty to be examined, and notice does not have a duty to be given. Only a party to a transaction can have a duty under the written document.

The Great Debate. Although most lawyers are blissfully unaware of it, drafting scholars are engaged in an ongoing debate over the correct use of the word "shall" as opposed to "must" or "will." Some highly regarded scholars have argued that THE ONLY proper use of the word "shall" is in the context of statutory duties.[11] They argue that the word "shall" should not be used AT ALL in contracts. They prefer the word "will" to "shall," based on the logic that a contract expresses what the parties have mutually **agreed** to do, rather than what they are **commanded** to do.[12]

Other scholars who are not so extreme as to claim that "shall" should never be used in contracts have nevertheless given up on using it because it is misused the vast majority of the time.[13] These scholars prefer "must" to shall. But "must" also has its critics, who argue that: 1) "must" does not have the imperative ring that "shall" does; 2) "shall" is itself the statement of the duty, while "must" infers that the duty is created elsewhere; 3) "must" should be used to create conditions; and 4) using "must" in place of "shall" would then necessitate finding yet another acceptable word to create conditions.

Until the debate is settled and consensus achieved, drafters can significantly improve their work product by using shall consistently. "Shall" should be used only to impose a duty on a named party.[14] If the word "shall" can be replaced with "has a duty to" and it imposes a direct duty on a specific party to the agreement, it is probably being used correctly.

Exercise 8.2:

Correct the following sentences and phrases by replacing "shall."

1. No attorney-in-fact shall be obligated to furnish bond or other security.

2. Except where the context indicates otherwise, words in the singular number shall include the plural, and words in the masculine gender shall include the feminine, and vice versa.

3. In the event a Shareholder shall file a voluntary petition, complaint or answer ...

4. The Specifications shall be deemed to be part of this Agreement.

5. This Agreement shall become effective upon execution by both parties and shall remain in full force and effect for the period of time specified in the Project Description unless terminated as described below.

8.3 Choose Correct Language for the Intended Consequence.

The primary purpose of a contract is to create legal consequences, but there are many different kinds of consequences. For example, contracts create **duties**, but they also create **rights**. The flip side of every duty to perform is the right to receive the performance. Contracts also create **privileges**—the option to do something in the future if the party so desires. Some contracts include **representations**, which are statements of fact made as of a specific point in time, and **warranties,** which provide remedies if the representations are not true. Most contracts include **policies** the parties have agreed upon, such as defined terms and most boilerplate provisions. And, of course, contracts are sometimes drafted to negate duties, rights or privileges, and to create other legal consequences as well.

One of the most important aspects of legal drafting involves choosing the proper words to create the intended consequences. This sounds easy enough, but even drafting scholars disagree as to which words create which consequences and courts have been known to interpret the same words differently. To complicate matters, most lawyers are unaware of the distinctions, so most contracts misuse words creating consequences at least as often as they use them correctly. When the words creating consequences are used inconsistently within the contract, even CORRECT usage is vulnerable because it has been contaminated by the inconsistent usages.

1.   Use "shall" to create duties. Only a party to a contract can have a duty under it, so unless the word "shall" appears directly after a named party, the usage is suspect. Even so, "shall" can appear directly after a named party without creating a duty. Consider the following examples where "shall" is used incorrectly:

> e.g.,   Employee shall be entitled to… [i.e., has a duty to be entitled]
>
> Company shall have the duty to… [i.e., has a duty to have the duty]
>
> Licensor shall have authority to… [i.e., has a duty to have authority]

2.   Use "is not required" to negate duties.

> e.g.,   Landlord is not required to improve the premises.

3.   Use "is entitled to" to create rights. Rights are the flip side of duties: A right does not exist unless the other party has a duty to act.

> e.g.,   Buyer is entitled to inspect the goods.

4.   Use "is not entitled to" to negate rights.

> e.g.,   Buyer may inspect the goods but is not entitled to return defective goods to seller without advance notice.

5.   Use "may" to create a privilege. A privilege is discretionary, but there is no corresponding duty on the other party, except the duty to accept the choice of the party exercising the privilege. A privilege is sometimes called a "no-right," meaning that the other party has no right to object to the exercise of the privilege.

e.g., Licensee may terminate the license upon 30 days' notice to Licensor.

The Indemnified Party may retain separate counsel at its sole expense.

6. Use "may not" to negate a privilege. Even in this sense, be very careful to avoid ambiguity using "may not." Add clarifying words like "after October 31" in the example below to ensure that the "may not" cannot be construed as "may or may not" — giving the party permission to make an election.

e.g., Company may not exercise the option after October 31.

7. Use "shall not" to create a duty not to act. Use "shall not" to prohibit a party from taking any action.

e.g., Company shall not assign its rights under this agreement.

8. Use a present-tense verb to perform an action. If the action is actually taken within the contract, use a present-tense verb and active voice to state the action. Do not use passive voice to perform an action, as in "the license is granted to Licensee."

e.g., Licensor grants ABC a limited license to use the Software.

Investor acknowledges that it has received the disclosure statement.

Buyer assumes the liabilities secured by the assets.

9. Use a present-tense verb to state a policy. Policies are rules that the parties must observe but do not require action or inaction by either party. Do not use "shall" in expressing policies, unless a specific duty is imposed directly on a party.[15]

e.g., This agreement is governed by the laws of the State of Georgia.

10. Use "must" to create an obligation on an unnamed party. If an obligation exists, but a named party is not the subject of the clause or sentence creating the duty, use "must."

e.g., Notice must be given within thirty days.

NOTES

1. SCOTT J. BURNHAM, DRAFTING AND ANALYZING CONTRACTS, 102 (2003); REED DICKERSON, THE FUNDAMENTALS OF LEGAL DRAFTING, 15 (1986).

2. RICHARD C. WYDICK, PLAIN ENGLISH FOR LAWYERS, 66 (5th 2005).

3. KENNETH A. ADAMS, A MANUAL OF STYLE FOR CONTRACT DRAFTING, 1 (2004).

4. J. G. Mackay, Some General Rules of the Art of Legal Composition, 32 J. of Juris. 169 (1888), cited in ROBERT N. COOK, LEGAL DRAFTING 26-36 (1951).

5. DAVID MELLINKOFF, LEGAL WRITING: SENSE AND NONSENSE, 23 (1982).

6. In Covington Square Asso. v. Ingles Markets, 641 S.E.2d 266 (Ga. App. 2007), the court construed the following provisions: "As used herein, "*Common Area Costs*" shall mean… *and shall include… but shall not include….*" And "Landlord shall maintain… the Common Areas in good repair, *including but not limited to*: . …" The court held that the use of the phrase 'but not limited to' in Section 6.3 and its absence in Section 6.4 implied a different operation of the word 'include.'

7. SEE Section 7.2.

8. MELLINKOFF, *supra* note 5, at 27.

9. DICKERSON, *supra* note 1, at 213-216; BRYAN A. GARNER, GARNER ON LANGUAGE AND WRITING, 174-176 (2009); ADAMS, *supra* note 3, at 22; WYDICK, *supra* note 2, at 63-64; THOMAS R. HAGGARD AND GEORGE W. KUNEY, LEGAL DRAFTING: PROCESS, TECHNIQUES, AND EXERCISES, 214 (2d 2007).

10. BURNHAM, *supra* note 1, at 257; TINA L. STARK, DRAFTING CONTRACTS: HOW AND WHY LAWYERS DO WHAT THEY DO, 133-152 (2007).

11. THOMAS R. HAGGARD, LEGAL DRAFTING IN A NUTSHELL, 411 (2d 2003). Note that the addition of Professor Kuney as a co-author seems to have brought a calming influence on Professor Haggard, because the assertion that the ONLY proper use of the word "shall" is in statutory drafting has been relaxed a bit in the third edition. Compare: THOMAS R. HAGGARD AND GEORGE W. KUNEY, LEGAL DRAFTING IN A NUTSHELL, 385 (3d 2007).

12. I disagree with this approach, simply because it seems to me that in modern times, "will" is used colloquially to signal a plan rather than an obligation. My observation is that the average person who says "I will" do something in casual conversation does not actually feel obligated to do it. "I will" expressed in casual conversation is generally understood and accepted to be subject to change if circumstances change. I believe stronger

language is needed to elevate a plan to an obligation, so I prefer to use "shall," precisely because it is not used often in every day conversation, and the difference in language conveys a stronger responsibility.

13. GARNER, GARNER ON LANGUAGE, *supra* note 9, at 179; WYDICK, *supra* note 2, at 64. BUT SEE ADAMS, *supra* note 3, at 24. Having successfully taught the correct use of the word "shall" to law students, I agree with Mr. Adams that the situation is not so bleak as to force the conclusion that the legal profession as a whole cannot also master the concept. I also agree with Mr. Adams that it is unlikely the American bar would adopt "must" as a viable alternative to "shall" without extreme coercion from the bench. While Mr. Garner prefers the ABC rule, the basic tenet of the ABC rule seems to be that the bar cannot be trusted to use the word "shall" correctly. SEE GARNER, GARNER ON LANGUAGE, *supra* note 9, at 176. Although I admire and appreciate Mr. Garner's zealous efforts to improve the writing skills of the entire American bar, it seems somewhat inconsistent to devote one's career to the pursuit of teaching excellence in legal writing, while at the same time deeming the pursuit to be futile! I hope we can prove ourselves worthy of his efforts.

14. BURNHAM, *supra* note 1, at 253; DICKERSON, *supra* note 1, at 214; STARK, *supra* note 10, at 133-152.

15. ADAMS, *supra* note 3, at 40.

Focus on Sentence Structure

Objective of this Lesson: To demonstrate how to structure sentences properly to enhance readability.

Key Techniques:
- Shorten average sentence length.
- Draft most performance provisions in active voice.
- Convert hidden verbs.
- Structure sentences logically.
- Structure complicated provisions AFTER the verb.
- Draft in parallel structure.
- Use tabulations to eliminate ambiguity.

For many generations, lawyers have routinely prepared legal documents that are convoluted, complicated, and virtually incomprehensible to all but the most sophisticated clients. Usually, the complexity of syntax in legal documents is a much greater barrier to comprehension than the concepts addressed within them. For more than 100 years, drafting scholars have been advising lawyers to use simplified sentence structures to enable end users to understand the legal documents they must consult and implement. Unfortunately, because relatively few practicing lawyers have been formally trained in the art of legal drafting, a new transactional lawyer will soon discover most standard form documents handed down in practice from one transaction to the next will need significant revision. This lesson will present several techniques for improving sentence structure in legal documents.

9.1 Shorten Average Sentence Length.

Lawyers sometimes seem to measure their ability on how long a sentence they can create. Unfortunately, long sentences make legal documents hard to understand. Separate, shorter sentences and clauses state the same topics with greater clarity and are much easier for the reader to comprehend.[1] Perhaps a more significant issue is this: The longer the sentence, the more likely it is that ambiguity is lurking within it.

To enhance readability and eliminate havens for ambiguity, replace long, complicated sentences with shorter ones. Strive for shorter sentences averaging 25 to 30 words.[2] (Note that this goal is expressed as an *average*; it will not be possible or even desirable to draft *every* sentence in a legal document with 30 words or less.) Even though a larger total number of words may ultimately be used by breaking complex sentences into shorter components, the readability of the document as a whole will be improved.

When the client you are representing is highly sophisticated, it may be possible to use longer sentences without sacrificing comprehension. Even so, beware that the audience of a legal document is often much broader than the client itself, and may include parties who are adversarial to your client's interests. Also, beware of the collaborative nature of drafting, and the fact that the document you draft for one transaction will likely be used again under different circumstances.

Rather than counting words, simply target sentences that are longer than three lines of text; each indented sub-paragraph or bullet-pointed phrase can be counted as a separate sentence. Sub-paragraphs and bullet-pointed phrases should be used liberally to simplify complex provisions.

Flesch Test of Reading Ease. One of the current standards for measuring the readability of a sentence is the Flesch Test of Reading Ease. This test was developed in 1951 by Rudolph Flesch, who studied law and later obtained a Ph.D. in English. The test measures the readability of a sentence based on the number of words it contains and the number of syllables per word. Readability scores under the test range from 0 to 100, with 100 designating very easy and 0 designating virtually incomprehensible. Many government agencies currently require documents or forms to meet specific readability standards based on the Flesch Test or a similar index.

Recommendations from drafting scholars regarding average sentence length of 25 to 30 words are based upon readability standards like the Flesch test, although sentences of that length actually do not meet the "plain English" standard under that test. Under the Flesch test, the minimum score for plain English is 60, which is roughly 20 words per sentence with an average of 1.5 syllables per word. For comparison purposes, consider that this Lesson 9 contains approximately 5750 words, 195 sentences and has a reading ease score of 38.8, which is considered "difficult" on the Flesch Reading Ease scale.[3] This book, written for lawyers and law students, does not even come close to meeting the readability recommendations for plain English!

Considering the daunting challenges presented by the Flesch Reading Ease test, how does a drafter shorten average sentence length?

- First, remove any unnecessary words using the drafting techniques discussed in Lessons 6, 7, and 8.

- Next, whittle down long sentences composed of multiple clauses that could be expressed more clearly as separate sentences.

- Then, set off lists of items, qualifications, or conditions with bullet points, paragraphs, or subparagraphs, which are counted separately.

9.2 Draft Most Performance Provisions in Active Voice.

Whenever Possible, Use Active Voice Rather than Passive in Drafting Performance Provisions. The English language has two "voices"—active and passive. "Voice" describes whether the subject of the sentence is acting or being acted upon. In active voice, the subject of the sentence is doing something; in passive voice, the subject of the sentence is having something done to it.

Sentences written in passive voice usually are formed using "is," "was," or another form of the helping verb "to be" along with a main verb that ends in -ed. Lawyers have grown quite fond of using passive voice because it seems somehow more polite. Passive voice does not point a finger, it merely says something has been done or will have to be done in the future. For example, "Mistakes were made," or "Payment will be made to Vendor." However, using passive voice improperly can cause several problems in legal documents. The first is that passive voice adds unnecessary words (a.k.a. "clutter") to sentences. Another problem is that sentences written in passive voice score lower on readability indexes like the Flesch Test of Reading Ease. The most serious problem is that use of truncated passive voice may cause ambiguity if the document fails to specify which party is required to act.

Active voice is preferred for most performance provisions in legal documents for several reasons:

- Active voice specifies "who" is responsible to act.
- Active voice uses stronger verb forms.
- Active voice eliminates clutter.
- Active voice is easier to follow, because the reader is able to visualize the party taking action.

Examples:

Passive:	If this contract is terminated by Licensee, a termination fee shall be paid.
Truncated Passive:	If this contract is terminated, a termination fee shall be paid.
Active:	If Licensee terminates this contract, Licensee shall pay a termination fee.

Better Active:	Licensee shall pay a termination fee if it terminates this contract.
Passive:	The premises will be occupied until March 31.
Active:	Tenant will occupy the premises until March 31.

Passive voice is usually preferable in boilerplate. Generally, passive voice is preferable for provisions that state policy, like boilerplate.

Example:

Passive:	This agreement is governed and construed according to the laws of the State of Delaware.
Active:	The parties shall govern and construe this agreement according to the laws of the State of Delaware.

Note that active voice for this provision makes no sense, because if the agreement is ever litigated, it will not be governed or construed by the parties, but rather by an independent tribunal, one who is not a party and therefore not bound by the terms of the agreement.

Passive voice may be preferable in representations and warranties. Passive voice may be preferable in representations and warranties, depending upon which party is giving the representation and which party is receiving it.

Example:

Passive:	No hazardous materials have been used upon the Premises.
Active:	Seller has not used hazardous materials upon the Premises.

Note that in this provision, passive voice allocates a greater risk to the seller. Written in active voice, the seller is only representing and warranting its own use of the premises; when passive voice is used, the seller is potentially liable if hazardous materials have been used on the premises by any prior owner in the chain of title.

Passive voice is preferable in uncertainty. Use passive voice where the identity of the actor is unknown—for example, "The tape was erased."

Avoid Beginning Sentences or Phases with "There is," "There are," or, Even Worse, "There shall be." Sentences that begin with "there is," "there are," or "there shall be" usually are written in passive voice. The reader will immediately be confused as to the focus of the sentence because the subject and predicate are out of order.

Exercise 9.2:

Redraft these sentences using active voice.

1. Goods or services may at any time be rejected for defects or defaults revealed by inspection, analysis or by manufacturing operations or use after delivery even though such goods or services may have previously been inspected and accepted.

2. The acceptance of said offer by the Company shall be made by the vote of a majority of the disinterested Directors.

3. The purchase price shall be paid, as the purchaser elects, either (A) in cash or by certified or cashier's check at the closing or (B) in installments as provided in subsection (ii) below.

4. The Plan has been established, maintained and administered in substantial compliance with its terms and with applicable provisions of ERISA.

5. Any payment to be made by Client pursuant to this Agreement not made in a timely manner shall bear interest at the rate of one and one-half percent per month or fraction thereof from the date due until the date of payment.

9.3 Convert Hidden Verbs.

Lawyers are fond of transforming action verbs into nominal (noun-based) constructions with helping verbs, articles, and prepositions,[4] but we can eliminate a few words, replace weaker verbs with stronger ones, and force the text to focus on "who" is required to do "what" by converting these nouns back to verb form. Noun forms of verbs often end in -al, -ance or -ence, -ancy or -ency, -tion or -sion, -ment, -ity, or -ure.[5] Legal drafting scholars recommend that words like decision, response, application, acceptance, occurrence, violation, cessation, failure, performance, etc., should be replaced with their verb forms, like decide, respond, apply, accept, occur, violate, cease, fail, perform, and so on.[6] Here are a few examples:

Instead of this:	Use this:
• Notice shall be given	Licensee will notify
• an application will be submitted	Seller will apply
• provide a response	Company will respond
• the failure of any party	If any party fails
• require performance	Licensor must perform
• upon the occurrence of	If this occurs
• provide indemnification	indemnify
• result in a violation of	violates
• commencement of any action	any action commences
• cessation of business	business ceases
• constitutes misappropriation	misappropriates
• impose any penalty or limitation	penalize or limit
• make a determination	determine
• is applicable	applies

Exercise 9.3:

Redraft these sentences to convert the hidden verbs.

1. In order to provide to the Executive assurances with respect to the protection provided against liabilities that he may incur in the performance of his duties to the Corporation, and to provide inducement for the Executive to serve as an officer of the Corporation, the Corporation has made the determination to enter into this agreement with the Executive.

2. Promptly after receipt by the Corporation of notice of the commencement of Services by Vendor, Corporation will make payment of the initiation fee, but omission by the Corporation to make prompt payment will not relieve Vendor from continuing the performance of the Services.

3. Indemnitee shall be entitled to indemnification of Expenses, and shall receive payment thereof, from the Company in accordance with this Agreement as soon as practicable after Indemnitee has made written demand on the Company for indemnification, unless the Indemnitee is not entitled to indemnification under applicable law.

9.4 Structure Sentences Logically.

In Lesson 5, we noted that topics and ideas should be arranged logically in legal documents. The same principle applies at the sentence level: The information presented in each sentence should be arranged in a logical order. Sentences that lack internal logic are difficult to read, understand, and remember. The reader should not have to read the entire sentence to figure out its purpose. The main idea should be readily apparent and not hidden in the middle or, worse, the end of the sentence.

In journalistic and creative writing, the author's objective is to challenge the audience and make the prose more interesting by varying sentence structures. Our objective as drafters is not to challenge the reader or make the document more interesting, but rather to ensure that the document is indisputably understood. The sentence should be easily accessible so the end user is free to focus on the content instead of the syntax. This means sentence structures should be simple and consistent. Whenever possible, start the sentence with information the reader already knows.

1. **Where a party has a duty to act, the sentence should identify the actor by using active voice. (See Section 9.2.)**

2. **The actor should be the grammatical subject of the sentence as well as the topic of it.**

   Before: The cost of goods, quality of work force, and availability of raw materials are what distinguish the two cities and will be determining factors in the company's decision to build a new plant.

   Better: The Company will decide whether to build its new plant in City A or City B based upon the following determining factors: cost of goods; quality of work force; and availability of raw materials.

3. The subject, verb and object should be close together at the beginning of the sentence. A reader reading a sentence for the first time is looking for the subject, verb and object of the sentence in order to understand it. If these grammatical components are set out close together at or near the beginning of the sentence, the reader will be able to understand it more quickly.

Before:	Subject only to the exclusions set forth in Section 2 hereof, and in addition to any other indemnity to which the Executive may be entitled under the State Statute or any bylaw, resolution or agreement (but without duplication of payments with respect to indemnified amounts), the Corporation hereby further agrees to hold harmless and indemnify the Executive, to the fullest extent permitted by law, including, but not limited to, holding harmless and indemnifying the Executive against any and all expenses. ...
Better:	The Corporation shall indemnify and defend the Executive to the fullest extent permitted by law against any and all expenses. ...

4. Modifiers should be located next to the word they are intended to modify.

Before:	Buyer shall remit payment by wire transfer to an account designated by Seller within five days after closing.
Better:	Buyer shall remit payment within five days after closing by wire transfer to an account designated by Seller.

Find a Logical Basis for Arranging Information in a Sentence. As you draft or revise each sentence, first consider its purpose. What information is this sentence intended to convey? Look for some logical basis on which to arrange the sentence that emphasizes that information. The order of the information could be based on time sequence, cause and effect, order of priority, or another method of categorizing that facilitates the reader's understanding.

9.5 Structure Complicated Provisions AFTER the Verb.

Lawyers are fond of drafting complicated provisions with many qualifications and conditions. While complicated provisions are familiar to practicing lawyers, these provisions are unfamiliar and often incomprehensible to the audience. Lawyers should draft complicated provisions with the audience in mind and make the information as accessible as possible to the unfamiliar reader. Avoid structuring sentences where a long laundry list of qualifications and conditions appear before the verb. Sometimes, it may be preferable to set out short exceptions or conditions at the beginning of the sentence, but it is never a good idea to draft long, complicated clauses before the subject, verb and direct object have been identified. Set out qualifications and conditions after the subject and verb to help the reader organize, understand, and remember the information presented in the sentence. (See Case Study 9A.)

9.6 Draft in Parallel Structure.

"Parallel structure" means that related words, phrases, or clauses are drafted in parallel, or similar, grammatical form. Drafting in parallel structure makes the content more apparent and more accessible to the reader, and also helps the drafter test the clarity of the text. The process of putting ideas into parallel structure reveals where concepts are dissimilar and prompts the drafter to deal with these concepts separately.

Parallel structure can be used to improve the language in lists, within a sentence, among sentences within a paragraph, and sometimes within an entire document. For example, the drafting techniques included in this book are drafted in parallel structure—each with an imperative verb (in this case, "draft") followed by a direct object (in this case, "structure").

Using parallel structure within a sentence helps reveal how the parts of the sentence are related and makes it easier for the reader to receive, organize, understand, and remember the content.

Examples:

Non-parallel Structure:	The old man fed the dog, then he had to go to the post office, and needed some groceries from the store.
Parallel Structure:	The old man fed the dog, went to the post office, and bought some groceries at the store.

Non-parallel Structure:	The partnership has the following options:

        (1) require an additional capital contribution;

        (2) liquidation of partnership assets; and7

        (3) the right to dissolve the partnership.

Parallel Structure:	The partnership may exercise any one or more of the following options:

        (1) require an additional capital contribution;

        (2) liquidate partnership assets; or

        (3) dissolve the partnership.

The non-parallel version in the second example contains a verb, a nominalized (noun-based) verb; and then a noun. In the parallel version, the options are all phrased as action verbs. Notice how much easier it is to follow the sequence of events in the parallel structured sentences.

9.7 Use Tabulations to Eliminate Ambiguity.

"Tabulation" is a fancy term for drafting a series of items in list form instead of paragraph form. Tabulation is a great device for curing ambiguity in situations where it may be otherwise unclear exactly what a modifying word or phrase modifies. You can also use it to show whether a modifier applies to all items in a list or only one of them.

If a tabulation starts with a complete sentence, the first letter of the first word in each item in the tabulation is capitalized, and each item ends with a period. The list does not include an "and" or "or" after the penultimate item in the list. For example, the third paragraph of Section 9.2 is a tabulation that begins with a complete sentence.

A tabulation may also start with a phrase that is not a complete sentence. In this case, the first letter of the first word in each item in the tabulation is not capitalized, and each item ends with a comma or semicolon except that an "and" or "or" is inserted after the penultimate item on the list, and a period follows the last item in the list. If a tabulation begins with a phrase, each item in the tabulation must match the phrase to form a complete sentence. (Unless the "left-over" language that follows the tabulation, called a "tail," is also part of the sentence; in this case, the introductory phrase, plus each item, plus the tail must equal a complete sentence.)[8] For example, in paragraph (iii) (a) of Case Study 9B on page 158, the phrase "and the Borrower's failure to pay causes or permits the holder or holders of the obligation (or a trustee on behalf of such holder or holders) to declare it due prior to its stated maturity;" constitutes a tail. In this multi-layered tabulation, when the beginning paragraph, the first and second level introductory phrases contained in (iii) and (a), listed item (1), and the tail are assembled, they form the following complete sentence:

> At the option of the Lender, this Note and all interest accrued on it will immediately become due and payable, without demand or notice, if/ the Borrower/ fails to pay the principal of or interest, as and when due and payable, before any applicable grace period expires, / on any other obligation for borrowed money /and the Borrower's failure to pay causes or permits the holder or holders of the obligation (or a trustee on behalf of such holder or holders) to declare it due prior to its stated maturity.

In a well-drafted tabulation:

1. all items within the tabulation are drafted in parallel structure;
2. all items are indented;
3. material preceding or following the tabulation must not be indented unless it is the beginning of a paragraph; and
4. all items must read appropriately with the prefatory language and with the tail.

Exercise 9.7:

Redraft in parallel structure, using tabulations to eliminate clutter and ambiguity.

1. Each Member hereby agrees to execute such other and further statements of interest and holdings, designations, powers of attorney and other instruments necessary to comply with any applicable laws, rules, or regulations. The Members each agree to cooperate, and to execute and

deliver in a timely fashion any and all additional documents necessary to effectuate the purposes of the Company and this Operating Agreement.

2. (b) <u>Initiation of Proceeding</u>. Notwithstanding anything in this Agreement to the contrary, Indemnitee shall not be entitled to indemnification pursuant to this Agreement in connection with any Proceeding initiated by Indemnitee against the Company or any director or officer of the Company unless (i) the Company has joined in or the Board has consented to the initiation of such Proceeding; (ii) the Proceeding is one to enforce indemnification rights under Section 5; or (iii) the Proceeding is instituted after a Change in Control (other than a Change in Control approved by a majority of the directors on the Board who were directors immediately prior to such Change in Control) and Independent Counsel has approved its initiation.

3. Confidential Information may be disclosed to any governmental, judicial or regulatory authority requiring such Confidential Information, provided that: (i) such Confidential Information is submitted under applicable provisions, if any, for confidential treatment by such governmental, judicial, or regulatory authority; and (ii) prior to such disclosure, the Owner is given notice of the disclosure requirement so that it may take whatever action it deems appropriate to prohibit such disclosure; and (iii) the Contractor shall endeavor to protect the confidentiality of any Confidential Information to the extent reasonable under the circumstances and use its good faith efforts to prevent the further disclosure of any Confidential Information provided to any government judicial or regulatory authority.

Case Study 9A

In the event of the happening of any one or more of the following events of default: (i) if the Borrower fails to pay, as and when the same shall become due and payable, any principal of or interest on this Note; (ii) if the Borrower fails to perform any of its duties or obligations as specified in any agreement now or hereafter existing between the Borrower and the Lender (including without limitation the Pledge Agreement (as defined below)); (iii) if the Borrower either fails to pay, as and when the same shall become due and payable, any principal of or interest on any other obligation for borrowed money or any obligation secured by purchase money mortgage or title retention lien beyond any period of grace provided with respect thereto, or fails to perform any other agreement, term or condition contained in an agreement under which any such obligation is created, if the effect of such failure is to cause, or to permit the holder or holders of such obligations (or a trustee on behalf of such holder or holders) to cause, such obligation to become due prior to its stated maturity; (iv) if at any time any representation, warranty, statement, certificate, schedule, or report made by the Borrower to the Lender shall prove to have been false or misleading in any material respect as of the time made or furnished; (v) should the Borrower, or any endorser or guarantor of the indebtedness evidenced by this Note, generally not pay its debts as such debts become due, or admit in writing its inability to pay its debts generally, or make a general assignment for the benefit of creditors, or should any proceedings be instituted by or against the Borrower or any such endorser or guarantor seeking to adjudicate it a bankrupt or insolvent, or seeking liquidation, relief or composition of it or its debt under any law relating to bankruptcy, insolvency, reorganization or relief of debtors, or seeking the entry of an order for relief or for any substantial part of its property (and, in the case of any such proceeding instituted against the Borrower or any such endorser or guarantor, should the same remain undismissed or unstayed for a period of 10 days), or should the Borrower or any such endorser or guarantor take corporate action to authorize any of the actions set forth in this clause (v); or (vi) if the Borrower, or any endorser or guarantor of the indebtedness evidenced hereby, is liquidated or dissolved or its articles of incorporation expire or are revoked, <u>then</u>, or at any time after the happening of such an event of default (but in the case of events referred to in items (ii) and (iii) of this paragraph, no default shall occur until the tenth (10th) business day after notice of such default has been given to the Borrower without such default's being cured), at the option of the Lender, **this Note**, together with all accrued interest thereon, **shall immediately become due and payable**, without demand or notice, anything contained in this Note to the contrary notwithstanding, TIME BEING OF THE ESSENCE. *[Emphasis added]*

Case Study 9A, Revised

Comments: Notice how much easier it is to read and understand this sentence when the conditions appear AFTER the verb. By structuring this sentence so the subject, verb, and direct object are readily apparent, and by using the white space on the page to allow the reader to focus on each paragraph separately, the readability of this complicated provision is instantly enhanced.

At the option of the Lender, this Note and all interest accrued on it will immediately become due and payable, without demand or notice, if any of the following events of default happen:

(i) if the Borrower fails to pay, as and when the same shall become due and payable, any principal of or interest on this Note;

(ii) if the Borrower fails to perform any of its duties or obligations as specified in any agreement now or hereafter existing between the Borrower and the Lender (including without limitation the Pledge Agreement (as defined below));

(iii) if the Borrower either fails to pay, as and when the same shall become due and payable, any principal of or interest on any other obligation for borrowed money or any obligation secured by purchase money mortgage or title retention lien beyond any period of grace provided with respect thereto, or fails to perform any other agreement, term or condition contained in an agreement under which any such obligation is created, if the effect of such failure is to cause, or to permit the holder or holders of such obligations (or a trustee on behalf of such holder or holders) to cause, such obligation to become due prior to its stated maturity;

(iv) if at any time any representation, warranty, statement, certificate, schedule, or report made by the Borrower to the Lender shall prove to have been false or misleading in any material respect as of the time made or furnished;

(v) should the Borrower, or any endorser or guarantor of the indebtedness evidenced by this Note, generally not pay its debts as such debts become due, or admit in writing its inability to pay its debts generally, or make a general assignment for the benefit of creditors, or should any proceedings be instituted by or against the Borrower or any such endorser or guarantor seeking to adjudicate it a bankrupt or insolvent, or seeking liquidation, relief or composition of it or its debt under any law relating to bankruptcy, insolvency, reorganization or relief of debtors, or seeking the entry of an order for relief or for any substantial part of its property (and, in the case of any such proceeding instituted against the Borrower or any such endorser or guarantor, should the same remain undismissed or unstayed for a period of 10 days), or should the Borrower or any such endorser or guarantor take corporate action to authorize any of the actions set forth in this clause (v); or

(vi) if the Borrower, or any endorser or guarantor of the indebtedness evidenced hereby, is liquidated or dissolved or its articles of incorporation expire or are revoked.

Time is of the essence of this Agreement.

Case Study 9B

Zero in on sub-paragraphs (iii) and (v) from the prior case study:

(iii) if the Borrower either fails to pay, as and when the same shall become due and payable, **any principal of or interest on** any other obligation for borrowed money or any obligation secured by purchase money mortgage or title retention lien **beyond any period of grace provided with respect thereto**, or fails to perform any other agreement, term or condition contained in an agreement under which any such obligation is created, if the effect of **such failure** is to cause, or to permit the holder or holders of such obligations (or a trustee on behalf of such holder or holders) to cause, such obligation to become due prior to its stated maturity;

(v) should the **Borrower, or any endorser or guarantor** of the indebtedness evidenced by this Note, generally not pay its debts as such debts become due, or admit in writing its inability to pay its debts generally, or make a general assignment for the benefit of creditors, or should any proceedings be instituted by or against the **Borrower or any such endorser or guarantor** seeking to adjudicate it a bankrupt or insolvent, or seeking liquidation, relief or composition of it or its debt under any law relating to bankruptcy, insolvency, reorganization or relief of debtors, or seeking the entry of an order for relief or for any substantial part of its property (and, in the case of any such proceeding instituted against the **Borrower or any such endorser or guarantor**, should the same remain undismissed or unstayed for a period of 10 days), or should the **Borrower or any such endorser or guarantor** take corporate action to authorize any of the actions set forth in this clause (v); or

Comments: Focus on sub-paragraph (iii). Note how the ambiguity in paragraph (iii) caused by the sentence length and convoluted sentence structure is resolved by breaking the long sentence into separate clauses and using tabulations. In the first version, it is unclear what "any principal of or interest on" refers to—does it modify "any other obligation for borrowed money" AND "any obligation secured by purchase money mortgage" AND "title retention lien"? Similarly, it is unclear whether "beyond any period of grace provided with respect thereto" modifies only "title retention liens." Another problem occurs with the words "such failure" as TWO failures have been mentioned: the failure to pay and the failure to perform. See how these ambiguities are resolved by using tabulations in the revised version.

Next, focus on sub-paragraph (v). First, note that this sub-paragraph is not drafted in parallel structure with the rest of this section. Also, note how the words "Borrower, or any endorser or guarantor" are repeated

four times in the same sentence! Finally, note how the sentence length and convoluted sentence structure render this sentence difficult to understand. See how these drafting errors are also resolved by using tabulations and parallel structure in the revised version.

Case Study 9B, Revised

At the option of the Lender, this Note and all interest accrued on it will immediately become due and payable, without demand or notice, if any one or more of the following occur:

(i) the Borrower fails to pay any principal of or interest on this Note, as and when due and payable;

(ii) the Borrower fails to perform any of its duties or obligations as specified in any agreement now or hereafter existing between the Borrower and the Lender;

(iii) the Borrower fails either:

(a) to pay the principal of or interest, as and when due and payable, before any applicable grace period expires, on:

(1) any other obligation for borrowed money; or

(2) any obligation secured by purchase money mortgage or title retention lien;

and the Borrower's failure to pay causes or permits the holder or holders of the obligation (or a trustee on behalf of such holder or holders) to declare it due prior to its stated maturity; or

(b) to perform any other agreement, term or condition contained in an agreement under which any other obligation is created;

(iv) the Borrower makes any representation, warranty, statement, certificate, schedule, or report to the Lender that is proven to have been false or misleading in any material respect when made;

(v) the Borrower, or any endorser or guarantor of the indebtedness evidenced by this Note, does any one or more of the following:

(a) becomes generally unable to pay its debts as such debts become due;

(b) admits in writing its inability to pay its debts generally;

(c) makes a general assignment for the benefit of creditors;

(d) institutes any proceedings seeking to:

(1) adjudicate it a bankrupt or insolvent;

(2) liquidate, relieve or compose it or its debt under any law relating to bankruptcy, insolvency, reorganization or relief of debtors; or

(3) obtain an order for relief for Borrower or for any substantial part of its property;

(e) has involuntary proceedings described in subparagraphs (1), (2) or (3) of clause (d) instituted against it that remain undismissed or unstayed for a period of 10 days; or

(f) takes corporate action to authorize any of the actions set forth in this clause (v); or

(vi) the Borrower, or any endorser or guarantor of the indebtedness evidenced in this Note, is liquidated or dissolved or its articles of incorporation expire or are revoked.

NOTES

1. SCOTT J. BURNHAM, DRAFTING AND ANALYZING CONTRACTS, 107 (3d 2003).

2. *Id.* at p. 290; RICHARD C. WYDICK, PLAIN ENGLISH FOR LAWYERS, 36 (5th 2005), recommending an average sentence length below 25 words; THOMAS R. HAGGARD and GEORGE W. KUNEY, LEGAL DRAFTING IN A NUTSHELL, 323 (3d 2007) recommending an average of 26 words; KENNETH A. ADAMS, A MANUAL OF STYLE FOR CONTRACT DRAFTING, 201 (2004) recommending an average of 20 to 25 words. Note that Adams' recommendation would be warranted according to the Flesch Test of Reading Ease.

3. The readability assessment is calculated for this lesson as a whole and is negatively impacted by the examples, exercises, and case studies.

4. Mark Mathewson, *Law Students, Beware*, 8 SCRIBES J. LEGAL WRITING 142 (2001-2002); WYDICK, *supra* note 2, at 23.

5. WYDICK, *supra* note 2, at 24; ADAMS, *supra* note 2, at 203; TINA L. STARK, DRAFTING CONTRACTS: HOW AND WHY LAWYERS DO WHAT THEY DO, 285 (2007); BURNHAM, *supra* note 1, at 290.

6. *Id.*

7. Note the ambiguous "and" in this example—can the partnership exercise all of these options, or are the options mutually exclusive?

8. SEE BURNHAM, *supra* note 1, at 103 and 291 for more discussion on using tabulations. But note that some legal drafting scholars advise against using "tails" in tabulations unless the use is absolutely necessary to avoid awkward sentence structures.

10

Identify Common Sources of Syntactic Ambiguity

Objective of this Lesson: To identify common sources of syntactic ambiguity.

Key Techniques:
- Eliminate clutter and redundant language.
- Avoid intrusive phrases and clauses.
- Avoid ambiguous phrasing.

10.1 Eliminate Clutter and Redundant Language.

In legal drafting, each word should serve a clear purpose. No word or phrase should appear in a document unless a good reason exists to include it. Question the utility of every word. If you do not know why a word is included in a legal document, look it up. If there is no good reason to include the word, it is clutter and should be eliminated.

Extra, unnecessary words do not just annoy the reader; they also create space where ambiguity can arise. Adopting the practices described in Lessons 7 through 9 will help eliminate some clutter in legal documents. Clutter also tends to accumulate in the following situations.

Get to the Point.

Lawyers sometimes seem to start drafting before their minds have worked out the point they are trying to convey. The result is a lot of unnecessary, beating around the bush, here's-what-I'm-going-to-tell-you-when-I-get-around-to-it, throat-clearing phrases like the following:

> "Subject to the foregoing…"
> "Notwithstanding any other provision to the contrary…"[1]
> "Except as otherwise provided in this Agreement…"
> "It is interesting to note that…"
> "It is important to remember that…"
> "It seems clear that…"
> "It is widely understood that…"
> "As noted above…"

Better to think first, then write. Figure out the point of the sentence and leave out unnecessary prefaces.[2]

Eliminate Repetitive Phrases of Agreement or Understanding.

If the document begins with a general statement of agreement, as it should (see Section 3.4), additional phrases of agreement are unnecessary sources of clutter, because the parties have already agreed to all of the terms that follow. Phrases like "the parties agree that" or "licensee understands that" in performance or boilerplate provisions are usually superfluous and can be excised without remorse. Particularly redundant are sentences that include a phrase of agreement coupled with "shall," as in "Employer agrees that it shall. …"

Instead of this:

"Each of Surviving Company and Acquired Company covenants and agrees that it shall hold all information received by it in connection herewith on a confidential basis."

Identify Common Sources of Syntactic Ambiguity

Use this:

"Surviving Company and Acquired Company shall keep confidential all information received in connection with this transaction."

Instead of this:

"The Members agree to take such actions as are necessary under the Delaware Act and any other applicable law to permit the purchase by the Company of the Shares of the Members in accordance with this Agreement."

Use this:

"The Members shall take the actions necessary under the Delaware Act and any other applicable law to permit the Company to purchase the Shares according to this Agreement."

Phrases of agreement can be used, sparingly, for emphasis, particularly with respect to provisions courts tend to disfavor, like liquidated damage provisions, restrictive covenants, and assignment of intellectual property rights.

e.g., "Client acknowledges and agrees that ASP's pricing for this Agreement is based upon a term of no less than 36 months, and this termination fee is a genuine estimate of ASP's damages for Client's early termination of this Agreement."

e.g., "Consultant acknowledges that Company is and will be considered the author of each work for hire produced by Consultant under this Agreement."

Eliminate Unnecessary Strings of Words.

Lawyers sometimes seem to be afraid to commit to a word choice. Instead of choosing one word to convey a thought, they toss in every possible choice in the genre to ensure that the point has been covered. This apparent word-commitment phobia may have originated in the 1700's when lawyers were paid by the word for legal documents, but there is no sensible purpose for the long strings of words that plague legal documents today.[3] In fact, using a string of words may have unintended, negative consequences, because the courts endeavor to give meaning to each word even in situations where no distinction

---

was intended. If one word covers the intended meaning, use only that word.

Example:

Before: Shareholder may not sell, give, bequeath, assign, alienate, set-over, devise, convey, transfer, hypothecate, pledge or otherwise encumber all or any part of the Shares.

Better: Shareholder may not transfer or otherwise encumber all or any part of the Shares.

Better Still: Shareholder may not transfer any interest in the Shares.

Eliminate Common Doublets and Triplets.

Another source of clutter in legal drafting arose during the Middle Ages, when drafters drew from English, French, and sometimes Latin to explain a single idea.[4] The drafters may have been uncertain which word best conveyed the concept, so they used several. Undoubtedly, the fact that they were paid by the word was also a factor for an unscrupulous few! Whatever the original purpose, legal doublets and triplets emerged from that era that are still commonly used in legal drafting today. Drafters use phrases like "null and void" where either word alone would be sufficient. If there is no distinction between the words, the drafter has merely doubled the words the reader must read.[5] Yet, as discussed, in interpreting contracts judges endeavor to give each word meaning and may strain to find distinctions between words where none were intended. If the legal doublet comes from a statute or case law, then it may be necessary to use it in the same form.[6] Absent some compelling reason to include the extra words, eliminate clutter by removing the redundant language typically included by habit.

Here are a few common legal doublets and triplets[7]:

aid and abet	keep and perform
alter or change	kind and nature
appropriate and proper	legal and valid
bind and obligate	liens and encumbrances
by and between	make and enter into
cancel, annul and set aside	name, constitute and appoint
cease and desist	null and void
convey, transfer and set over	over and above
covenant and agree	part and parcel
deem and consider	perform and discharge

demise and lease	power and authority
due and payable	remise, release, and forever quit claim
final and conclusive	rest, residue and remainder
full and complete	right, title and interest
full faith and credit	sale or transfer
furnish and supply	sole and exclusive
give, devise, bequeath	successors and assigns
grant, bargain, sell	terms and conditions
have and hold	then and in that event
indemnify and hold harmless	true and correct

Exercise 10.1:

Revise these sentences to eliminate the unnecessary words.

1.   The Corporation hereby further agrees to hold harmless and indemnify the distributor to the fullest extent permitted by law, including but not limited to, holding harmless and indemnifying the distributor against any and all expenses (including attorneys' fees), judgments, fines, liabilities, costs, and amounts paid in settlement actually and reasonably incurred by distributor.

2.   The Indemnitee shall qualify for such Expense Advances upon the execution and delivery to the Company of this Agreement which shall constitute an undertaking providing that the Indemnitee undertakes to repay such Expense Advances.

3.   If Indemnitee is entitled under any provision of this Agreement to indemnification by the Company for some or a portion of Expenses, but not, however, for the total amount thereof, the Company agrees that it shall nevertheless indemnify Indemnitee for the portion thereof to which Indemnitee is entitled.

4.   In case any one or more of the provisions contained in this Agreement shall for any reason be held to be invalid, illegal or unenforceable in any respect, such invalidity, illegality or unenforceability shall not affect any other provision of this Agreement and this Agreement shall be construed as if such invalid, illegal or unenforceable provision were limited or modified, consistent with its general intent, to the extent necessary so that it shall be valid, legal and enforceable, or if it shall not be possible to so limit of modify such invalid, illegal or unenforceable provision, this Agreement shall be construed as if such invalid, illegal or unenforceable provision had never been contained herein, and all other provisions hereof shall be and remain unimpaired and in full force and effect.

5.   I give, devise and bequeath all the rest, residue and remainder of my estate, wherever situated, including real and personal property and any other property I own in whole or part at the time of my death. ... [8]

10.2 Avoid Intrusive Phrases and Clauses.

Lawyers tend to pack too much information into a single sentence by inserting details in phrases set off by commas. These additions, exceptions, and incidental information disrupt the logical flow of the sentence, distract the reader, and make it more difficult for the reader to digest the main point of the sentence. Avoid drafting sentences where the subject, verb, and object are separated by intrusive material. Put the details and peripheral language into separate sentences if necessary.

Example:

Before: Subject only to the exclusions set forth in Section 2 hereof, and in addition to any other indemnity to which the Executive may be entitled under the State Statute or any bylaw, resolution or agreement (but without duplication of payments with respect to indemnified amounts), the Corporation hereby further agrees to hold harmless and indemnify the Executive, to the fullest extent permitted by law, including, but not limited to, holding harmless and indemnifying the Executive against any and all expenses. ...

Better: The Corporation shall indemnify and defend the Executive to the fullest extent permitted by law against any and all expenses. ...

Example:

Before: The invoice, which must, on or before the 5th day of each calendar month, be prepared, must, unless otherwise agreed in writing, include all charges, authorized, but solely to the extent authorized, under this agreement, incurred by client during the preceding calendar month, and must be delivered to client, on the same day, by facsimile, at 404-123-4567, or courier.

Better: An invoice must be prepared on or before the 5th day of each calendar month. The invoice must include all charges incurred by client during the preceding calendar month that are authorized under this agreement. The invoice must be delivered to client on the 5th day of each calendar month by courier or by facsimile at 404-123-4567.

Better Still: Company shall deliver an invoice to client on or before the 5th day of each calendar month by courier or by facsimile at 404-123-4567. The invoice must include all charges authorized under this agreement that are incurred by client during the preceding calendar month.

Case Study 10.2

You should be able to identify many problems with this provision.

(c) <u>Change in Control</u>: shall be deemed to have occurred if (i) any "person" (as such term is used in Sections 13(d) and 14(d) of the Securities Exchange Act of 1934, as amended (the "Exchange Act")) (other than a trustee or other fiduciary holding securities under an employee benefit plan of the Company or a corporation owned directly or indirectly by the stockholders of the Company in substantially the same proportions as their ownership of stock of the Company, and other than any person holding shares of the Company on the date that the Company first registers under the Act or any transferee of such individual if such transferee is a spouse or lineal descendant of the transferee or a trust for the benefit of the individual, his spouse or lineal descendants), is or becomes the "beneficial owner" (as defined in Rule 13d-3 under the Exchange Act), directly or indirectly, of securities of the Company representing 30% or more of the total voting power represented by the Company's then outstanding Voting Securities, or (ii) during any period of two consecutive years, individuals who at the beginning of such period constitute the Board and any new director whose election by the Board or nomination for election by the Company's stockholders was approved by a vote of at least two-thirds (2/3) of the directors then still in office who either were directors at the beginning of the period or whose election or nomination for election was previously so approved, cease for any reason to constitute a majority of the Board, or (iii) the stockholders of the Company approve a merger or consolidation of the Company with any other entity, other than a merger or consolidation that would result in the Voting Securities of the Company outstanding immediately prior thereto continuing to represent (either by remaining outstanding or by being converted into Voting Securities of the surviving entity) at least 80% of the total voting power represented by the Voting Securities of the Company or such surviving entity outstanding immediately after such merger or consolidation, or (iv) the stockholders of the Company approve a plan of complete liquidation of the Company or an agreement for the sale or disposition by the Company (in one transaction or a series of transactions) of all or substantially all of the Company's assets.

Comments: Although this provision deals with a complicated concept, much of the complexity is caused by the syntax. The defined terms stuffed in the provision add unnecessary layers of complexity. These sentences are packed with intrusive phrases and clauses that cause the sentences to ramble unnecessarily. Item (i) is structured so almost nine lines of text separate the subject ("person") and verb (is or becomes). The syntax can be simplified and improved by 1) pulling the defined terms out; 2) adding a few key definitions; 3) structuring sentences logically; 4) moving the intrusive phrases to separate, shorter sentences; and 5) using the white space to focus the reader's attention on one clause at a time.

(c) <u>Change in Control</u> means that any one or more of the following have occurred:

  (i) any Person becomes the Beneficial Owner, directly or indirectly, of 30% or more of the Company's then outstanding Voting Securities;

  (ii) during any consecutive two year period, the Original Directors plus Added Directors cease to constitute a majority of the Board of Directors;

  (iii) the Stockholders approve a merger or consolidation of the Company with any other entity, except that a Change in Control is not deemed to occur if the Stockholders retain at least 80% of the combined voting power of the merged or consolidated entity; or

  (iv) the Stockholders approve a plan to liquidate the Company, or agree to sell or dispose of, in one transaction or a series of transactions:

  • the stock of the Company; or
  • all or substantially all of the Company's assets.

(#) <u>Added Director</u> means any Person who becomes a member of the Board of Directors during any consecutive two-year period and whose nomination was approved by at least two-thirds of the Original Directors.

(#) <u>Beneficial Owner</u> has the meaning given in Rule 13d-3 of the Exchange Act.

(#) <u>Exchange Act</u> means the Securities Exchange Act of 1934.

(#) <u>Original Director</u> means a Person who was a Director of the Company at the beginning of any period of two consecutive years.

(#) <u>Person</u> has the meaning given in Sections 13(d) and 14(d) of the Exchange Act.

(#) <u>Stockholders</u> means all Persons owning common stock of the Company.

•••

10.3 Avoid Ambiguous Phrasing.

Contract litigation often centers around ambiguous references to specific dates and times. Drafters use many words and phrases that seem clear but are construed by the parties, and the courts, in different ways. Sometimes, the legal interpretation is inconsistent with how non-lawyers would understand the language.

The simplest way to avoid ambiguity in provisions that contain date references is to specify a time of day for each beginning and ending date. Note that if the contract is to be performed between parties located in different time zones, it should always specify what time zone is to be used.

1. Between ... and ...

The closing must take place between December 1, 2010 and January 1, 2011.

Courts generally construe this language literally, so that December 1 and January 1 are EXCLUDED, and the closing must take place within the range of days starting with December 2 and including December 31.[9] Non-lawyers would most likely assume that December 1 and January 1 are INCLUDED, so this expression may be counter-intuitive to the audience of the contract. Note that no time would exist **between** December 30 and December 31.[10] Eliminate ambiguity by including a time reference: "The closing must take place between 9:00 a.m. on December 1, 2010 and 5:00 p.m. on January 1, 2011."

2. After ... before

The parties shall close the transaction after December 1, 2010.

The parties shall close the transaction before January 1, 2011.

The parties shall close the transaction after December 1, 2010 and before January 1, 2011.

Although it may seem counterintuitive to non-lawyers to define a time period by dates that are not included in the period, the courts consistently hold that December 1 and January 1 in the examples above are EXCLUDED. Avoid confusion by including "on or" in the expression, as in "The parties shall close the transaction **on or** after December 1, 2010."

3. From ... to

The parties may close the transaction from December 1, 2010 to January 1, 2011.

The courts are completely divided as to what this expression means. Some conclude that both specified dates are EXCLUDED; some conclude that both are INCLUDED, and some conclude that the "from" is EXCLUDED but the "to" date is INCLUDED. With interpretation as uncertain as this, it is far better to choose language that is more definitive in the drafting stage than argue about it in litigation!

4. Until

The parties have until December 31, 2010 to close the transaction.

The majority view is that "until" includes the date December 31, but some courts construe it differently. To avoid litigation on the issue, the drafter should explicitly state a date and time, e.g., "The parties have until noon, eastern standard time, on December 31, 2010 to close the transaction."

5. By

The closing must take place by December 31, 2010.

Most courts have construed this language to INCLUDE December 31, but especially in cases where a great deal of money is at risk, the drafter should choose language more carefully. E.g., "The closing must take place by noon on December 31, 2010."

6. Starting

The closing may take place at any mutually convenient time starting December 1, 2010.

Most courts would construe December 1 to be INCLUDED. Use "on or after" to eliminate ambiguity: "The closing may take place at any mutually convenient time on or after December 1, 2010."

---

7. Through

The closing may take place at any mutually convenient time through January 1, 2011.

Most courts would construe January 1 to be INCLUDED, but clarifying words eliminate doubt: "The closing may take place at any mutually convenient time through company's regular business hours on January 1, 2011."

8. Within

The closing must take place within 30 days.

Drafters should avoid using "within" in this context for many reasons. First, "within" can run forwards or backwards, which means that this language could be construed to include the 30-day period before or after the specified date. Second, the usage in this particular example is ambiguous because the audience cannot tell when the 30 day period begins. Use "no later than" instead, and specify the start of the period.

NOTES

1. Most often, this phrase is included out of bad habit as a "catch all" protection when the drafter has not taken the time to determine whether contrary provisions exist. The drafter certainly ought to know whether provisions to the contrary have been intentionally included before the client signs the document, and, instead of a generic excuse like this, contrary provisions should be specifically identified. The same is true of "Except as otherwise provided in this Agreement. ..."

2. HENRY WEIHOFEN, LEGAL WRITING STYLE, 55 (1961).

3. KENNETH A. ADAMS, A MANUAL OF STYLE FOR CONTRACT DRAFTING, 204 (2004); RICHARD C. WYDICK, PLAIN ENGLISH FOR LAWYERS, 61 (5th 2005); THOMAS R. HAGGARD AND GEORGE W. KUNEY, LEGAL DRAFTING IN A NUTSHELL, 299 (3d 2007).

4. WYDICK, *supra* note 3, at 18; HAGGARD/KUNEY NUTSHELL, *supra* note 3, at 300; BRYAN A. GARNER, THE REDBOOK: A MANUAL ON LEGAL STYLE, 163 (2002); DAVID MELLINKOFF, LEGAL WRITING: SENSE & NONSENSE, 4, 189-190 (1982).

5. LAUREL CURRIE OATES, ET AL., THE LEGAL WRITING HANDBOOK, 690 (3d 2002).

6. *Id.*

7. For more exhaustive lists of common doublets and triplets, *see* GARNER, REDBOOK, *supra* note 4, at 163; REED DICKERSON, THE FUNDAMENTALS OF LEGAL DRAFTING, 207-208 (1986); HAGGARD/KUNEY NUTSHELL, *supra* note 3, at 302.

8. Even the most stringent drafting scholars encourage considerable caution in determining which words are unnecessary in wills. "A lawyer has reason to be especially careful in wording a will. It is a mournful characteristic of probate cases that the testator [or testatrix] is always dead, and so is not available to explain what he [or she] meant. The draft[er] should therefore take care to express [the] client's wishes without ambiguity." HENRY WEIBOFEN, LEGAL WRITING STYLE 47 (1961).

9. HAGGARD/KUNEY NUTSHELL, *supra* note 3, at 256.

10. BRYAN A. GARNER, A DICTIONARY OF MODERN LEGAL USAGE, 106 (2d 1995).

11

Start from a Winning Position

Objective of this Lesson: To demonstrate which provisions from a prior transaction should be included in the current draft, and how to draft provisions to allocate risk.

Key Techniques:
- Understand whether provisions are required, essential, strongly recommended, or optional.
- Start with provisions that favor your client.
- Draft to allocate risk.
- Identify the range of risk.

11.1 Understand whether provisions are required, essential, strongly recommended, or optional.

One interesting quirk of a transactional practice is that the methods and procedures of drafting a contract are almost completely unregulated by statute or case law. Unlike a litigation practice, where the time frame for filing, format, content, length, type size, and even the size of paper of a brief or pleading are dictated by statute and court rules, very little about drafting a contract is "required." Although contracts are based upon the law, most are completely unregulated in terms of language or format. Contracts are not even "required to be clear, or even legible, and too many of them are neither."[1]

Little drafting is done completely from scratch. Drafting scholar David Mellinkoff mused that, "No one who makes frequent use of the law will ever live long enough to live without forms."[2] Most drafting projects begin with a template document that was used in a previous transaction. The genealogy and original purpose of the template, or distinct provisions included in the template, are seldom known. Some—if not all—of the provisions included in the template have been negotiated by the parties to previous transactions and may not represent either party's best interests.

Drafters should understand why each substantive provision was included in the template in order to discern whether those provisions are appropriate for the contract they are currently drafting. Substantive provisions may be required, essential, strongly recommended, or optional. Too often, irrelevant provisions are included in contracts because the drafter is uncertain why they were included in the template, and it is easier simply to include the language than to figure out whether it is relevant. Besides being annoying to the users, unnecessary language creates havens for ambiguity to thrive.

If you are not sure why a provision was included in the template, look it up. An excellent resource for determining the etymology of legal concepts is *A Dictionary of Modern Legal Usage* by Bryan A. Garner. Also be sure to carefully research a treatise on applicable law. New drafters should consult more seasoned drafters before deleting suspicious language. If no reason currently exists for including the provision, it should be eliminated.[3] Beware that errors can occur at both ends of the spectrum, so take as much care not to include unnecessary provisions as not to eliminate necessary ones.

1. Required. Although there are surprisingly few statutory requirements for contracts, they tend to pop up in the most unlikely places, and the failure to comply with these statutory requirements is usually fatal to the contract. For example, in employment and severance agreements, if the employee is asked to waive possible age discrimination claims, according to federal law, the contract must inform the employee of the right to consult with counsel before signing the agreement. The waiver is legally ineffective and unenforceable if this language is not included. Similarly, in government contracts, the vendor is required to comply, and require its vendors to comply, with a host of government regulations, all of which must be specified in the contracts with those vendors. Another trap for the unwary is that in certain circumstances, such as employment agreements, arbitration clauses must be initialed in order to be enforceable under state law. Obviously, the drafter must identify relevant statutory requirements before drafting. (See Section 2.4.)

2. Essential. These are the substantive provisions that, although not required by statute, are required to make the contract legally effective. For example, a license agreement is not effective without a provision that actually grants rights. A contract for the sale of goods must identify the parties and what goods are to be sold. Unless the parties have agreed to the essential terms, the contract will not be enforceable; however, the laws of each jurisdiction differ as to what constitutes an "essential term." The drafter must determine what terms are essential under applicable law, and be sure the contract contains them.

3. Strongly Recommended. These substantive provisions are not required or essential, but are those that, in the drafter's assessment and experience, are important to the transaction. For example, although they are not required or essential, most experienced lawyers would strongly recommend that restrictive covenants be included in employment agreements, especially where key executives have access to sensitive proprietary information. The drafter's experience in dealing with this client or with similar matters usually helps identify substantive provisions that SHOULD be included, even though they are not required or even essential. Strongly recommended provisions often have to do with avoiding or remedying problems that could arise if the transaction does not go as planned.

4. Optional, Based on the Drafter's Assessment. After the drafter has included required, essential, and strongly recommended substantive provisions, the client's goals and objectives may suggest optional provisions. For example, in a software license agreement, after the drafter has granted the license and described how deficiencies will be handled, the drafter may need to include provisions dealing with derivative works if the transaction encompasses the possibility of incorporating the software into new products in the future.

Exercise 11.1:

Determine whether the following provisions are required, essential, strongly recommended, or optional. Note that your conclusions may vary based on assumptions regarding the underlying circumstances and based on which party you represent.

1. Contractor must send to each labor union or representative of workers with which it has a collective bargaining agreement or other contract or understanding, a notice to be provided by Company's designated representative, advising the labor union or workers' representative of the Contractor's commitments under section 202 of Executive Order 11246 of September 24, 1965. Contractor must post copies of the notice in conspicuous places available to employees and applicants for employment.

2. No shareholder may transfer all or any part of the rights and incidents of ownership of the Shares. Any transfer in violation of this Shareholder Buy-Sell Agreement is null.

3. This paragraph does not limit my right to challenge the validity of this Severance Agreement in a legal proceeding under the Older Workers Benefit Protection Act, 29 U.S.C. 626 Section (f) with respect to claims under the Age Discrimination in Employment Act.

4. THE WARRANTIES AND REMEDIES PROVIDED IN THIS AGREEMENT ARE EXCLUSIVE AND IN LIEU OF ALL OTHER WARRANTIES, EXPRESS OR IMPLIED, INCLUDING BUT NOT LIMITED TO THE IMPLIED WARRANTIES OF MERCHANTABILITY AND FITNESS FOR A PARTICULAR PURPOSE. NO ORAL OR WRITTEN INFORMATION OUTSIDE OF THIS AGREEMENT WILL IN ANY WAY EXTEND OR MODIFY THE FOREGOING WARRANTY.

5. If Consultant creates any works protectible under the copyright law, including, but not limited to, computer software programs and

applications, textual, audio, or visual works ("Works"), each Work will be deemed specially commissioned by the Company for use as a "collective work," and considered a "work made for hire," as those terms are defined in the United States Copyright Act.

6. The closing for the sale and purchase of the Assets will take place at a mutually agreeable time and place on or before December 31, 2007.

7. Employee may participate in bonus incentive plans offered by the Company.

8. This Agreement is governed and construed according to the laws of the State of Georgia.

9. Vendor hereby grants Customer a non-exclusive and non-transferable license to use the Software.

10. Supplier agrees to perform the services described in the Statement of Work according to the terms of this Agreement.

11.2 Start with provisions that favor your client.

Virtually every sentence in a contract can be drafted so it favors one party or the other. Most provisions can also be drafted more neutrally, so the right or obligation is reciprocal. The objective of this lesson may be better stated in a negative manner: don't start from a losing position! It's surprising how often in actual practice a client's "standard form" actually favors the other party. For example, purchase agreements for goods and services routinely exclude the warranty of fitness for particular purpose, yet this UCC warranty only comes into effect when the seller is *aware* of the buyer's intended use, and the buyer *relies* on the seller's recommendation to purchase it. Why would a buyer who has relied on the seller's advice that the product is appropriate for buyer's purposes *automatically* exclude this warranty?[4] Sometimes, the parties negotiate to exclude the warranty, but too often it is excluded simply because the drafter inserted familiar language from another form without considering the *raison d'être*, namely, to exculpate seller from responsibility.

Clients differ in their approach to the bargaining process, and lawyers are obligated under the Model Rules of Professional Conduct to follow the client's reasonable directives concerning the objectives of

---

representation, within certain parameters.[5] Some clients prefer that all provisions be drafted as strongly as possible in their favor, while others prefer a more paternalistic, "I'm o.k., you're o.k.," approach where provisions are drafted in a more neutral manner that is considered equitable to both parties.

Documents should be drafted according to the client's objectives, but in no event should the *starting position* be detrimental to the client's interests. Where the client adopts a more paternalistic approach, the provision should be drafted so it is more neutral, but not in a manner that favors the other party. For example, an indemnification provision can be drafted so either party is required to indemnify the other, or so both parties undertake a reciprocal obligation to indemnify. Absent a compelling reason, do not draft an indemnification provision that requires your client to indemnify the other party without receiving a reciprocal promise, because this is a losing position.

A lawyer should be aware of the client's philosophical approach to business relationships before drafting because the client's policies should permeate every sentence. Some clients might take a different approach with different types of contracts, or when dealing with different business partners. For example, a company might adopt a more aggressive approach to protect its intellectual property rights, but the same company might adopt a more paternalistic approach in other types of agreements, or when its business partners are small businesses. The best way to learn the client's objectives is to ask during the interview process. While a lawyer can certainly offer advice and make recommendations, it is not ethically appropriate to ignore the client's preferences or to substitute your own.

11.3 Draft to allocate risk.

Contracts serve to allocate risk among the parties to a transaction. For most contract provisions, there is an approach that allocates more risk to the party receiving assets, goods, or services; an approach that allocates more risk to the party providing them; and a range of possibilities between the extremes. The way a provision is drafted affects the level of risk and responsibility each party undertakes in the contract. Sometimes a single word or phrase can have an enormous impact. For example, insertion of the phrase "to the extent that" in an indemnification provision activates proximate cause limitations to reduce the indemnifying party's risk.

Consider the following clauses:

1. Seller shall deliver the goods on or before July 31.

2. Seller shall use best efforts to deliver the goods on or before July 31.

3. Seller shall use best efforts to deliver the goods on or before July 31. For purposes of this Agreement, "best efforts" means that Seller will obtain the goods on the open market and absorb any additional costs incurred to fulfill its delivery obligations on a timely basis.

4. Seller shall use commercially reasonable efforts to deliver the goods on or before July 31.

5. Seller will attempt to deliver the goods on or before July 31.

The risk allocation between buyer and seller varies in each of the examples given above. Relatively simple edits in the language shift the risk from the Seller in the first sentence to the Buyer in the last. In the first sentence, the Seller has more risk because in order to comply with the terms of the agreement, the goods have to be delivered by July 31 without exception.[6] The second example provides a small exception: the Seller will not breach the agreement if it uses best efforts but is unable to deliver the goods by July 31. The Seller still has the risk of ensuring that its efforts rise to the level of being "best efforts," which can be a tough standard. "Best efforts" implies that the Seller will do anything within its power to see that the goods are delivered on or before July 31, which may be financially unfeasible. The third example whittles away from the Seller another small degree of risk because the term "best efforts" is defined within the contract. In the fourth example, the risk is shifting more towards the Buyer, because Seller is only obligated to use "commercially reasonable" efforts to deliver the goods, which means the Seller is not obligated to use efforts that are financially unfeasible. In the last example, the Buyer has assumed the risk because the Seller has only agreed to attempt to deliver by July 31, meaning that the Buyer will have no recourse if the Seller attempts but is unable to deliver the goods.

It is your responsibility as drafter to ensure that your client assumes the correct level of risk. While your buyer client may ultimately wind up accepting no more than an attempt at delivery by the seller as a result of negotiations, by no means should you START the negotiation process at this position. This is a losing position because the buyer has absorbed all risks if the goods are not delivered.

Case Studies:

Notice how the risk shifts between the parties based on relatively small changes to the wording of each provision.

Warranties:

1. Warranty. Seller warrants that the goods will conform to buyer's specifications.

2. Warranty. Seller warrants that the goods will conform in all material ways to buyer's specifications.

3. Limited Warranty. Seller warrants that the goods are merchantable. Seller specifically disclaims the warranty of fitness for particular purpose.

4. Limited Warranty. Seller warrants that it will use commercially reasonable efforts to comply with the terms of this Agreement. Seller specifically disclaims all other warranties, including the warranty of merchantability and the warranty of fitness for particular purpose.

5. No Warranty. Seller disclaims all warranties under this Agreement, including the warranty of merchantability and the warranty of fitness for particular purpose.

Comments: In the first example, Seller has assumed a large risk for three reasons: first, this is a full warranty with no limitations, so UCC warranties of merchantability and fitness for particular purpose apply; second, there is no materiality limitation, so the goods must conform in every detail, not just in every material way; and third, because the buyer's specifications are not defined and limited in the agreement. Presumably, the buyer may change its specifications from time to time during the term of the agreement, and the seller has absorbed the risk of conforming, no matter what those specifications may be. The Seller's risk is reduced in the second example because a materiality limitation has been added. In the third example, Seller's risk is reduced and Buyer's risk is increased because this is no longer a full warranty and the UCC warranty of fitness for particular purpose is disclaimed. How does the risk allocation shift in the fourth and fifth examples?

Conditions of Transfer:

1. The Transferring Owner shall have delivered to the Company a written opinion of counsel for the Company substantially in the form attached to this Agreement as Schedule 14.1 that the Transfer will not result in a violation of applicable law.

2. The Transferring Owner shall have delivered to the Company a written opinion of counsel for the Company or of other counsel satisfactory to the Company substantially in the form attached to this Agreement as Schedule 14.1 that the Transfer will not result in a violation of applicable law.

3. The Transferring Owner shall have delivered to the Company a written opinion of counsel reasonably satisfactory to the Company that the Transfer will not result in a violation of applicable law.

4. The Transferring Owner shall have delivered to the Company a written opinion of counsel that the Transfer will not result in a violation of applicable law.

Comments: The transferring owner has a higher degree of risk in the first example because counsel for the company is going to be highly protective of its client's interests and the form attached is likely to be one-sided in advancing the Company's rights. In the second example, the transferring owner may be able to obtain an opinion of counsel from its own representatives (if the Company deems them satisfactory), who will advocate the owner's interests. How does the risk allocation shift in the third and fourth examples?

Grant of a License:

1. Licensor grants Company all intellectual property rights in the Software.

2. Licensor grants Company the right to use the Software and all rights appurtenant to use of the Software, including the right to modify the Software and the right to create derivative works.

3. Licensor grants Company the right to use the Software in any manner consistent with the terms of this Agreement.

4. Licensor grants Company the right to use the Software for the specific purposes described in this Agreement. Except as stated in this Agreement, no other rights are granted by Licensor to Company.

Comments: Who has more risk in the first example, and why? How does risk allocation shift among the parties in this case study?

Assignment:

1. Seller may not assign any rights or duties under this Agreement.

2. Seller may not assign any rights or duties under this Agreement without the consent of Buyer, which consent may be withheld for any reason or no reason.

3. Seller may not assign any rights or duties under this Agreement without the consent of Buyer, which consent may not be unreasonably withheld.

4. Neither party may assign any rights or duties under this Agreement without written consent of the other party.

5. Neither party may assign any rights or duties under this Agreement except to a parent, affiliate or subsidiary or except to a successor in interest in the event of a change in control.

Comments: Who has more risk in the first example, and why? How does risk allocation shift among the parties in this case study? How would the range of risk extend beyond the fifth example?

11.4 Identify the range of risk.

The biggest challenge for the new drafter is to determine the parameters of the range of risk for each contractual obligation. In other words, when you begin "marking up" a document to fit the current transaction, how do you determine whether a provision is neutral or whether it favors one of the parties over the other? Where does this particular provision fall in the overall range of risk as currently written? Does it advance your client's interests, or is it more favorable to the other party? If your client prefers a more aggressive approach, how do you know whether the provision is one-sided enough or whether it needs to be tightened up?

To some extent, this knowledge is gained through experience, which is why it is called the "practice" of law, and why partners' billing rates are substantially higher than new associates' rates. For the diligent, however, some sources exist that can help identify the range of risk. The best source for identifying the range of risk for a particular provision is an experienced mentor. If a reliable mentor is not available, the next best source is your law firm's or law department's form files. Try to find a contract where your firm represented the buyer and compare it to a contract where your firm represented the seller. The final forms most likely have been heavily negotiated, so the best source is the first draft submitted to opposing counsel, if your firm drafted the contract, or the first revision, if your firm reviewed an initial draft prepared by opposing counsel. Study the revisions requested by counsel for each party and observe how experienced lawyers have fine-tuned the language to shift risk from one party to the other.

Although experienced drafters usually avoid them, some form books are well written and often include forms labeled as to which party they favor, like this: "Software License Favoring Licensee."[7] Sometimes, form books are annotated with a running commentary as to why each provision is phrased a certain way, with alternative language included. By comparing forms favoring a licensee and a licensor side by side, for example, a new drafter can begin to identify the range of risk for each provision.

Exercise 11.4:

Identify the range of allocating risk between a buyer and seller with respect to an indemnification provision. Start with a simple provision more favorable to the Buyer, develop into a provision that is neutral, and end with a provision more favorable to Seller.

NOTES

1. DAVID MELLINKOFF, LEGAL WRITING: SENSE AND NONSENSE, 77 (1982).

2. *Id.*, at 102.

3. New drafters may find it helpful to maintain a list of provisions omitted from the prior draft, which can be quickly reviewed by supervising lawyers.

4. A buyer client may have made the decision that it would rather give up its UCC warranty rights in every purchase than to have to negotiate the provision on a case by case, but this should be based on an intentional decision of someone having appropriate authority, not on happenstance or ignorance.

5. **RULE 1.2 SCOPE OF REPRESENTATION**

   (a) A lawyer shall abide by a client's decisions concerning the objectives of representation, subject to paragraphs (c), (d) and (e), and shall consult

with the client as to the means by which they are to be pursued. A lawyer shall abide by a client's decision whether to accept an offer of settlement of a matter. In a criminal case, the lawyer shall abide by the client's decision, after consultation with the lawyer, as to a plea to be entered, whether to waive jury trial and whether the client will testify.

(b) A lawyer's representation of a client, including representation by appointment, does not constitute an endorsement of the client's political, economic, social or moral views or activities.

(c) A lawyer may limit the objectives of the representation if the client consents after consultation.

(d) A lawyer shall not counsel a client to engage in conduct that the lawyer knows is criminal or fraudulent, nor knowingly assist a client in such conduct, but a lawyer may discuss the legal consequences of any proposed course of conduct with a client and may counsel or assist a client to make a good faith effort to determine the validity, scope, meaning or application of the law.

(e) When a lawyer knows that a client expects assistance not permitted by the rules of professional conduct or other law, the lawyer shall consult with the client regarding the relevant limitations on the lawyer's conduct.

The maximum penalty for a violation of this Rule is disbarment.

Comment

Scope of Representation

[1] Both lawyer and client have authority and responsibility in the objectives and means of representation. The client has ultimate authority to determine the purposes to be served by legal representation, within the limits imposed by law and the lawyer's professional obligations. Within those limits, a client also has a right to consult with the lawyer about the means to be used in pursuing those objectives. At the same time, a lawyer is not required to pursue objectives or employ means simply because a client may wish that the lawyer do so. A clear distinction between objectives and means sometimes cannot be drawn, and in many cases the client-lawyer relationship partakes of a joint undertaking. In questions of means, the lawyer should assume responsibility for technical and legal tactical issues, but should defer to the client regarding such questions as the expense to be incurred and concern for third persons who might be adversely affected.

[2] In a case in which the client appears to be suffering mental disability, the lawyer's duty to abide by the client's decisions is to be guided by reference to *Rule 1.14: Client under a Disability*.

Independence from Client's Views or Activities

[3] Legal representation should not be denied to people who are unable to afford legal services, or whose cause is controversial or the subject of popular disapproval. By the same token, representing a client does not constitute approval of the client's views or activities.

Services Limited in Objectives or Means

[4] **The objectives or scope of services provided by a lawyer may be limited by agreement with the client or by the terms under which the lawyer's services are made available to the client. For example, a retainer may be for a specifically defined purpose.** Representation provided through a legal aid agency may be subject to limitations on the types of cases the agency handles. When a lawyer has been retained by an insurer to represent an insured, the representation may be limited to matters covered by the insurance policy. The terms upon which representation is undertaken may exclude specific objectives or means. Such limitations may include objectives or means that the lawyer regards as repugnant or imprudent.

[5] An agreement concerning the scope of representation must accord with the Rules of Professional Conduct and other law. Thus, the client may not be asked to agree to representation so limited in scope as to violate *Rule 1.1: Competence,* or to surrender the right to terminate the lawyer's services or the right to settle litigation that the lawyer might wish to continue. The agreement should be in writing.

[6] For purposes of this discussion, we assume that time is of the essence of the agreement, although that is not the case for contracts for the sale of goods under the UCC, which applies a reasonableness standard. In some states, it is necessary to state in the agreement that time is of the essence if the parties intend it to be. For example, under O.C.G.A. § 13-2-2, time is not of the essence of the agreement, but the parties can so stipulate. This means that if the parties do not stipulate in the agreement that time is of the essence, delivery on August 1st or 2nd would be satisfactory in most situations under "reasonableness" standards. This is the reason a "time is of the essence" clause is often included in the boilerplate.

[7] Look for form books that are subject-matter specific, but avoid form books that contain thousands of forms covering a multitude of legal practice areas.

12

Eliminate Contextual Ambiguity

Objective of this Lesson: To explain the causes of contextual ambiguity and how to avoid it.

Key Techniques:
- Organize documents properly.
- Keep related documents consistent.
- Flow-chart money and alternative outcomes.
- Proofread strategically to ensure schedules, exhibits, and appendices are attached.

Contextual ambiguity derives primarily from two sources: inconsistent provisions and omitted information. When two provisions that are part of the same document or related documents contain inconsistent language or terms, ambiguity arises because two or more interpretations are equally plausible. For example, if the parties decide to insert a provision that includes a defined term which has been already been defined elsewhere in the document, ambiguity arises as to which definition controls. Contextual ambiguity also arises when a document omits necessary information.

12.1 Organize documents properly to avoid contextual ambiguity.

Section 5.4 discussed the need to organize documents logically to assist the readers in finding needed information as the transaction is implemented. Organizing documents properly also yields another benefit: it helps avoid contextual ambiguity. If a document is poorly organized, inconsistent provisions are much harder to spot. As the parties negotiate long, complicated documents, one party may insert additional language, unaware that the topic has been addressed elsewhere in the document. In the best case scenario, if the additional language and the original language are identical, the provisions are merely redundant—and therefore, unnecessary. If, however, the additional language and the original language are not identical, the inconsistent provisions cause ambiguity when the parties try to determine which provision controls. When related concepts are grouped and arranged properly, overlapping provisions should appear side by side, and inconsistencies are easily identified.

New lawyers are particularly prone to creating contextual ambiguity by copying sections from one document into another without carefully integrating the new material into the existing text. Scrutinize every inserted provision to ensure it is consistent with the rest of the document. Make sure the terms of the inserted language do not conflict with the terms of the document and that the defined terms and other terminology are used consistently.

12.2 Keep Related Documents Consistent.

Sometimes, several different documents are all part of the same transaction. For example, if a client hires a new employee and grants a stock option, the parties may enter into an employment agreement, a stock option agreement, and a shareholders' agreement. To the greatest extent possible, avoid drafting the same subject matter into multiple documents. If the subject matter is addressed in more than one document, it is crucial that the overlapping provisions match identically. If the overlapping provisions are not identical, you have created contextual ambiguity that a highly-trained professional will be happy to exploit.

Examples:

Shareholder Agreement: "Shareholder separately covenants and agrees with the Company that, for so long as he holds the Shares and **for a period of six (6) months following cessation** as a Shareholder, he will not, either directly or indirectly, on his own behalf or in the services of others in the United States, engage in the Business of the Company as an officer, director, executive, managerial employee, consultant to. ..."

Employment Agreement: "**For one (1) year following termination**, neither Employee nor any Affiliate will, without the prior written consent of Company, engage in any Competing Business. ..."

[Note: in this example, the shareholder agreement stated that upon termination of employment, the shares in question must be sold back to the Company—which means both non-compete provisions will come into effect at the same time, one with a six month term and the other with a one year term. Which prevails?]

Articles of Incorporation: "Any action which *[read "that"]* may be taken at a meeting of the shareholders may be taken without a meeting if a written consent, setting forth the actions so taken, shall be signed by those shareholders entitled to vote with respect to the subject matter thereof having voting power to cast not less than the minimum number (or numbers, in the case of voting by classes) of votes that would be necessary to authorize or take such action at a meeting at which all shareholders entitled to vote were present and voted."

Bylaws: "Any action required or permitted to be taken at a shareholders' meeting may be taken without a meeting if all the shareholders entitled to vote on such action, or the appropriate percentage of shareholders necessary to approve the action at a meeting of the shareholders at which all shareholders entitled to vote were present and voted, sign one or more written consents."

The excerpt from the Bylaws is syntactically ambiguous because it is not clear whether *all* of the shareholders or *less than all* of the shareholders are required to take action by written consent. This language is contextually ambiguous as well because the language of the related provision in the Articles differs from the language in the Bylaws. Both problems could have been avoided with careful editing.

12.3 Track money and alternative outcomes.

One of the distinctions between legal drafting and legal writing discussed in Lesson 1 is that legal drafting must anticipate and provide for future events. Contextual ambiguity can arise where the terms of a document are incomplete with respect to all possible outcomes of a transaction or a particular provision. For example, a distribution agreement may grant an exclusive territory and provide a bonus if the distributor meets or exceeds certain required sales objectives. What happens if the distributor fails to achieve the sales objectives? If the agreement fails to provide for this outcome, contextual ambiguity may arise between the parties as to the distributor's fate.

One tool to avoid contextual ambiguity caused by incomplete terms is to flow-chart potential outcomes. A flow chart is basically a diagram that helps the drafter visualize how the transaction as a whole or a particular provision operates. A substantive provision is broken down into a series of simple yes or no questions. Each question is written in a box with arrows indicating the next step whether the answer is "yes" or "no" until the ultimate conclusion is reached.

Although computer programmers use specific flow-charting symbols, arrows, and decision blocks to answer a series of yes/no questions, it's not necessary to master flow-charting as an art form to obtain the chart's benefits of logic and to visualize potential outcomes. A simple flow chart that tracks the potential flow of money or alternative outcomes is sufficient to help the drafter identify substantive gaps in either the terms of the transaction or the document itself.

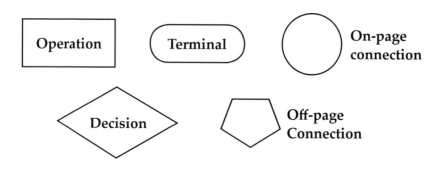

Consider the following provision:

"The husband agrees that upon the sale of the marital residence, or on April 1, 2001, whichever event first occurs, he shall pay from the proceeds of the sale to the wife all of the net proceeds from the sale of the house, but not more than $50,000."[1]

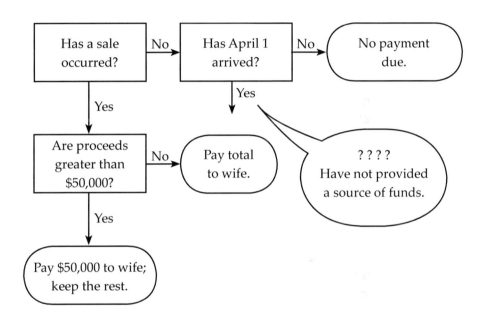

A flow chart illustrates in pictorial form all of the alternative outcomes that should be addressed in a provision. Errors can be more easily spotted in that picture than in 1,000 words! Flow-charting a complicated provision helps the drafter visualize and clarify its substantive components. A flow chart can identify omissions or duplications that are potential sources of contextual ambiguity. A flow chart may also illustrate that a particular provision has been poorly organized. Be sure to compare your flow chart to the facts gathered during the client interview to ensure that the provision is substantively accurate and complete.

Exercise 12.3:

Flow-chart the flow of funds described in the following provision. Have all possible outcomes been addressed? What other revisions would you recommend?

8.6 Price. If any Member who is employed by the Company ceases to be employed within 365 days of the Effective Date of this Agreement, the purchase price of the Membership Interests purchased pursuant to Section 8.5 shall be equal to the amount of said Member's initial capital contribution as reflected in Exhibit A. After the first anniversary of the Effective Date of this Agreement, the purchase price for the Membership Interests purchased pursuant to Section 8.5 shall be calculated as follows: Gross sales for the twelve calendar months preceding (a) the termination date; (b) the bankruptcy; (c) the inception of the Disability; or (d) the date of death, times the Ownership Interest to be purchased expressed as a percentage of the total of all Ownership Interests as of the same date. The Purchase Price for such Membership Interests shall be paid in cash or by certified or cashier's check at the closing, or, at the Company's option, shall be paid by the execution of a promissory note to the Member or legal representative from the Company. The promissory note shall be dated as of the date of the Closing and shall provide for (i) equal monthly payments of principal plus interest over a period of up to sixty (60) consecutive calendar months, (ii) payments commencing one (1) month after the date of the Closing (iii) a rate of interest equal to the One-year T-Bill rate as published in the Wall Street Journal on the Closing Date (or the next business day), plus two percent (2%); and (iv) the right to prepay in whole or in part without premium or penalty. Notwithstanding the foregoing, if the Company receives life insurance proceeds as beneficiary of a life insurance policy on the life of a deceased Member, the Company shall have the obligation to purchase the Membership Interest and shall pay for the Membership Interests in cash at Closing for at least that portion of the Purchase Price as life insurance proceeds are received.

12.4 Proofread strategically to ensure schedules, exhibits, and appendices are attached.

Most legal documents include information which is "incorporated by reference." Instead of listing details, facts, or specifications in the text of the document, drafters sometimes refer to the information included in a schedule, exhibit, attachment or elsewhere—possibly a statute, a request for proposal, or other existing documentation. Drafters use the phrase "incorporated by reference" to make the information part of the document: i.e., the information is *incorporated* into the document, and hence, into the agreement of the parties, by the *reference* to it.

If the primary document incorporates information included in a schedule, exhibit, or attachment, it is crucial that the information is actually attached. If important information is omitted, the parties must supply and interpret the missing pieces, and when the parties make differing assumptions regarding the missing information, contextual ambiguity arises. For example, a software license agreement may refer to the software's performance capabilities and specifications attached as Exhibit A. If the exhibit is not attached to the final agreement, the parties may disagree as to what performance capabilities and specifications were agreed upon. If an asset purchase agreement provides that the seller will be released from all the personal guarantees listed on Schedule 1 but no schedule is actually attached, the result could be disastrous and seller's lawyers may rightfully be sued for malpractice!

Develop a strategy to ensure that referenced information is actually attached or at least can be found where indicated. For example, one excellent law firm has implemented a policy requiring that each reference is highlighted in bright yellow utilizing the function available in most word-processing software. Before the document is signed, an employee of the firm physically marks each reference with a check-mark to ensure the information is attached or available where indicated in the text. And while this function is usually performed by a paralegal or administrative assistant, remember, it is ultimately the lawyer's responsibility.

NOTES

1. **Horwitz v. Weil**, 275 Ga. 467 (2002). The ambiguity and litigation in this matter arose because all possible outcomes were not addressed in the settlement agreement. The husband did not sell the residence before April 1; hence, there were no proceeds from a sale to distribute to the wife. The appellate court held that the provision was not ambiguous, but it was unenforceable because it was contingent upon a sale. The Georgia Supreme Court reversed, saying that the provision IS contextually ambiguous because the requirement to pay exists in two separate events, whereas the source of payment funds only exists upon the occurrence of one of the events. Under these circumstances, there is an ambiguity as to the rights and responsibilities when April 1, 2001 passes and there are no sales proceeds. The contextual ambiguity arose because a vital piece of information—how the purchase price was to be paid if the house had not been sold by April 1, 2001—was omitted.

13

Consider These Issues

> **Objective of this Lesson:** To introduce miscellaneous topics to be considered in drafting legal documents.
>
> **Key Techniques:**
>   - Consider alternative dispute resolution clauses.
>   - Draft gender free.
>   - Use numbering conventions consistently.
>   - Omit Consideration Recitals.
>   - Consider Contracts Under Seal.
>   - Amend with care.

13.1 Consider alternative dispute resolution clauses.

Despite our best efforts to control the future, disputes sometimes arise between the parties to a contract. Litigation can be costly, time consuming, and destructive to the parties' long term business relationship. Drafters should anticipate what types of problems are likely to arise and consider how best to address them so appropriate methods of dispute resolution can be built into the contract. Consider whether disputes are likely to be minor but frequent; to be based on facts more than interpretation of law or regulations; to require special expertise or collection of information for resolution; or to be potentially severe disputes which go to the very core of the contractual relationship. For example, a freight company that delivers furniture is likely to have frequent, minor disputes regarding scratches and dents. Whether a vendor's goods and services meet buyer's specifications is usually based more on the facts than an interpretation of law. A contractor who builds high-rise office buildings will need someone with special expertise in construction matters if disputes arise as to whether a particular project meets building standards. Partners who disagree as to how their business should be managed may eventually have to sever their relationship.

In an effort to avoid litigation, lawyers have developed several alternative methods to resolve disputes, including step negotiation, mediation, arbitration, and standing neutral, but no solution devised to date is perfect for every situation. Arguments can be made for and against each alternative form of dispute resolution. In addition, some lawyers are diametrically opposed to ANY method of dispute resolution that involves waiving constitutional rights to a trial by judge and jury. Convincing arguments can be made that in certain situations litigation remains the best alternative, particularly by lawyers who make their living litigating! The drafter needs to be aware of the alternatives available and consider the advisability of each in context of the transaction and the nature of potential disputes. It is just as short-sighted automatically to INCLUDE the same ADR provisions in every contract as it is automatically to EXCLUDE them.

1. Step Negotiation. The parties agree that each dispute will be addressed at their respective first levels of management having authority to resolve the dispute. If this level of management is not able to resolve the dispute within a given time frame, the dispute is elevated through higher levels of management until it is resolved or the parties conclude that it cannot be resolved by negotiation. To some degree, step negotiation is inherent in doing business even without a written provision, but a step negotiation provision forces management to move the dispute up the chain of command in situations where they might otherwise be reluctant to do so. One unique advantage of this method is that each level of management is motivated to try to resolve the dispute while it is in their hands, without having to pass it up through the executive hierarchy. Potential disadvantages are that: 1) the negotiations are non-binding; and 2) step negotiation may not work well in situations where a great disparity exists between the sizes of the entities. For example, a mom-and-pop entity would not have as many levels of management to refer the matter to as a Fortune 500 company, and may not be satisfied with the decision of a mid-level manager of the other party when its own hierarchy is exhausted. Step negotiation may be used in combination with other forms of dispute resolution. For example, the alternative dispute resolution provision may require the parties to attempt to resolve the dispute through step negotiation and require mediation or binding arbitration for disputes that cannot be resolved internally.

Example:

The parties shall attempt in good faith to resolve any dispute arising out of or relating to this Agreement promptly by negotiation between executives who have authority to settle the controversy and who are at a higher level of management than the persons with direct responsibility for administration of this contract. The parties shall elevate the issues to their respective upper management levels as necessary to resolve the dispute. If the parties are unable to resolve within 60 days any dispute arising out of or relating to this Agreement, or the breach thereof, the parties shall submit the dispute to final, binding arbitration administered by the American Arbitration Association.

2. Mediation. The parties agree that each dispute will be referred to a mediator who will work with the parties to try to achieve a compromise. Advantages are: 1) mediation is usually less expensive than litigation and arbitration; 2) matters are usually resolved much quicker than in litigation; 3) the dispute can be referred to a person knowledgeable in the subject matter; 4) mediation tends to be less destructive to the relationship of the parties than litigation or arbitration; and 5) it is not necessary for either party to admit fault in order to resolve the problem. The disadvantages are that mediation is not binding, and the parties cannot be forced to agree.

Example:

The parties shall submit any dispute or claim in law or equity arising out of this agreement to neutral, non-binding mediation before beginning arbitration, litigation, or any other proceeding before a trier of fact. The parties shall act in good faith to identify a mutually acceptable mediator. If a mediator cannot be agreed upon by the parties, each party shall designate a mediator and those mediators will select a third mediator who will act as the neutral mediator, assisting the parties to mediate in good faith to reach a resolution. The parties to the mediation shall share equally in its cost. If the dispute or claim is resolved successfully through the mediation, the resolution will be documented by a written agreement executed by all parties. If the mediation does not successfully resolve the dispute or claim, the mediator will provide written notice to the parties and the parties may then seek an alternative form of resolution of the dispute or claim, according to the remaining terms of this agreement and other rights and remedies afforded to them by law.

3. Arbitration. The parties agree that each dispute will be referred to an arbitrator or panel of arbitrators under the rules of the American Arbitration Association or similar entity. Advantages are: 1) arbitration is *usually* less expensive than litigation; 2) the dispute can be referred to a person or panel knowledgeable in the subject matter; and 3) the decision of the arbiter can be binding if the parties agree in the contract to make it so. The primary disadvantages of arbitration are that: 1) the parties in arbitration are usually represented by lawyers who are likely to insist on "adequate" preparation and discovery; and 2) the arbitrators may not have the discretion to hear only part of the dispute, as would be the case of a hearing for summary judgment or declaratory judgment within the judicial system, so the lawyers may have to prepare and present the entire case.

Example:

The parties shall settle any controversy or claim arising out of or relating to this contract, or its breach, by arbitration administered by the American Arbitration Association in accordance with its commercial arbitration rules, and judgment on the award entered by the arbitrator(s) may be entered in any court having jurisdiction.

4. Standing Neutral. At the inception of the contract, the parties appoint a standing neutral who functions throughout the term as a counselor of sorts. The parties keep the standing neutral informed as the transaction progresses, and the standing neutral is essentially "on call" to propose a solution to any disputes that arise. The advantages are: 1) the process is usually less expensive than litigation; 2) the standing neutral can be a person knowledgeable in the subject matter; 3) the standing neutral is available to respond immediately so that disputes are quickly resolved before they escalate into more complicated problems; 4) the standing neutral is—neutral!; and 5) the arrangement helps the parties work as a team and avoid damage to ongoing business relationships. The primary disadvantages are: 1) the standing neutral is paid a fee regardless of whether a dispute actually arises; and 2) the decision is not binding, although the standing neutral's decision can be entered as evidence in a judicial proceeding.[1]

Example:

The parties shall endeavor to settle any dispute arising under or related to this Agreement by mediation under the CPR Mediation Procedure in effect on the date of this Agreement. The parties have selected [insert name] as the mediator in any such dispute, and [he][she] has agreed to serve in that capacity and to be available on reasonable notice. If [mediator] becomes unwilling or unable to serve, the parties have selected [insert name] as the alternate mediator. If neither person is willing or able to serve, the parties will agree on a substitute with the assistance of CPR. Unless otherwise agreed, the parties will select a mediator from the CPR Panels of Distinguished Neutrals.

13.2 Draft Gender Free.

During the 1960's and 1970's, the legal profession faced the issue of handling gender-specific language, as feminists waged a campaign against latent sexism lurking in legal documents. Certainly, a document that offends, annoys, or distracts half its audience is less effective than one that does not. Even so, lawyers who have struggled to find suitable language may be more tolerant of gender-specific language than those who have not tried to draft a contract without it!

Many alternatives have been attempted with varying degrees of success, and no alternative works in every situation. The first attempts at gender-free language came in the form of boilerplate clauses essentially stating that "he" means "she" when the context requires. Next, drafters experimented with he/she, s/he, alternating he and she, or using both—"he or she." With practice, drafters have found ways of drafting gender free without using these passé methods.

Whatever your personal views along the "politically correct" spectrum, be aware that it is no longer considered appropriate to use a masculine form with the assumption that both genders are included,[2] and that gender-specific language is considered "old fashioned."[3] Drafters have to be persistent in recognizing and eliminating gender-specific references or risk criticism from peers for failing to do so. But the good news is that gender-neutral drafting eliminates the need to replace gender-specific references to suit the transaction and therefore may save drafting time in the long run.[4] Consider the following example:

A lawyer must handle gender references carefully to avoid offending his client.

1. Plural Nouns. Try using a plural noun so you can use a plural pronoun. Plural pronouns are gender neutral (they, them, their):

Lawyers must handle gender references carefully to avoid offending their clients.

2. Second Person. Try drafting in second person (you) so you can use a second person pronoun—but don't shift from third person to second in the same sentence:

You lawyers must handle gender references carefully to avoid offending your clients.

But not: You lawyers must handle gender references carefully to avoid offending their clients. Or: Lawyers must handle gender references carefully to avoid offending your clients.

3. Articles. Try using an article (the, this, these) instead of a pronoun:

A lawyer must handle gender references carefully to avoid offending the client.

4. Repeat the Noun. Though it causes some redundancy, try repeating the noun to avoid use of gender specific pronouns. It is better to have repetition than language that is offensive or old fashioned:

A lawyer must handle gender references carefully to avoid offending the lawyer's clients.

5. **Omit It?** Try omitting the pronoun unless it causes ambiguity:

A lawyer must handle gender references carefully to avoid offending clients.

6. **Indefinite Pronouns.** Try using indefinite pronouns—"all, another, any, both, each, either, every, few, many, most, much, neither, nobody, none, no one, nothing, one, ones, other, others, several, some, and words that end with suffixes –one, –body, and –thing."[5]

A lawyer must handle gender references carefully to avoid offending any clients.

Also, be sure to avoid gender-specific titles:

Fireman	Fire fighter
Chairman	Chair, chairperson
Foreman	Foreperson
Policeman	Police officer
Businessman	Business Executive
Craftsman	Artisan
Spokesman	Spokesperson
Salesman	Salesperson

13.3 Use Numbering Conventions Consistently.

Nearly all contracts contain numbers used in some fashion, whether to specify a purchase price, a percentage interest, or a span of time for performance. The most formal forms of writing spell out all numbers—for example, many wedding invitations even spell out the year. Although legal drafting is formal, most lawyers don't spell out all numbers.[6] Several conventions for dealing with numbers have evolved over the years, including spelling all, spelling none, spelling AND using numerals, and spelling numbers up to 10, 11, or 12 but using numerals for the rest. One of the reasons given for spelling numbers is that spelling makes typographical errors less likely to occur. On the other hand, numbers expressed in numerals are easier to read.[7] Apparently, the logic in not spelling smaller numbers is that because smaller amounts are involved (hence, the smaller numbers), the potential harm is less if a typographical error is made and the benefit of the brevity and clarity of the numerals outweighs the risk of error.[8]

According to drafting scholars, there is no right or wrong way to use numbers; the trick is to **use whatever convention you choose consistently.**[9] Even so, drafting scholars recommend against spelling AND using numerals because it is redundant. Using both may also result in ambiguity, because some studies have shown that people (including careless proofreaders) tend to skip over the spelled out version and focus only on the numerals, which may result in discrepancies between the spelled out and numeric versions.[10] This writer's personal preference is to spell out numbers from 1 through 10 and use numerals for the rest, but like so many drafting conventions, this preference is based on nothing more than the habits and preferences of the lawyers who trained me. The following are additional guidelines for using numbers:

1.   If one item in a list should be in numerals, use numerals for all items within that list.

e.g., Please revise sections 4, 15, and 21; (not four, 15, and 21)

2.   If numbers refer to the same type of thing in proximity, then use numerals for all.

e.g., In 1960 there were 5 lawyers in this county; now there are 125.

3.   If two numbers that are not of the same kind appear right next to each other, avoid confusion by spelling one—usually, but not always, the first.

e.g., There are 15 five-star hotels in Illinois.

4.   Don't begin a sentence with a numeral—try to reword the sentence if possible, and if not, spell the number out.

5.   Use numerals for citations, statutes, addresses, dates and times, money, decimals, percents, fractions, ratios, and units of measurement.

e.g., 248 N.E. 2d 515

§2-618 of the UCC

1500 Wall Street

November 15, 2012 at 6:30 p.m.

$1,523,717.25

51 percent (or 51%)

7/8ths

a ratio of 5 to 1

23 tons

6. For a number in the millions or more, unless a precise number is required, round it off to a decimal and spell out million, billion, trillion, etc.

e.g., $32.6 million.

7. Use commas to break down large numbers. Arrange the digits in groups of 3 from the left of the decimal. Use figures for numbers with decimals. Do not use commas to the right of the decimal. Do not use commas in addresses, telephone numbers, years, or military time (e.g., 1700 hours).

e.g., 5,246.09674

8. Do not use .00 cents or 00 minutes (e.g., 6:00) unless necessary to match another usage in proximity.

e.g., 8:30; 12:00 and 5:30

9. When the word "o'clock" is used for the time of day, express the time in words.

e.g., three o'clock (not 3 o'clock)

10. Use numbers to reference specific pages.

e.g., page 234 (not page two hundred thirty four)

13.4 Omit Consideration Recitals.

Consideration Recitals. Consideration recitals are usually included in contracts to *eliminate* ambiguity as to whether consideration has been exchanged by the parties. For example, these are typical (though not recommended) consideration recitals:

> "In consideration of the mutual promises herein[11] contained..."

"For consideration of $10.00 in hand paid, and other good and valuable consideration, the receipt and sufficiency is hereby acknowledged..."

Transactional lawyers have even been known to accuse each other of committing malpractice[12] for failing to include the recital in standard contracts, but is the *recital* of consideration *itself* an essential element of most contracts? No: A simple statement that "the parties agree" is sufficient to evidence a *bargain*, and hence, consideration, in virtually all bilateral contracts. Drafting scholars concur that in most instances, the recital of consideration is superfluous and should be omitted, based on the assumption under the law of a majority of states that merely stating consideration exists does not make it so.[13]

The most useful place for a recital of consideration seems to be in unilateral contracts, such as option agreements, and promissory notes, which are based on the promises of only one party.[14]

13.5 Consider Contracts Under Seal.

What is a Contract Under Seal? Under common law, a contract signed under seal was afforded special treatment because of the formality and apparent authority associated with affixing the seal. The origins of the seal are humorous: Lord Coke reports that King Edward III sealed deeds by biting them with his foretooth.[15] Fortunately, fewer germs were exchanged shortly thereafter, when aristocrats and "gentlemen of the better sort" affixed their seals by applying their signet rings to softened wax.[16] In the 19th century, a seal was affixed by pressing a mechanical device onto a foil-like "wafer" attached to the page. In modern times, seals can be affixed simply by having the word "seal" appear on the page.

The practice of signing documents under seal was criticized as having no value many generations ago:

"The only reason ever urged at this day, why a seal should give greater evidence and dignity to writing is, that it evidences greater deliberation, and therefore should impart greater solemnity to instruments. Practically we know that the art of printing has done away with this argument. For not only are all official, and most individual deeds, with seals appended, *printed* previously, and filled up at the time of their execution, but even merchants and business men are adopting the same practice as it respects their notes. ... for myself I am free to confess, that I despise all forms having no sense or substance in them."[17]

Imagine how distraught Justice Lumpkin would have been had he known we would still be grappling with this atavistic practice over 150 years after he first attempted, "for the good of the country," to rid us of it![18] Many state legislatures, however, have concurred with the gravamen of Justice Lumpkin's argument, and at least 25 states have passed statutes purporting to abolish private seals.[19]

Drafters should have a clear understanding of the effect of signing under seal, particularly when the law of another jurisdiction governs the contract. One effect of signing a contract under seal in jurisdictions where seals have not yet been abolished is that the statute of limitations for contracts signed under seal may be much longer. For example, in Georgia, Delaware, Maine, New Hampshire, Pennsylvania, Rhode Island, South Carolina, and possibly South Dakota, the statute of limitations for contracts signed under seal is 20 years, unless a statutory exemption exists.[20] Many other states impose 10 or 15 year statutes of limitation for contracts signed under seal.[21] Another concern is that in some jurisdictions, it is possible that one party can sign under seal, but not the other. If the word "seal" appears after one party's signature, but not the other, the former is subject to a 20 year statute of limitations, although the latter is not. This means the party that signed under seal can be sued even after potential counterclaims are extinguished. So let the litigators rejoice, and drafters beware!

For some contracts, signing under seal may be advantageous; for others it is not. The determination of whether a contract should be signed under seal may depend upon which party you represent. Bank loan documents and real estate transactions are almost always signed under seal in jurisdictions where the concept survives. For example, if you represent the buyer in a real estate transaction, a 20-year statute of limitation would be advantageous although the seller would prefer the regular statute of limitations, which is typically about three years but varies from state to state. Similarly, in a merger situation, a 20-year statute of limitations would be advantageous for the surviving company to cover latent liabilities that might not arise until years after the closing, like asbestos or hazardous materials in the acquired company's property. A 20-year statute of limitations could also be advantageous for shareholders of the acquired company if it is ultimately discovered that a representation and warranty given by the surviving company at closing was fraudulent. If, however, you represent the licensor in a technology agreement, a 20-year statute of limitations could be highly disadvantageous to your client. Similarly, a manufacturer of goods would prefer a shorter window to be sued for defective products.

13.6 Amend With Care.

The parties sometimes desire to make changes to a contract after it has been signed. The contract may contain mistakes that need to be corrected, one or both parties may desire to change the terms of the deal, or new circumstances might arise that need to be addressed. Amendments can be used to add new provisions or to modify existing contract terms. Ordinarily, neither party is obligated to amend the contract, although the contract may require them to negotiate amendments in good faith if certain circumstances occur. (In these instances, if the parties negotiate in good faith but DO NOT reach agreement, no breach has occurred.)

An amendment is essentially a new contract between the parties and requires as much thought and care as the original document. If amendments are not properly drafted, the amended provisions can cause contextual ambiguity which may be used to defeat the terms of the underlying contract.

The first step in drafting an amendment is to consult the original contract to determine what is required to amend. Although under common law, some contracts can be amended orally, most contracts contain boilerplate language stating that amendments must be in writing and signed by both parties. If the underlying contract specifies how amendments can be made, the amendment must satisfy those requirements. General principles of contract law apply equally to amendments. For example, consideration is a required element of the underlying contract, so consideration must also be exchanged in the amendment.

The drafter should carefully consider the terms of the amendment in light of the existing contract. First of all, language used in the amendment, including any defined terms, should be consistent with the underlying contract. The drafter must also consider whether any other provisions in the underlying contract are impacted by amending a specific provision. For example, if the parties amend a contract to extend a deadline by 15 days, are any other provisions in the contract impacted by the extension?

Each amendment should be numbered so the parties can account for all amendments if it turns out that there are many. You likely will not know when you draft the first amendment whether there will be 1 or 20 amendments, so identify even the first amendment as "First Amendment to the Agreement Dated…" Most lawyers use ordinal numbers (first, second, seventh, twentieth, etc.) but cardinal numbers work just as well (Amendment No. 1, Amendment No. 2, etc.). Whether you choose ordinal or cardinal numbers, be sure to use them consistently.

When only a few changes are being made, it is usually most practical to amend rather than restate the contract. Conversely, if many changes are made, it may be better to restate the contract entirely and incorporate the amendments into the text.

The amendment should specify exactly what provisions are being changed, and identify what changes are being made: whether language is replaced in its entirety, modified to read as follows, modified by inserting the following words, or so on.

Case Study

Form of Amendment
First AMENDMENT TO

GENERAL SERVICES AGREEMENT

This First Amendment to the General Services Agreement is entered into between Company and Contractor pursuant to Section 12.5 of the GSA. The parties desire to amend the terms of the GSA as indicated below. The parties, intending to be legally bound, agree as follows:

1.   The parties desire to modify Section 1.2 by deleting that section in its entirety and inserting the following new Section 1.2 in its place:

"1.2   Insert Text Here."

2.   Except as specifically modified in this First Amendment, all other provisions of the GSA remain the same. Defined terms used in this amendment have the meanings ascribed to them in the GSA. If any of the terms of this Amendment conflict with the GSA, the terms of this Amendment control.

The duly authorized representatives of the parties have executed this Amendment to be effective on the date indicated below.

Company:	Contractor:
By:	By:
_____	_____
Name:	Name:
_____	_____
Title:	Title:
_____	_____
Date:	Date:
_____	_____

NOTES

1. James P. Groton, Beijing Workshop Materials (2006) on alternative dispute resolution methods. I am grateful to Mr. Groton for sharing this information and for his tireless efforts over at least two decades to promote the concept of alternative dispute resolution within the legal profession.

2. BRYAN A. GARNER, THE REDBOOK: A MANUAL OF STYLE, 276 (2001).

3. KENNETH A. ADAMS, CONTRACT DRAFTING: A MANUAL OF STYLE, 213 (2004).

4. SCOTT J. BURNHAM, DRAFTING AND ANALYZING CONTRACTS, 253-255 (3d 2003).

5. GARNER, REDBOOK, *supra* note 2 at 127.

6. *Id.*, at 75.

7. ADAMS, *supra* note 3, at 171.

8. *Id.*

9. THOMAS R. HAGGARD AND GEORGE W. KUNEY, LEGAL DRAFTING IN A NUTSHELL, 316 (3d 2007); GARNER, REDBOOK, *supra* note 2 at 75.

10. HAGGARD/KUNEY NUTSHELL, *supra* note 9, at 316.

11. According to legal drafting scholars, the word "herein" is inherently ambiguous and should not be used in contracts. See Lesson 7.

12. Those lawyers will remain nameless to protect the guilty, but they know who they are!

13. Kenneth A. Adams, *Drafting a New Day: Who Needs that Recital of Consideration?*, Business Law Today, Mar.-Apr. 2002, at 47; BRYAN A. GARNER, A DICTIONARY OF MODERN LEGAL USAGE, 434 (2d 1995); HAGGARD/KUNEY NUTSHELL, *supra* note 9, at 48-49.

14. HAGGARD/KUNEY NUTSHELL, *supra* note 9, at 45-48.

15. CORBIN ON CONTRACTS, § 10.2 (1993).

16. *Id.*

17. Lowe v. Morris and another, 13 Ga 147, 153-156 (1853); Lumpkin, J. concurring.

18. See Drumright and others vs. Philpot, 16 Ga 424, 428 (1854) "Having discharged my duty to the country, by doing what I could in Lowe vs. Morris and another, to bring the modern scrawl, misnamed a seal, into merited contempt, I shall content myself with what I have now said. ..."

19. Note that some states, such as Georgia, make no distinction between private and corporate seals. Louisiana and Puerto Rico never adopted the concept of seal; according to Corbin on Contracts, the following states have abolished distinctions between sealed and unsealed contracts: Alaska,

Arizona, Arkansas, California, Illinois, Indiana, Iowa, Kansas, Kentucky, Minnesota, Mississippi, Missouri, Montana, Nebraska, New York, North Dakota, Ohio, Oklahoma, Oregon, South Dakota, Tennessee, Texas, Utah, Washington, Wyoming, and the U.S. Virgin Islands. Corbin on Contracts, §10.18. Massachusetts has apparently joined the list. Knott v. Racicot, 442 Mass. 3314, 812 N.E. 2d 1207 (2004).

20 Corbin on Contracts, §10.18. An exemption does exist for contracts for the sale of goods under the UCC in some states.

21. *Id.*

Edit or Review Effectively

Objective of this Lesson: To introduce effective strategies for editing drafted documents or reviewing documents prepared by opposing counsel.

Key Techniques:
- Edit documents effectively.
- Review documents prepared by opposing counsel effectively.

14.1 Edit Documents Effectively.

Note: The editing strategy described in this section applies to documents you control. As a matter of professional courtesy, editing strategy should be curtailed for documents prepared by opposing counsel that you merely review. In reviewing documents prepared by opposing counsel, focus on eliminating ambiguity but avoid edits that are primarily a matter of stylistic preference.

The best way to edit effectively is to allow enough time in the drafting process to let the document sit for at least two days after the initial draft is complete. When you go back to the document with fresh eyes, mistakes will practically leap off the page. The second most effective way to edit is to have someone else edit the document.

However you approach the editing process, it is unlikely that all of the techniques recommended in this book can be incorporated in a single pass through a document. Editing should involve several passes through the document and each pass should focus on a few of the specific techniques described in this book.

Divide editing into four levels: substantive, mechanical, semantic, and syntactic. As you become more proficient in implementing these drafting techniques, editing will be proportionately less tedious.

Substantive Edit. The primary purpose of the substantive edit is to ensure that the necessary legal provisions have been included in the document. Consider each section separately. Take time to think through what information should be included in the section. Without looking at the document, brainstorm and jot a rough outline of the key provisions. Compare the terms of documents used in similar transactions to be sure you have addressed all the important issues. Search for sources of contextual ambiguity. Has any important information been omitted? Does the document reveal the who, what, when, where, how and why of the transaction? Are the risks and liabilities properly allocated? Are the terms of the document internally consistent? Are overlapping provisions in related documents identical? The first and most important step in editing is to ensure that your document is substantively complete. Be sure to review notes taken during the client interview to ensure all of the client's concerns have been addressed.

Mechanical Edit. The mechanical edit can be done by experienced paralegals and younger lawyers. The mechanical edit should include the following:

a) Eliminate archaic customs—replace useless legalese like "witnesseth" and a string of "whereas" clauses with a more modern statement of purpose. Eliminate phrases like "know all men by these presents," and "in witness whereof, Contractor has hereunto set his hand and seal."

b) Check visual format—is the document formatted consistently? Do the headings and paragraphs follow the same formatting conventions such as bold text, italics, underlining, font, and style? Is the text justified consistently throughout the document? Have widows/orphans been eliminated to prevent single lines of text at the top or bottom of the page?

c) Check spelling—use the Spell Check function to identify some misspelled words, but be aware that this function is not foolproof. Proofread carefully to find words that are spelled correctly but used incorrectly.

d) Check basic grammar—be sure that the document is grammatically correct. Look for subject/verb agreement, sentence fragments, and pronouns used incorrectly.

e) Check all cross references.

f) Check the organization of the document—are related topics grouped together? Does the order progress in a logical manner? Are related provisions ordered from the general to the specific? Is the physical layout correct as far as indented paragraphs and subparagraphs? Does the document contain headings and subheadings to aid the reader in locating relevant provisions?

Semantic Edit. The semantic edit should focus on word choice.

a) Replace lawyerly phrases with simple words.

b) Check Defined Terms—do a global search for each defined term to ensure that it is used, is used consistently, and is not used except as defined. Check to ensure that all defined terms appear in the glossary. Challenge each defined term to be certain it is necessary. Use "means" instead of "shall mean" or "includes" instead of "shall include," and do not use "means and includes."

c) Check every "shall"—do a global search to ensure that the word is only used to impose a duty on a party to the document.

d) Check every "only"—do a global search to ensure that the word appears in the correct place in the sentence to produce the intended meaning.

e) Eliminate imprecise words and phrases and legalese:
   - And/or;
   - Provisos;
   - Herein or therein;
   - Here-, there-, where- words and other gobbledygook;
   - Such, said, and same; and
   - Foreign phrases.

f) Check recurring words and phrases to ensure consistent use.

g) Eliminate elegant variations.

h) Search for and replace ambiguous words.

Syntactic Edit. The syntactic edit should focus on improving sentence structure.

a) Turn passive-voice sentences into active where doing so improves clarity.

b) Review and consider each sentence to be sure it is organized logically to convey its point. Rearrange intrusive information into separate sentences.

c) Convert hidden verbs (nouns ending in -tion, -sion, -ment, -ity, -ance) and replace with actual verbs.

d) Eliminate unnecessary or redundant language:
   a. Doublets and triplets;
   b. Repetitive statements of agreement;
   c. Throat-clearing phrases; and
   d. Unnecessary strings of words.

e) Use parallel structure and tabulations for lists.

f) Structure complicated provisions so the conditions appear after the subject and verb.

g) Target long sentences. Try to reduce them to an average of 30 words.

h) Search for and eliminate sources of syntactic ambiguity:
   - Squinting modifiers;
   - Dangling or misplaced modifiers;
   - Uncertain pronoun reference;
   - Misplaced prepositional phrases; and
   - Ambiguous conjunctions.

14.2 Review contracts prepared by opposing counsel effectively.

In most negotiated transactions, both parties are involved in crafting the language that memorializes the agreement of the parties, but one party has to begin the process by creating the initial draft. Although you ultimately have more control over documents that you create, about half of the time your responsibility will be to review the drafts prepared by opposing counsel. Sometimes, the initial draft is created specifically for the transaction but other times you will be called upon to review a more or less "standard" form prepared for your client's business partner.

Most new lawyers and their clients are surprised to learn that it usually takes longer to review a contract prepared by someone else than to draft it yourself, particularly where your practice area is very narrow and you handle the same types of contracts on a recurring basis. Because clients tend to underestimate the amount of time involved in reviewing a contract properly, they will often ask for review within an excruciatingly short time frame. It is not uncommon to have a client call on the way to a closing and ask the lawyer to review the document for the first time! In that situation, the client has already made the decision to go forward with the transaction and is looking for a scapegoat to blame if something goes wrong. Accept this representation at your own peril!

In this lesson, we will look at ways to streamline the review process, but in some situations where there is not enough time to complete a proper review, lawyers may be required by ethical standards to decline the representation to the extent they are able to do so. In this regard, in-house lawyers may have a distinct disadvantage because their continued employment may depend upon meeting impossible demands of their employer client.

Proper review of a contract involves much more than casual, or even studious, reading. Proper review requires several passes through the document, especially for newer lawyers and especially for more complicated transactions. Experienced lawyers may be able to compress some of the steps described below, but this writer has not met a lawyer who could effectively review a complicated contract in a single pass, and, fortunately, hasn't met many who even tried!

Reviewing contracts is more of an art than a science, and you will eventually develop a more personalized approach that incorporates the components described below. The basic mechanics of contract review involve the following steps:

1. Prepare;
2. Familiarize;

3. Identify key business terms;
4. Identify legal issues;
5. Identify ambiguous language;
6. Discuss with client;
7. Revise; and
8. Proofread.

Before you make any marks on a document, make a copy of it!

1. Prepare.

Just as you prepare to draft a contract, so you must prepare to review one. Preparation includes understanding:

- your client's objectives for the transaction;
- the law related to the transaction, including gap fillers and industry standards; and
- typical legal issues associated with this type of transaction.

If you are reviewing a particular type of agreement for the first time, it is very helpful to look at contracts prepared for similar transactions, either from your firm's form file or form books. Try to review at least one contract favoring each party to the transaction. For example, in a purchase situation, try to review a contract that favors the buyer and then review another contract that favors the seller. Compare the ranges of how similar provisions are drafted if one party is favored verses the other, as discussed in Lesson 11.

2. Familiarize.

Before you begin to review the language of a contract, start by quickly flipping the pages to get an idea of what provisions are included and where they are located. How long is the document? What is the subject matter? Who are the parties? Where do the defined terms appear? Are schedules and exhibits attached, and are key performance-based terms included in them? Are confidentiality provisions included? Is there a termination section, a limitation of liability, a warranty, an indemnification provision? Knowing what types of provisions are included in the document will help streamline the review process because you won't waste time searching for related provisions while you're trying to review the language. You also won't waste time adding provisions that already appear further in the text.

Edit or Review Effectively

3. Confirm Key Business Terms.

The next step is to locate the key business terms and ensure they conform to your client's description of the transaction. Key business terms usually involve who does what, how payment is made, and who owns the end result. In most cases, if there is a discrepancy in the key business terms, the client should work out the differences directly with the business partner. Discrepancies in business terms can occur for many different reasons—misunderstanding between the parties, miscommunication between one of the parties and its lawyer (possibly you!), rapid market fluctuations, advice from counsel against the terms previously agreed upon, typographical error, a better offer, a change of mind, etc. Where there is a discrepancy in key business terms, it may very well be that your work on the project is finished until the parties have resolved the discrepancy. At a minimum, you should put the client on notice immediately so the client can work simultaneously to resolve the discrepancy as you continue to review the document.

4. Identify Legal Issues.

This is the step where the lawyering really begins and where most of your time will be spent. Read the entire contract from start to finish and begin spotting legal issues. Jot notes in the margin, underline, circle, highlight—use whatever method works best for you to flag attention to issues that need further consideration. Mark with a check mark, question mark, asterisk, or other symbol every representation or promise given by your client so you can verify its accuracy with the client. Note any provisions that are too one-sided that need to be revised to be more neutral or reciprocal. Re-read provisions that affect your client's liability and remedies, such as representations and warranties, indemnification, warranty, limitations of liability, and termination. Be sure to refer to the definitions when you read a substantive provision where defined terms appear. If a glossary of defined terms is used, pull those pages out for convenient reference.

In addition to reading the provisions that appear in the document, be sure to compare to other forms to determine whether any typical provisions have been omitted. Prepare a flow chart using "yes" and "no" questions to ensure that all aspects of a provision have been addressed.

Understand that if the contract has been well-written by experienced and knowledgeable opposing counsel, the first draft

---

does not usually represent the opposing party's actual expectations or requirements—it's more of a wish list! If you don't object to something, opposing counsel hasn't asked for enough. This is a very good point to keep in mind when YOU prepare the initial draft.

5. Identify Ambiguous Language.

After you have spotted key legal issues, review the contract again to identify ambiguous language. It is generally considered among the legal community to be inappropriate to make changes that are nothing more than a matter of style, but if a particular provision can be interpreted two or more ways, it is ambiguous and needs to be revised. Focus most of your attention on provisions where ambiguity potentially affects your client's risk and responsibility.

6. Discuss key issues with the Client.

After you've reviewed the contract but, in most cases, BEFORE you start making revisions, discuss the legal issues and recommended changes with the client. Note again the lawyer's ethical obligation to ensure that the client understands the important provisions of the document before signing under Model Rule 1.4 (discussed on page 100). Be sure the client is aware of each representation and promise made in the document and that they are accurately stated. Don't be surprised if some of the issues you've spotted are of no concern to the client. Most clients will instruct you as to what issues you should pursue and what issues you should ignore. If you've explained the legal basis for the issues and are sure the client understands according to the criteria of the Model Rules, you are obligated to follow the client's directives unless to do so would constitute malpractice.

7. Revise.

After your client agrees with the changes you've recommended, the next step is to revise the initial draft. There are several ways of doing this.

- If opposing counsel provides the document by word processor in an electronic format, you can make revisions directly into the file. It's best to track your changes using the word processor's "track changes" feature, typing in a different color, using brackets, or in some other way setting your revisions apart.

- If opposing counsel provides the document on paper, you can make revisions manually on the page.

- If opposing counsel provides the document in pdf or other electronic format that you can't revise, you can either make changes by hand on a printed copy or make changes on a separate document. For example, lawyers often use an attachment called "special stipulations" to alter provisions in a contract. (See Case Study 14A.)

- If opposing counsel provides the document in pdf or other format you can't revise, you can request changes verbally, either via in person conference or telephone conference.

8. Proofread.

After all revisions have been made, proofread the contract carefully.

CASE STUDY 14A

See how specific provisions are modified using special stipulations.

SPECIAL STIPULATIONS

The terms of the Certified Vendor Agreement ("Vendor Agreement") between FIRST OPTION SOFTWARE, INC. of 3015 Pacific Boulevard, Seattle, WA 98101 ("First Option") and TLC Consulting, LLC of 1801 Rose Avenue, Dallas, Texas 75201 ("TLC") are accepted by TLC as of June _____, 2012, subject to the following Special Stipulations. Defined terms used in these Special Stipulations have the same meaning ascribed to them in the Vendor Agreement.

1. The defined term "Vendor" is modified to include subsidiaries and "Affiliates" of TLC.

2. Section 1.5 is revised to read as follows: "Order" means an electronic or written request submitted to First Option by Vendor pursuant to the terms and conditions of this Agreement 1) requesting Option to grant a license to a prospective End User for the use of one or more Products; or 2) for First Option to provide Services to an End User; or 3) both.

3. The first sentence of Paragraph 2.2 of the Vendor Agreement is modified to read as follows: "Vendor will use commercially reasonable efforts to monitor compliance with all License Agreements."

6. Paragraph 4.5 is modified by adding the phrase "except as otherwise provided in this Vendor Agreement" at the end of the sentence.

10. Paragraph 5 is modified by adding the phrase "upon 30 days written notice to Vendor" at the end of the second sentence.

13. Paragraph 7.4 (b) is modified by inserting the phrase "Unless any End User License Agreement specifies otherwise" at the beginning of the second sentence. Paragraph 7.4 (b) is further modified by inserting this sentence "If First Option is unable to cure any defect it will issue a full refund of all fees and charges paid under this Vendor Agreement."

14. Paragraph 7.4 (c) is modified by inserting the phrase "Unless any End User License Agreement specifies otherwise" at the beginning of that paragraph.

15. Paragraph 7.6 is modified by deleting the phrase ", up to the price paid by the Vendor for Software,".

16. Paragraph 8.2 is modified by inserting the word "undisputed" between "any" and "sum" and by replacing the phrase "without further" with the word "upon" each time that phrase appears in the paragraph.

17. Paragraph 8.3 is modified by inserting the word "voting" between "of" and "control" in item (iii).

Vendor   FIRST OPTION SOFTWARE, INC.

BY: _____   BY: _____
PRINT NAME: _____   PRINT NAME: _____
TITLE: _____   TITLE: _____

CASE STUDY 14B

This case study demonstrates how the changes made by Special Stipulation in Case Study 14A would be marked on the document itself. The original document was prepared by First Option Software and has been "marked up" by counsel for TLC. Counsel for TLC may have suggested other changes, but the changes reflected here are the ones TLC wanted to pursue. Note that counsel for TLC did not revise all drafting flaws but focused instead on editing where the language was ambiguous and could lead to disputes between the parties. Counsel for TLC also did not make changes that should have been recommended by counsel for First Option. Note that the warranty provisions and the limitation of liability provisions in the original draft are unenforceable in most jurisdictions. (See Lesson 4.1.)

CERTIFIED VENDOR AGREEMENT

THIS CERTIFIED VENDOR AGREEMENT ("Agreement") is made and entered into on _____, 2012 (the "Effective Date") between First Option Software, Inc. of 3015 Pacific Boulevard, Seattle, WA 98101 ("First Option") and

TLC Consulting, LLC
1801 Rose Avenue
Dallas, Texas 75201

(TLC consulting, LLC, its subsidiaries, and affiliates are referred to in this Agreement as "Vendor").

The parties agree as follows:

1. **Definitions.** As used in this Agreement, the following terms have the meanings described below.

   1.1 **"Designated System"** means a computer system identified in writing to First Option by the manufacturer's serial number or other verifiable means of identification and which is in the possession and control of Vendor.

   1.2 **"End User"** means a third party that has executed a License Agreement that has been accepted by First Option for the authorized use of one or more Products.

   1.3 **"First Option Marks"** means any and all trademarks, service marks, tradenames, insignias, trade dress, logos and other source of origin indicators that are designated by First Option for use in the Software or Documentation.

   1.4 **"License Agreement"** means First Option's then-current Master License Agreement, as provided to Vendor by First Option from time to time, that has been executed by an End User and accepted in writing by First Option. A copy of First Option's current Master License Agreement is attached hereto as Exhibit D.

   1.5 **"Order"** means an electronic or written request submitted to First Option by Vendor pursuant to the terms and conditions of this Agreement: **1)** requesting First Option to grant a license to a prospective End User for the use of one or more Products; ~~and/~~or **2)** for First Option to provide Services to that End User: **or both 1) and 2).**

   1.6 **"Price List"** means the then-current suggested retail price list for the Products, as updated by First Option from time to time in accordance with Section 6.3. The current Price List is attached hereto as Exhibit C.

   1.7 **"Products"** means the Software and all related Documentation identified on Exhibit A attached to this Agreement, as updated from time to time and executed by both parties referencing this Agreement.

   1.8 **"Services"** means training, maintenance and support, or consulting services for the installation and adaptation of the Software authorized to be performed by Vendor pursuant to this Agreement and made generally available to an End

Edit or Review Effectively

User pursuant to the terms and conditions of a License Agreement.

1.9 **"Software"** means all or any portion of the software programs made commercially available by First Option, in object code form only, as specified on Exhibit A, and all modifications, corrections, improvements, enhancements and updates thereto made commercially available from time to time by First Option.

1.10 **"Term"** means the initial term plus renewal terms.

2. **Scope of Agreement and Grant of Licenses.**

2.1 **Grant of Rights.** During the Term and subject to the terms and conditions of this Agreement, First Option hereby grants to Vendor, and Vendor hereby accepts, the non-exclusive, non-transferable right and license, at Vendor's sole cost and expense unless stated otherwise herein to use internally in object code form only on its Designated System to provide to End Users those services that are more completely described in Exhibit G (consulting services), Exhibit H (training services) and/or Exhibit I (first level support services), to the extent that any such exhibit is initialed by both parties and attached to this Agreement.

2.2 **License Agreement Enforcement.** Vendor will <u>use commercially reasonable efforts to </u>monitor compliance with all License Agreements. If Vendor becomes aware that any End User is violating the terms of a License Agreement with respect to use of the Software, Vendor shall promptly notify First Option.

2.3 **Use of First Option Web Sites.** Pursuant to Exhibits to this Agreement, First Option may permit Vendor to access First Option websites. Access to such First Option sites may require the use of PIN's and/or passwords. Vendor agrees to keep confidential and not to disclose any PIN's or passwords to third parties, nor will Vendor use a PIN or password that was not issued to Vendor by First Option. Vendor is solely responsible for any and all activities that occur using the PIN's and passwords that are issued to Vendor hereunder. Vendor agrees to abide by any terms and conditions or other policies located on the First Option sites, as modified in First Option's discretion from time to time.

---

3. **Obligations of Vendor.**

   3.1 **Sales and Marketing Obligations.** Vendor will perform its sales and marketing obligations set forth on Exhibit F.

   3.2 **First Option Name.** Vendor will maintain the formal name of the Products (with its appropriate First Option Mark designations) in all advertising and other printed materials relating to the Products. Upon First Option's request, Vendor will furnish to First Option in advance for review and approval any and all promotional, advertising and other materials which refer to the Products or which use or display any First Option Mark. In the event First Option does not approve promotional, advertising or other materials referring to First Option or the Products, upon First Option's request, Vendor will immediately discontinue use of any such materials.

   3.3 **Export Control.** Vendor shall be solely responsible for complying with all laws relating to the export, re-export or importation of the Products. Vendor shall keep such books and records and take such other actions as may be required by such laws. Vendor shall be responsible for obtaining all import and export permits and licenses required by any government agency to permit the importation of the Products for Vendor's use in the Target Market. If any laws or regulations require that the Products, any portions thereof, or this Agreement be registered with or approved by a governmental entity, Vendor shall comply with such requirements after prior written notice to First Option specifying the required registration or approval; provided, however, that no such registration shall claim an ownership interest in any of First Option's property. Such compliance shall be at Vendor's sole expense and solely for the benefit of First Option. First Option shall provide to Vendor reasonable assistance in Vendor's compliance with the above requirements.

   3.4 **Compliance with Laws.** Vendor shall be solely responsible for compliance and will strictly comply with all applicable U.S. and foreign laws relating in any way to Vendor's performance under this Agreement. Vendor will also strictly comply with all the prevailing laws and regulations pertaining to the advertising, promotion, and marketing of the Products. Vendor shall give First Option immediate prior written notice of any steps to be taken by Vendor to comply with any legal requirements that may affect First Option's intellectual property rights in the

Products, or other interests of First Option, and Vendor shall, at its expense, fully cooperate with First Option to minimize and/or eliminate any adverse impacts of any such compliance on First Option's interests.

4. **Orders and Delivery.**

   4.1 **Orders.** Vendor will place Orders directly with First Option.

   4.2 **Fulfillment.** Upon receipt of Orders from Vendor that comply with all requirements of this Agreement, First Option will, unless Vendor is delinquent in its payments or in breach of any agreement with First Option, make reasonable efforts to fill such orders for the Products.

   4.3 **Delivery.** First Option will deliver the Products ordered by an End User through Vendor to the point of delivery designated in the Order, F.O.B. shipping point. First Option shall not be liable to Vendor, or to any other person, for First Option's failure to fill any Orders, or for any delay in delivery or error in filling any Orders.

   4.4 **Other Terms.** No terms or conditions in Vendors' purchase orders, license agreements or in any other business forms shall add to or supersede the terms and conditions of this Agreement, even if signed and returned, unless both parties hereto expressly agree in a separate writing to be bound by such different or additional terms or conditions.

   4.5 **No Return.** Vendor acknowledges and agrees that First Option will not accept returns of Products and neither Vendor nor any End User will be entitled to any refund or credit of any amounts due to First Option from Vendor **except as otherwise provided in this agreement**.

5. **Software Changes.** First Option may, in its discretion, inform Vendor of First Option's plans related to new product development, enhancements, upgrades, and other changes associated with the Software. First Option reserves the right to make changes to, or discontinue altogether, any Product **upon 30 days written notice to vendor**.

6. **Fees and Charges.**

6.1 **End User License Fees.** Vendor shall establish the license fees, maintenance fees and other fees and charges payable by End Users with respect to the Products and Services ordered from First Option pursuant to this Agreement. Vendor shall collect all such fees payable by End Users.

6.2 **Vendor's License Fees.** Vendor will pay the license fees set forth in Exhibit B for each copy of the Software licensed from First Option by an End User pursuant to an Order placed by the Vendor.

6.3 **Price List.** First Option may update the price list, a current version of which is attached as Exhibit C, from time to time upon written notice to Vendor. The updated price list will be effective thirty (30) days from the date of the notice unless otherwise agreed by First Option in writing.

6.4 **Payments.** First Option shall invoice Vendor for an Order upon acceptance by First Option of such Order. Vendor shall pay all invoices from First Option within thirty (30) days of the date of the invoice. Vendor shall make all payments in U.S. dollars to First Option's address for payment as otherwise indicated on First Option's invoice to Vendor.

6.5 **Late Payments.** In addition to such other rights as First Option may have, Vendor shall, on any invoice not paid when due until such payment is made, pay a late charge equal to the lesser of one and one half percent (1.5%) of the outstanding amount or the maximum amount allowed by law.

6.6 **Taxes.** All fees are exclusive of taxes. Upon presentation of invoices by First Option, Vendor shall pay any and all taxes. In the event Vendor or an End User claims exemption from such taxes, Vendor will immediately provide First Option a tax exemption certificate and other proper documentary evidence requested by First Option.

7. **General Terms and Conditions.**

7.1 **Term of Agreement.** The initial term of this Agreement shall commence on the Effective Date and shall continue for a period of twelve (12) months from such date, unless sooner terminated as provided in Section 8. After the initial term, the Agreement shall be automatically renewed on an annual

Edit or Review Effectively

basis, each a renewal term, unless sooner terminated as provided in Section 8.

7.2 **Records and Reports.** During the Term and for a period of one (1) year thereafter, Vendor shall keep full, true and accurate records and accounts in accordance with generally accepted accounting principles to show the amount of license fees payable to First Option.

7.3 **Equitable Remedies.** Vendor acknowledges that (i) any use or threatened use of the Products in a manner inconsistent with this Agreement, or (ii) any other misuse of the Proprietary Information will cause immediate irreparable harm to First Option for which there is no adequate remedy at law. Accordingly, Vendor agrees that First Option shall be entitled to immediate and permanent injunctive relief from any court of competent jurisdiction (notwithstanding the provisions of Section 9.2) in the event of any such breach or threatened breach by Vendor. The parties agree and stipulate that First Option shall be entitled to such injunctive relief without posting a bond or other security; provided, however that if the posting of a bond is a prerequisite to obtaining injunctive relief, then a bond in the amount of $1000 shall be sufficient. Nothing contained herein shall limit First Option's right to any remedies at law, including the recovery of damages from Vendor for breach of this Agreement.

7.4 **Warranty.**

    (a) Both parties represent and warrant that they have the right to enter into this Agreement.

    (b) First Option warrants solely for the benefit of Vendor for the Term of this Agreement that the then-current, unmodified version of the Software will perform the functions or generally conform to the then-current version of the published Documentation relating to such Software. ~~If~~ **Unless any End User License Agreement specifies otherwise, if** it is determined that the Products do not perform as warranted, First Option's sole responsibility and Vendor's sole remedy will be to use reasonable efforts consistent with industry standards to cure the defect. **If First Option is unable to cure any defect, it will issue a full refund of all fees and charges paid under this Vendor Agreement.** First Option does not represent that the Software is error free or will satisfy all of Vendor's or its End User's requirements.

(c) **Unless any End User Agreement specifies otherwise,** Vendor shall report each warranty claim based on Section 7.4(b) to First Option within the lesser of 30 days after shipment of the Product with respect to which such claim is made. In its report Vendor shall describe in reasonable detail the Product affected, the End User, the date of shipment of the Product and the nature of the claim. Vendor shall be entitled to no remedy under this Agreement at law or in equity with respect to any claim that Vendor fails to report with such limitations period.

(d) THE WARRANTY SET FORTH IN SECTION 7.4(b) IS IN LIEU OF ALL OTHER WARRANTIES. TO THE MAXIMUM EXTENT PERMITTED UNDER APPLICABLE LAW, ALL OTHER WARRANTIES, CONDITIONS AND REPRESENTATIONS, WHETHER EXPRESSED OR IMPLIED, VERBAL, STATUTORY OR OTHERWISE AND WHETHER ARISING UNDER THIS AGREEMENT OR OTHERWISE ARE HEREBY EXCLUDED, INCLUDING, BUT NOT LIMITED TO, THE IMPLIED WARRANTIES OF MERCHANTABILITY, FITNESS FOR A PARTICULAR PURPOSE, SYSTEM INTEGRATION, NON-INFRINGEMENT OR NON-INTERFERENCE WITH ENJOYMENT. FIRST OPTION SHALL NOT BE BOUND BY OR LIABLE FOR ANY REPRESENATIONS OR WARRANTIES, WHETHER WRITTEN OR ORAL, WITH RESPECT TO THE PRODUCTS MADE BY DISTRIBUTOR OR ITS AGENTS, EMPLOYEES OR REPRESENTATIVES.

7.5 **Limitation of Liability.** EXCEPT FOR THE INDEMNIFICATION SET FORTH BELOW, FIRST OPTION'S MAXIMUM LIABILITY FOR DAMAGES UNDER THIS AGREEMENT (REGARDLESS OF THE FORM OF ACTION, WHETHER IN CONTRACT OR TORT) SHALL NOT EXCEED THE AMOUNT PAID BY VENDOR TO FIRST OPTION FOR THE SOFTWARE TO WHICH THE CLAIM RELATES. IN NO EVENT WILL FIRST OPTION BE LIABLE TO VENDOR OR ANY OTHER PARTY, WHETHER IN CONTRACT OR TORT, FOR ANY INCIDENTAL, INDIRECT, SPECIAL, OR CONSEQUENTIAL LOSS OR DAMAGES (INCLUDING, WITHOUT LIMITATION, LOSS OF PROFITS, REVENUE OR DATA), THAT MAY ARISE FROM THE USE, OPERATION OR MODIFICATION OF THE PRODUCTS, EVEN

IF ADVISED OF THE POSSIBILITY OF SUCH LOSS OR DAMAGES BEING INCURRED.

7.6 **First Option Indemnification.** First Option, at its expense, shall defend any action brought against Vendor to the extent that it is based on a claim that any Software infringes a third party's copyright or a patent duly issued by the United States of America. First Option shall pay all damages and costs~~, up to the price paid by the Vendor for Software,~~ finally awarded against Vendor in such action provided that First Option is notified in writing of the existence of such claim against Vendor within seven (7) days of Vendor's first learning of the same.

8. **Default and Termination.**

8.1 **Termination for Convenience.** Either party may terminate this Agreement, with or without cause and without liability therefore, on sixty (60) days written notice to the other party.

8.2 **Termination for Breach.** If Vendor fails to pay any **undisputed** sum of money due and owing under this Agreement within ten (10) days of written notice thereof from First Option, First Option shall have the right to suspend its own performance hereunder or terminate this Agreement ~~without further~~ **upon** notice to Vendor. If either party breaches any of the terms, conditions, or provisions of this Agreement and fails to cure such breach within thirty (30) days after written notice thereof, the other party shall have the right to terminate this Agreement ~~without further~~ **upon** notice.

8.3 **Other Termination.** This Agreement may be immediately terminated by First Option if (i) Vendor violates any of the conditions of Section 2 or 7.3; (ii) Vendor ceases business, files for bankruptcy, is adjudged bankrupt or insolvent or commits any other act of bankruptcy; (iii) there is a sale or transfer, whether by operation of law or otherwise, or direct or indirect change of **voting** control of Vendor; or (iv) there is an attempt by Vendor to assign this Agreement or any right or obligation hereunder without First Option's prior written consent.

9. **Miscellaneous.**

9.1 **Entire Agreement.** Each party is bound by the terms of this Agreement. This Agreement is the complete and exclusive statement of the agreement between the parties, which supersedes and merges all prior proposals, understandings and all other agreements with respect to software maintenance. This Agreement may not be modified or altered except by a written instrument duly executed by both parties.

9.2 **Governing Law.** This Agreement must be governed by and construed according to the laws of the State of North Carolina. Any and all proceedings relating to the subject matter hereof must be brought and maintained in the state or federal courts of Durham, North Carolina which courts have exclusive jurisdiction for such purpose. Each of the parties waives any objection to venue or in personam jurisdiction, provided that service is effective.

9.3 **Severability.** If any provision of this Agreement is held to be invalid, illegal or unenforceable, the validity, legality and enforceability of the remaining provisions is not affected or impaired.

9.4 **Assignment.** Neither party may assign its rights, duties or obligations under this Agreement to any other person or entity, in whole or in part without the prior written consent of the other party. This Agreement is binding upon and inures to the benefit of the parties' respective successors and permitted assigns.

9.5 **Waiver.** The waiver or failure of either party to exercise in any respect any right provided in this Agreement may not be deemed a waiver of that or any other right.

Each party has caused this Agreement to be signed as of the date written above by its duly authorized representative.

Vendor   First Option Software, Inc.

By: _____   By: _____
Its: _____   Its: _____

A:

Traditional Form Contract

NON-DISCLOSURE & INTELLECTUAL PROPERTY PROTECTION AGREEMENT

This Non-Disclosure & Intellectual Property Protection Agreement (the "Agreement"), between Xyz, LLC ("Firm") and _____ ("Company") is effective as of _____, 2010.

STATEMENT OF PURPOSE

Firm and Company are interested in pursuing discussions concerning possible future transactions between them. Firm and Company desire to obtain further information from each other that could involve interaction and discussions between their respective personnel. Company possesses information that it considers confidential and proprietary, and during the course of these discussions, Company may find it necessary or desirable to disclose proprietary or confidential information to Firm. Similarly, Firm possesses information that it considers confidential and proprietary and may find it necessary or desirable to disclose portions of it to Company. In order to properly safeguard the proprietary and confidential information belonging to each other, Firm and Company agree as follows.

1. **Definitions.** As used in this Agreement:

- "Confidential Information" means information, other than Trade Secrets, that is of value to its owner and is treated as confidential.

- "Derivatives" means any new material, inventions, improvements, upgrades, updates, translations, abridgements, revisions or other form in which existing Proprietary Information may be adapted, modified, transformed, or recast.

- "Owner" means the party disclosing the Proprietary Information or owning the products.

- "Proprietary Information" includes Trade Secrets and Confidential Information. Proprietary Information may include, but is not limited to, functions and components of products and services, data, survey questions, profiles, computer programs, future business plans, marketing strategies, lists of actual and potential customers, and intellectual property. Proprietary Information includes all Trade Secrets and Confidential Information disclosed to Recipient, whether now owned or developed in the future.

- "Recipient" means the party receiving the Proprietary Information.

- "Trade Secrets" means information that is a trade secret as defined under applicable law.

2. **Non-disclosure; Permitted Use.**

2.1 Use of Proprietary Information. All Proprietary Information disclosed by Owner to Recipient during the term of this Agreement must be retained in confidence by Recipient. Recipient shall use the Proprietary Information for the purposes authorized by this Agreement and for no other purpose. Recipient shall not disclose the Proprietary Information (a) to any employee, contractor or representative of Recipient unless disclosure to that person is reasonably related to accomplishing the objective of this Agreement; or (b) to any third party. Recipient shall hold the Proprietary Information in strictest confidence and take all actions necessary to protect it against any unauthorized disclosure, publication, or use.

2.2 Duration of Obligations. Recipient's obligations under this Agreement with regard to Trade Secrets remain in effect for as long as the information remains a trade secret under applicable law. Recipient's obligations with regard to Confidential Information remain in effect for five years from the date of this Agreement.

2.3 Excluded Information. The obligations contained in this Section do not apply if and to the extent Recipient can prove the Proprietary Information:

- is publicly available, other than through a breach of this Agreement by Recipient;
- is developed by Recipient independently of, or was known by Recipient before, any disclosures made by Owner to Recipient of the information;
- becomes available to Recipient on a non-confidential basis from a source that is not prohibited from disclosing the information;
- is disclosed with written consent of Owner;
- is disclosed by Recipient pursuant to an order of a court of competent jurisdiction or administrative agency, a validly enforceable subpoena, applicable regulatory or professional standards, or any other legal or administrative process but only if Recipient provides notice to Owner of the request or requirement; or
- is disclosed by Recipient in connection with any judicial or other proceeding involving Firm and Company relating to this Agreement, but only if Recipient uses reasonable efforts to get confidential treatment of any information disclosed.

2.4 No Rights Granted. No provision in this Agreement may be deemed to grant either party any license or intellectual property right in the Proprietary Information of the other party. Neither party by virtue of this Agreement is obligated to purchase or use any products, materials, or services of the other party.

2.5 Derivatives. Any Derivatives of Proprietary Information, whether created by Owner or Recipient, remain the sole property of Owner.

3. Return.

Upon written request, Recipient shall promptly return to Owner all copies of the Proprietary Information of Owner, including computer software applications and any other information stored on computers.

4. Remedies.

The protections afforded by this Agreement are in addition to, and not in lieu of, protections available under applicable law. Disclosure or use of any Proprietary Information by Recipient in breach of this Agreement may give rise to irreparable injury to Owner. Owner may seek injunctive relief against the breach or threatened breach of this Agreement in addition to any other legal remedies that may be available.

5. Miscellaneous.

5.1 Applicable Law. This Agreement is governed by and construed in accordance with the laws of the State of Georgia without regard to its rules governing conflicts of law.

5.2 Dispute Resolution. The parties shall diligently negotiate efforts through negotiation to settle any disputes arising out of or related to this Agreement. Any controversy or claim not able to be settled by negotiation must be settled by final and binding arbitration administered by the American Arbitration Association under its Commercial Arbitration rules, and judgment on the award may be entered in any court having proper jurisdiction. The arbitrator may award reasonable attorneys fees and costs to the prevailing party.

5.3 Relationship of the Parties. The parties are independent principals. Nothing in this Agreement constitutes or may be deemed to constitute a partnership between the parties, or to constitute one party as agent of the other for any purpose. Neither party has authority or power to bind, to contract in the name of, or to create a liability for the other party.

5.4 Assignment. Neither this Agreement nor the rights or obligations of either party may be transferred or assigned by either party without the prior written consent of the other party.

5.5 Entire Agreement. This Agreement represents the entire understanding between the parties with respect to the subject matter contained in it and supersedes all other written or oral agreements made by or on behalf of Firm or Company. This Agreement may be changed only by written agreements signed by the authorized representatives of each party.

5.6 Severability. If any provision of this Agreement is declared invalid by a court of proper jurisdiction, the provision is affected only to the extent of the invalidity so the remainder of that provision and all remaining provisions of this Agreement will continue in full force and effect.

The parties have caused this Agreement to be duly signed as of the effective date first indicated above.

Xyz, LLC

By: _____

Name: _____

Title: _____

Company:

By: _____

Name: _____

Title: _____

B:

Schedule Agreement

AGREEMENT TO PROVIDE SERVICES
between
Xyz, LLC
and

_____
("Client")

This Agreement to Provide Services is entered into as of the Effective Date below, by and between Xyz, LLC, a Georgia limited liability company ("Consultant"), and the Client identified above.

Client desires to engage Consultant to provide the specific services described on the attached Schedule I on the terms and conditions set forth in this Agreement. This Agreement includes the General Terms and Conditions and Schedules listed below, which are incorporated by reference. Client and Consultant have read and fully understand this Agreement and, intending to be legally bound, agree as follows.

General Terms and Conditions
Schedule 1—Project Description
Engagement Letter

_____

_____

Xyz, LLC: Client:

By: _____   By: _____
Title: _____   Title: _____
Mailing Address: Mailing Address:

_____   _____

_____   _____

Telephone: Telephone:

_____   _____

Fax: Fax:

_____   _____

                                                 Form of Business:

                                                 _____ Individual
                                                 _____ Partnership
                                                 _____ Corporation
                                                 _____ Limited Liability Company

Effective Date: _____

GENERAL TERMS AND CONDITIONS
FOR SERVICES

1. Services. Consultant has developed a system for evaluating product effectiveness. Consultant will provide advice and recommendations to improve effectiveness and performance of Client's products. From time to time, Client may request Consultant to provide additional services. If Consultant agrees to perform these additional services, the parties will supplement this Agreement with an Addendum describing the additional services to be provided.

---

2. Ownership.

2.1 Rights Granted. Consultant owns all copyrights, trademarks, service marks and other intellectual property rights in and to the Xyz system. The Xyz system includes any manuals, tests, training materials and any written or electronic materials supplied by Consultant, and any modifications to them, including custom modifications requested by Client, if any. Client has no rights in the Xyz system, except as specifically granted in this Agreement. During the term and as long as client complies with the terms of this Agreement, Consultant grants client a perpetual, non-exclusive license to use and employ all data, reports, advice and recommendations prepared by Consultant pursuant to this Agreement.

2.2 Rejection of Limitations. Client acknowledges that Consultant is in the business of providing consulting services to many different organizations. Consultant specifically rejects any terms in any form submitted by Client that may be construed as precluding or limiting in any way Consultant's right:

- to provide consulting or other services of any kind or nature to any person or entity as Consultant in its sole discretion deems appropriate; or

- to develop for itself, or for others, materials that are similar to those produced as a result of the services provided pursuant to this Agreement.

3. Payment for Services.

3.1 Standard Fees. A retainer of 50% of the estimated total project fees is due and payable by Client upon execution of this Agreement. Client shall remit the balance of total project fees on a bi-weekly basis upon receipt of Consultant's invoices for services. Client shall pay Consultant's invoices within 30 days of receipt.

3.2 Expenses. Consultant may incur out-of-pocket expenses in rendering the services described in this Agreement. Expenses may include, but are not limited to, travel expenses (including transportation, lodging, and meals), photocopying, long distance charges, and charges for special supplies and equipment. Client shall pay or reimburse Consultant for all reasonable expenses incurred within 30 days after receipt of Consultant's invoice.

3.3 Fees for Additional Services. All additional services will be provided at Consultant's then current standard rates plus expenses. Client shall pay the additional fees and expenses within 30 days of receipt of Consultant's invoices.

3.4 Interest on Past Due Balances; Collection. Consultant may collect interest on overdue balances at the rate of one and one half percent per month. If any amounts due Consultant are collected by or through an attorney at law, Client shall pay the costs of collection, including actual attorneys' fees. Without limiting other rights or remedies, Consultant may temporarily suspend providing services without liability to Client until payment is received on past due invoices.

4. Responsibilities of Client.

4.1 Project Manager. Upon signing this Agreement, Client shall designate an employee of Client who will be responsible for communicating with Consultant on Client's behalf and for providing information and assistance reasonably requested by Consultant to enable Consultant to provide the services contemplated in this Agreement. Consultant may rely upon all decisions made and information provided by the project manager.

4.2 Cooperation. Client shall cooperate with Consultant by providing access to personnel and equipment and any information reasonably requested by Consultant in a timely manner.

4.3 Implementation. Client is solely responsible for making all decisions with respect to implementation of the recommendations made by Consultant pursuant to this Agreement.

5. Warranties; Limitation on Warranties and Liability.

5.1 WARRANTY; EXCLUSION OF WARRANTIES. CONSULTANT WARRANTS THAT IT WILL PERFORM ALL SERVICES PROVIDED UNDER THIS AGREEMENT IN A COMMERCIALLY REASONABLE MANNER. ALL IMPLIED WARRANTIES AND CONDITIONS INCLUDING, BUT NOT LIMITED TO, THE IMPLIED WARRANTIES OF MERCHANTABILITY AND FITNESS FOR A PARTICULAR PURPOSE ARE EXCLUDED FROM THIS AGREEMENT.

5.2 EXCLUSION OF CERTAIN DAMAGES. CONSULTANT IS NOT LIABLE FOR DAMAGES ARISING OUT OF DECISIONS

MADE BY CLIENT WITH RESPECT TO IMPLEMENTING, OR WHETHER TO IMPLEMENT, CONSULTANT'S ADVICE AND RECOMMENDATIONS. CONSULTANT IS NOT LIABLE FOR INDIRECT, SPECIAL, INCIDENTAL, OR CONSEQUENTIAL DAMAGES, INCLUDING, BUT NOT LIMITED TO LOSS OF PROFITS OR ANTICIPATED PROFITS OR LOSS OF DATA ARISING FROM OR IN CONNECTION WITH THE USE, DELIVERY, PERFORMANCE OR NON-PERFORMANCE OF ANY SERVICES TO BE PROVIDED UNDER THIS AGREEMENT, EVEN IF CONSULTANT HAS BEEN ADVISED OF THE POSSIBILITY OF SUCH DAMAGES OR COSTS.

5.3 LIMITATION OF DAMAGES. IN NO EVENT WILL CONSULTANT BE LIABLE TO CLIENT UNDER THIS AGREEMENT OR OTHERWISE, REGARDLESS OF THE FORM OF CLAIM OR ACTION IN AN AMOUNT THAT EXCEEDS, IN THE AGGREGATE, THE TOTAL FEES PAID TO CONSULTANT UNDER THIS AGREEMENT DURING THE THREE (3) MONTH PERIOD IMMEDIATELY PRIOR TO THE DATE OF THE EVENT, ACT, OR OMISSION GIVING RISE TO THE LIABILITY.

5.4 Limitation on Bringing Action. No action of any form arising under or related to this Agreement may be brought by either party more than one year after the cause of action has accrued, except that an action for non-payment may be brought by Consultant not later than one year after the due date of any payment due Consultant.

6. Indemnification.

Consultant shall indemnify Client against claims for bodily injury, death, or damage to real or tangible personal property to the extent directly and proximately caused by the gross negligence or willful misconduct of Consultant while performing the services described in this Agreement. The indemnification set forth in this Section is conditioned upon:

- Client's providing Consultant notice of any claim or cause of action upon which Client intends to base a claim of indemnification with sufficient promptness to avoid prejudicing Consultant's defense;
- Consultant's having the sole control of the defense and settlement of the claim or cause of action;

- Client's providing reasonable assistance and cooperation to enable Consultant to defend the action or claim; and
- Client's refraining from making prejudicial statements associated with the claim without the prior written consent of Consultant.

7. Term; Termination; Obligations Upon Termination.

7.1 Term. This Agreement is effective when signed by both parties and remains in full force and effect for [the period of time specified in the Project Description] unless terminated by either party.

7.2 Termination. This Agreement may be terminated at any time by mutual agreement. This Agreement may be terminated by either party at any time upon 30 days notice to the other party.

7.3 Post-termination Obligations. Upon termination of this Agreement for any reason, Consultant will immediately cease providing services. Consultant will prepare a final invoice for all fees and expenses incurred prior to the effective date of termination. Client shall pay the final invoice within 15 days of receipt. Within 10 days after termination, Client shall deliver to Consultant any written manuals or materials provided to Client by Consultant, any copies of them, and a certification signed by an officer of the Client stating that all written manuals and materials have been returned.

7.4 Survival of Terms. Upon termination or expiration of this Agreement, Sections 2, 3, 5, and 6 and Paragraph 7.3 continue and survive in full force and effect.

8. Miscellaneous Provisions.

8.1 Force Majeure. Consultant is not liable for any delays resulting from circumstances or causes beyond its reasonable control, including, without limitation, fire or other casualty, act of God, strike or labor dispute, war or other violence, or any law, order, or requirement of any governmental agency or authority.

8.2 Applicable Law. This Agreement is governed by and construed in accordance with the laws of the State of Georgia without regard to its rules governing conflicts of law.

8.3 Dispute Resolution. The parties shall diligently negotiate to settle any disputes arising out of or related to this Agreement. Any controversy or claim not able to be settled by negotiation must be settled by final and binding arbitration administered by the American

Arbitration Association under its Commercial Arbitration rules, and judgment on the award may be entered in any court having proper jurisdiction. The arbitrator may award reasonable attorneys fees and costs to the prevailing party.

8.4 Relationship of the Parties. The parties are independent principals. Nothing in this Agreement constitutes or may be deemed to constitute a partnership between the parties, or to constitute on party as agent of the other for any purpose. Neither party has authority or power to bind, to contract in the name of, or to create a liability for the other party.

8.5 Assignment. Neither this Agreement, nor the rights or obligations of either party may be transferred or assigned by either party without the prior written consent of the other party.

8.6 Entire Agreement. This Agreement represents the entire understanding between the parties with respect to the subject matter contained in it and supersedes all other written or oral agreements made by or on behalf of Consultant or Client. This Agreement may be changed only by written agreements signed by the authorized representatives of each party.

8.7 Severability. If any provision of this Agreement is declared invalid by a court of proper jurisdiction, the provision is affected only to the extent of the invalidity, so that the remainder of that provision and all remaining provisions of this Agreement will continue in full force and effect.

SCHEDULE I
PROJECT DESCRIPTION

1. **Names of Project Coordinators**

   Client:

   Consultant:

2. **General Description of Services and Project Deliverables**
3. **Anticipated Duration of Project:** _____Weeks
4. **Start Date:** _____

5. **Schedule and Performance Milestones:** The following schedule sets forth the target dates and performance milestones for the preparation and delivery of the Project Products.

Performance Milestone	**Responsible Party**	**Target Date**

6. **Job Site:** _____

7. **Payment Schedule:** Consultant will invoice Client on a _____ basis for Services performed at the rate of ($) per _____.

APPENDIX C:

Letter Agreement

[Date]

Best Choice Securities, Inc.
[Address]

Attention: _____

Re: Proprietary Information Agreement

Ladies and Gentlemen:

First Option Investors, Ltd., a Delaware corporation ("First Option"), desires to engage in discussions with Best Choice Securities, Inc., a New York corporation ("Best Choice") concerning a potential merger or acquisition. We desire to obtain from you and share with you further information that could involve interaction and discussions between our respective personnel. In the course of these discussions, Best Choice may find it necessary or desirable to disclose to First Option information that is proprietary and confidential in nature related to its business operations and procedures. In order to facilitate our discussions, First Option may also find it necessary or desirable to disclose proprietary and confidential information to Best Choice.

To safeguard the proprietary and confidential information belonging to each of us, we propose the following:

1. For purposes of this Agreement:

    • "Trade Secrets" means information, without regard to form, including but not limited to technical or nontechnical data, compilations, programs, devices, methods, techniques, processes, inventions, know-how, or algorithms, which is not commonly known by or available to the public and which information (a) derives economic value, actual or potential, from not being generally known to other persons who can obtain economic value from its disclosure or use and (b) is the subject of efforts that are reasonable under the circumstances to maintain its secrecy or confidentiality;

- "Confidential Information" means information, other than Trade Secrets, that is of value to its Owner and is treated as confidential;

- "Owner" means the party who owns and discloses the Proprietary Information;

- "Proprietary Information" means Trade Secrets and Confidential Information; and

- "Recipient" means the party that receives the Proprietary Information.

2.   The Recipient shall not use the Owner's Proprietary Information except to the extent necessary to negotiate, discuss and consult with personnel or representatives of the Owner regarding the proposed transaction. The Recipient shall not disclose any Proprietary Information received from the Owner during the term of this Agreement to any third party except as provided in Paragraph 8 (e). The Recipient shall not disclose the Proprietary Information to any employee, contractor, agent or representative of the Recipient unless disclosure to that person is reasonably related to accomplishing the objectives described above. The Recipient shall not disclose any Proprietary Information to any person located outside the United States of America without the express written consent of the Owner.

3.   The Recipient shall treat the Owner's Proprietary Information with the same degree of care it uses to protect its own Proprietary Information. The Recipient shall instruct its employees, contractors and representatives that the Proprietary Information belongs to the Owner and is to be held in confidence. The Recipient shall ensure that all employees, contractors and representatives to whom the Proprietary Information is disclosed take reasonable precautions to safeguard the confidential status of the Proprietary Information. Upon written request of the Owner, the Recipient shall require any employee, contractor, or representative who has access to the Proprietary Information to sign

a non-disclosure agreement with respect to the Owner's Proprietary Information. The Recipient shall immediately notify the Owner of any unauthorized use or disclosure of the Owner's Proprietary Information.

4. The Owner shall mark Proprietary Information disclosed in written or other tangible form with an appropriate legend, like "Confidential," "Proprietary," or "Trade Secret," but only material that the Owner believes in good faith to be Proprietary Information may be marked.

5. If the Owner desires to extend the protections of this Agreement to any Proprietary Information that is disclosed orally or visually (e.g., as a result of an office visit), the Owner shall provide a written summary of that information to the Recipient within 60 days from the date of the visual or oral disclosure.

6. The Recipient shall not reverse engineer, decompile, disassemble, re-engineer or otherwise recreate the Owner's Proprietary Information.

7. The Recipient's obligations with respect to the Owner's Confidential Information continue for a period of five years from the date the information is disclosed. The Recipient's obligations with respect to the Owner's Trade Secrets continue for so long as the information remains a Trade Secret under applicable law.

8. The Recipient's obligations under this Agreement do not apply to any portion of the Proprietary Information that the Recipient can prove with written evidence:

    (a) was known to the Recipient before the disclosure was made by the Owner;

    (b) was known to the public or generally available to the public before the Recipient received it;

    (c) becomes known to the public or generally available to the public after it was received by the Recipient through no act or failure to act on the Recipient's part;

    (d) corresponds in substance to information disclosed or made available to the Recipient at any time by a third party having a bona fide right to disclose the information to the Recipient; or

(e) is required to be disclosed in a judicial proceeding or governmental investigation if the Recipient gives the Owner advance notice of the required disclosure and allows the Owner an opportunity to oppose disclosure or seek a protective order.

9. Upon written request, the Recipient shall promptly return to the Owner all copies of Proprietary Information (including information on computers or computer software).

10. Neither party may disclose any information to the other if the disclosure would violate the proprietary rights of any third party.

11. This Agreement terminates on _____, 20__ unless sooner terminated by written notice by one party to the other. All obligations arising under this Agreement before termination survive termination.

12. This Agreement may not be assigned by either party.

13. If any provision of this Agreement is determined by a court having jurisdiction to be unenforceable under applicable law, the parties request that the remainder of this Agreement be interpreted so as to accomplish the objectives of the unenforceable provision within the limits of applicable law.

If the foregoing is acceptable to you, kindly sign the duplicate copy of this letter and return same to First Option.

FIRST OPTION INVESTORS, LTD.

By: _____

Title: _____

Date: _____

ACCEPTED AND AGREED TO THIS ____ DAY OF _____,
2012.

BEST CHOICE SECURITIES, INC.

By: _____

Name: _____

Title: _____

Suggested Answers to Exercises

The best answer to any question depends on assumptions made regarding underlying facts and circumstances. These suggested answers are not the only "correct" responses and are not intended to be exhaustive of all possible responses.

Exercise 1:

Tadpole may need any combination of the following: partnership or corporate formation documents; operating agreement or shareholders' agreement with buy-sell provisions; license agreement; manufacturing agreement; limited warranty; employment agreement; non-competition and confidentiality agreement; commercial lease agreement; architectural engagement agreement; finance and loan documents; subcontractor agreement; consulting agreement; distribution or sales representative agreement; purchase agreement; derivative works agreement; value-added reseller agreement; and marketing agreement.

Exercise 1.2:

1) brevity; simplicity
2) accuracy (employee); clarity
3) simplicity; brevity
4) tone; simplicity
5) clarity
6) clarity

Exercise 3.1:

The partners as well as their personal lawyers and accountants; employees, bankers, the bookkeeper; the partnership's accountants, estate representatives if any partners die during the term; bona fide purchasers for value; IRS auditors.

Exercise 4.2:

15.3; 15.9, 15.10, 15.16, 15.18, and 15.19 relate specifically to the relationship of partners or members to the LLC and to each other. These provisions are irrelevant in a software license, except that 15.9 could be modified to address more general assignment issues not involving "heirs." Sections 15.4 and 15.5 should be deleted for the reasons mentioned in the text at Section 4.2. The remaining provisions should be revised to include references to a software license instead of an operating agreement. Other boilerplate provisions specific to software licenses may need to be added, depending on the terms of the transaction.

Exercise 5.2:

Commercial Lease: Who are the parties to the lease? Is the landlord regularly engaged in property management with a good track record? Who is responsible for maintaining any common areas? Is construction to be done to comply with lessee's specifications? Who are nearby tenants? Are personal guarantees required? Is the property currently available or is it still occupied by another tenant? Is the property new or has it been used in the past? If so, by whom? Were hazardous materials used on the premises? Is this a sublease, an assignment of rights, or a new contract? What is the term of the lease? How can the lease be terminated? What are events of default? Can the tenant assign rights? Where is the property physically located? Are there any geographical problems, like a flood plain or earthquake fault line, that might make the property susceptible to acts of God? When is rent due? Will rent be adjusted periodically for changes to the CPI? What happens if rent is late?

Partnership Agreement:

Who are the partners? Will the partnership have general and limited partners? If so, who are they? What is the background of each partner? Will each partner be actively engaged in the business or are there passive investors? Are any partners party to an outside agreement that would prevent them from entering this one? What will be the ownership interest of each partner? Do all partners have authority to act on behalf of the partnership? Do certain matters require consent of all partners? What type of business will the partnership conduct? What is the capital contribution of each partner? Will separate financing be obtained? When will the partnership begin? What is the initial term of partnership? Where will the partnership's business be conducted? How will the partners be compensated? How will income be distributed among the partners? How will income and expense be allocated for tax purposes? Will there be restrictions on transfer of ownership interests? Will partners be subject to restrictive covenants?

Exercise 5.3A

Merger agreement topics:

Defined terms: 5, 8, 17, 23

Performance: 2, 3, 4, 6, 7, 19

Reps and warranties: 9, 18 (of the surviving co); 10, 16 (of the acquired co)

Indemnification: 14, 24

Termination: 13, 15, 20

Boilerplate: 1, 11, 12, 21, 22

Exercise 5.3B

Service agreement topics:

Supplier's duties: 2, 3, 8, 15

IP Rights: 4, 6, 9, 10, 11, 16

Payment Terms: 12, 19, 24

Warranties: 5, 17, 21, 22

Termination: 18

Boilerplate: 1, 7, 13, 14, 20, 23, 25

Exercise 6.1:

1. which

2. such business combinations (does "business combinations" include start-up businesses?)

3. promptly

4. frequently

5. only

6. only

7. he (note the dangling modifier; hopefully the judge is not ignorant of the law)

8. that

9. which

10. contextual—is it "all" or "the appropriate percentage?"

Exercise 7.1:

turns 21; during; if; enough; too many; under; because; immediately; begin; next to or adjacent to; may

Exercise 7.4:

1. The world is full of obvious things ~~which~~ **that** nobody by any chance ever observes.

2. We have developed a plan for operating a business~~,~~ ~~which~~ **that** sells printed business products and services.

3. The Company may elect to purchase the Membership Interest or Economic Interest ~~which~~ **that** is the subject of the proposed Transfer for the same price and on the same terms and conditions as described in the Transfer notice.

4. A Member may not voluntarily withdraw or take any other voluntary action ~~which~~ **that** directly causes a withdrawal event.

5. "Reserves" means funds set aside or amounts allocated during any fiscal period to reserves, which will be maintained in amounts deemed sufficient or necessary by the holders of a Majority in Interest to meet the needs of the business of the Company.

C 6. Any and all printed, written, or electronic material that Distributor obtains, produces, or prepares in performing services under this Agreement will be and remain the exclusive property of Owner, subject to paragraph 9.3 (c) of this Agreement.

7. The Members will decide any questions arising with respect to the Company and this Operating Agreement~~,~~ ~~which~~ **that** are not specifically or expressly provided for in this Operating Agreement.

Exercise 8.2:

1. No attorney-in-fact is obligated to furnish bond or other security.

2. Except where the context indicates otherwise, words in the singular number include the plural. *Note: The reciprocal gender clause should be omitted entirely; See Section 13.2.*

3. If a Shareholder files a voluntary petition, complaint or answer. . . .

4. The Specifications are part of this Agreement.

5. This Agreement is effective when signed by both parties and remains in full force and effect for the period of time specified in the Project Description unless terminated as described below. *[Note: Execution = performance, which is not what the drafter intended in this provision. See glossary.]*

Exercise 9.2

1. Buyer may reject defective goods and services at any time even if Buyer has previously inspected or accepted the goods or services.

2. The Company may accept the offer by affirmative vote of a majority of the disinterested Directors.

3. The purchaser may pay the purchase price at closing or in installments as provided in subsection (ii).

4. The Plan has been established, maintained, and administered in substantial compliance with its terms and with applicable provisions of ERISA. *[Note: A trick question! This representation and warranty is better stated in passive voice.]*

5. Client shall pay interest on any past due amount at the rate of 1-1/2 percent per month from the due date until paid.

Exercise 9.3

1. Hidden verbs: assurances, protection, performance, inducement; determination; agreement. The Corporation desires to protect Executive against liabilities he may incur while performing duties on its behalf and to induce Executive to serve as its officer. The parties agree as follows.

2. Hidden verbs: receipt, notice, commencement, payment, omission, payment, performance. Vendor shall notify Corporation when Vendor begins providing Services. Corporation will promptly pay the initiation fee after receiving this notice, but Vendor may not discontinue performing Services if Corporation fails to pay promptly.

3. Hidden verbs: indemnification, payment, accordance, demand, indemnification, indemnification. Company shall indemnify Indemnitee against Expenses. Upon written notice from Indemnitee, Company shall promptly reimburse Expenses according to this Agreement unless [Company] determines that Indemnitee is not entitled to be indemnified under applicable law.

Exercise 9.7:

1. Upon written request, each Member shall execute and deliver in a timely fashion:

- statements of interest and holdings;

- statements of designation;

- powers of attorney; and

- any other instruments

deemed by the Company necessary to comply with applicable law and to effectuate the purposes of this Operating Agreement.

2. The Company shall not idemnify Indemnitee in connection with any Proceeding initiated by Indemnitee against the Company or any officer or director of the Company <u>unless Independent Counsel approves initiation</u> of the Proceeding and any one or more of the following occur:

    (i) the Company has joined in or the Board consents to the Proceeding;

    (ii) Indemnitee initiates the Proceeding to enforce indemnification rights under Section 5; or

    (iii) Indemnitee initiates the Proceeding after a Change in Control (other than a Change in Control approved by a majority of the directors on the Board who were directors immediately before the Change in Control).

3. Contractor may disclose Confidential Information when requested to do so by any governmental, judicial, or regulatory authority if Contractor:

    (i) requests confidential treatment of the Confidential Information;

    (ii) notifies Owner in advance of the request so Owner may take any action it deems appropriate to prevent the disclosure;

    (iii) endeavors to protect the Confidential Information to the extent reasonable under the circumstances; and

    (iv) uses its good faith efforts to prevent any further disclosure of the Confidential Information.

Exercise 10.1:

1. The Corporation shall indemnify the distributor to the fullest extent permitted by law against:

> all expenses (including attorney's fees); and

> all liabilities

> actually and reasonably incurred by distributor....

2. Indemnitee may receive Expense Advances upon written request but shall repay Expense Advances if [a court of law] subsequently [determines that Indemnitee is liable.]

3. Company shall indemnify Director for Expenses as provided in this Agreement.

4. If any provision of this Agreement is declared unenforceable [by a court having jurisdiction], the provision is ineffective only to the extent declared unenforceable. The remainder of the provision and all other provisions of this Agreement will continue in full force and effect.

5. I give the remainder of my estate...

Exercise 11.1:

[Note: Answers to this exercise depend heavily upon the assumptions made and may vary widely depending on the party represented.]

1. required; 2. essential; 3. required if severed employee is an older worker; could be recommended if the client has a habit of re-using forms; otherwise, optional if employee is young; 4. required if the client intends to avoid the implied warranties; otherwise, recommended for the seller but not necessarily for the buyer; 5. required under copyright laws if company is to acquire rights in the work; essential in an assignment of rights agreement; otherwise, recommended for company and optional for consultant; 6. recommended if timing is important, otherwise optional; 7. optional from company's perspective but possibly essential from employee's; 8. usually recommended but could be optional; 9. essential; 10. essential.

Exercise 11.4:

1. Seller shall indemnify Buyer against all claims arising under this Agreement.

2. Seller shall indemnify Buyer against all claims arising under this Agreement to the extent caused by Seller's actions.

---

3. Seller shall indemnify Buyer against all claims arising under this Agreement to the extent caused by Seller's actions. Buyer shall indemnify Seller against all claims arising under this Agreement to the extent caused by Buyer's actions.

4. Buyer shall indemnify Seller against all claims arising under this Agreement to the extent caused by Buyer's actions.

5. Buyer shall indemnify Seller against all claims arising under this Agreement.

Exercise 12.3:

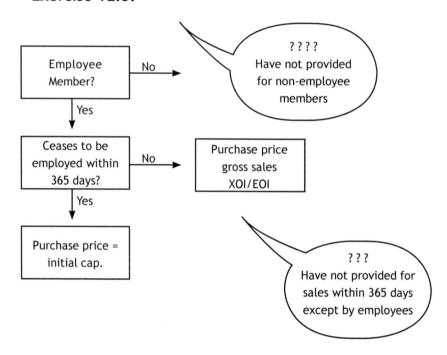

Glossary

This glossary contains two kinds of words: 1) words that are used to describe contracts or specific provisions in contracts; and 2) words that might be used in a variety of typical contracts. This list is not intended to be exhaustive of either kind.

AAA: American Arbitration Association

absent manifest error: without clear evidence of an obvious mistake

abstract of title: a summary of conveyances, liens, and encumbrances in the chain of title for a particular parcel of real property

acceleration clause: language in a contract that causes obligations to become due immediately rather than at the agreed upon time of performance, usually due to an event of default or breach

acceptance: the unqualified, final expression of an offeree agreeing to the terms of an offer. A qualified acceptance is usually considered to be a counteroffer and not an acceptance, except under certain conditions in the UCC. The acceptance of an offer forms a contract.

accord and satisfaction: an alternative method of performance that is deemed by the parties to discharge a contractual obligation

accounts receivable: the sum of amounts that are due from customers within one year

accredited investors: persons having sophisticated business acumen or a specified amount of net worth; see "non-accredited investor"

acquisition: a transaction in which substantially all of the equity or assets of another entity are acquired

act of God: an unforeseeable occurrence in nature that is beyond the control of humans

additional insured endorsement: a certificate which allows a third party beneficiary to be insured under the holder's insurance policy

ADR: alternative dispute resolution

ad valorem: a tax that is based on the value of property rather than income

allonge: a certificate physically attached to a negotiable instrument that contains one or more endorsements or permits other changes to the original terms of the instrument

alternative dispute resolution: refers to various methods of resolving disputes without resorting to the judicial system

amended and restated: a document that has been re-written to incorporate collectively all of the changes in multiple amendments into a single form

amendment: a separate contract that makes changes or corrections to the original document

American Arbitration Association: a nonprofit corporation which provides services to resolve disputes out of court

amortization: the process of charging capital expenditures, bond premiums, or loan payments proportionally over time

anchor tenant: the key tenant that gives stability to a shopping center by drawing a steady stream of customers

annual meeting: a gathering of shareholders or directors required to be held by a company each year at a time stated in the bylaws

antecedent debt: an obligation existing before a transaction takes place

anticipatory breach: a breach of contract that occurs before the required time of performance when a party indicates that it will not be able to perform

anti-dilution provision: in a transaction that arranges for a future issuance of stock or other equity interest, a protection against events that would cause the stock or equity to become less valuable by issuing other equity in the interim. For example, an anti-dilution provision might provide that if the grantee is entitled to receive 10,000 shares out of 100,000 authorized common stock, the issuer may not authorize an additional 100,000 shares without granting 10,000 additional shares to the grantee.

antitrust law: statutes, regulations, and case law designed to prevent monopolies and other methods of restraining free trade

appendix: in drafting, an attachment to a contract that contains supplementary information that is indirectly related to the current transaction. An appendix is usually attached as a matter of convenience or as a matter of record rather than as a part of the contract itself.

appropriate, appropriation: setting aside property for specific purposes, sometimes without permission. Can be used in a negative sense, i.e., a partner or shareholder may not appropriate company assets for personal use; or in a positive sense, e.g., the City Council appropriated funds for parks and recreation.

appurtenance: something added to another more important thing, like an easement that passes to successive owners of a parcel of land

APR: annual percentage rate

arbitration: a method of dispute resolution where the parties present their facts and arguments to one or more neutral arbiters, whose decision is binding upon the parties

arm's length: an adjective that describes a transaction between related parties that is conducted as though the parties were independent of each other

arrears: 1) the state of being behind in making payments; 2) an arrangement where payments are to be made after services are rendered. Most salaries are paid in arrears meaning that payment is made following the time period in which the employee has worked, while rent is usually paid in advance.

articles of incorporation: a document prepared by or on behalf of a company to request that a corporation be formed under state law. The articles of incorporation must comply with requirements of state law and must be filed with the secretary of state. If the filing is accepted, a corporation will be formed when a certificate of incorporation is issued by the secretary of state, but the articles of incorporation alone do not form a corporation.

articles of organization: a document prepared by or on behalf of partners or members to request that a limited liability company or partnership be formed under state law. See articles of incorporation.

artisan: a person manually skilled in some type of trade, craft, or art, e.g., a carpenter or plumber. An artisan may file an artisan's lien against property if not paid on a timely basis.

"as is": sold without implied or express warranties

asset-based loan: a loan that is based upon a certain percentage of the borrower's assets, usually current assets like accounts receivable and inventory.

assets: all property of any form owned by a person or entity. Tangible assets include items like cash, real estate, equipment, and inventory; intangible assets include items like goodwill and trademarks.

assign: to transfer property, rights, or interests

assignee: the person or entity to whom property, rights, or interests are assigned

assignment: the transfer of property, rights, or interests to another

assignment for the benefit of creditors: the transfer of property by a trustee in bankruptcy to satisfy the debtor's obligations

assignor: the person or entity who assigns property, rights, or interests to another

associate: in a law firm, a lawyer who is not a partner. Typically, associates receive a salary but do not participate in profits. "Associate" may have a different connotation in the business world, where the word might be used to describe someone having equal status and privileges.

assumption of risk: the concept that a person who undertakes an inherently risky venture has accepted the risk of loss, damage, or injury. E.g., a company assumes the risk of utilizing new, untested technology or equipment.

attach: a creditor's security interest in the borrower's property is said to "attach" when it becomes enforceable

attachment: 1) the taking of a borrower's property to satisfy an obligation; 2) in drafting, any document that is attached to the primary document, including appendixes, exhibits, and schedules

attest: to confirm as true, correct, or genuine. E.g., a corporate secretary might attest that the person signing on behalf of the corporation has authority to do so and that the transaction has been properly approved.

attorney, attorney-in-fact: a representative who is legally appointed to act on behalf of another. The person may or may not be a lawyer. E.g., power of attorney may be granted to someone who is not licensed to practice law.

attorney-at-law: a lawyer who is legally appointed to act on behalf of a client

"at will" employee: a person whose employment may be terminated by either party at any time

authorized stock: the number of shares permitted to be issued by the articles of incorporation

bad faith: acting in a way that is dishonest, misleading, or contrary to contractual obligations

balance sheet: a financial statement that summarizes assets, liabilities, and net worth as of a specific point in time.

bank draft: a check drawn by a bank on its own funds

bankruptcy: a process under federal or state law that allows an insolvent person or entity to reorganize or discharge debts

bargain: 1) promises exchanged among two or more people; 2) to negotiate the terms of an agreement or contract for the sale of assets, goods, or services, as in "a bargained-for exchange."

basis point: a unit of measure used to describe either a change in interest rate or a change in valuation. One basis point equal $1/100^{th}$ of a percent, or 0.0001 in decimal form. E.g., if a bank raises its floating interest rate by 25 basis points, the rate would increase from 5.5% to 5.75%

bearer instrument, bearer paper: a negotiable instrument that is payable to any person who has possession of it

beneficial owner: the person who has the right to receive proceeds and other benefits of ownership, which is distinguished from the "record owner," who is publicly recognized as the owner but may be holding the investment as an agent

beneficiary: a person who benefits from the actions of another; a person who is not a party to but receives benefits under a will, a trust, or a contract

benefit of the bargain: the advantage, outcome, or gain expected by a party entering into an agreement

bilateral contract: an agreement that contains promises from two or more parties

bill of lading: a document listing goods included in a shipment which is acknowledged by the carrier that transports the goods

bill of sale: a document by which the seller assigns or transfers its rights in the goods sold to the buyer

board of directors: the persons elected by the shareholders to advise and monitor the management of a corporation

boilerplate: in drafting, language that can be used in a variety of contracts to cover miscellaneous topics that is not heavily negotiated. "Boilerplate" may have a different connotation in the business world, which tends to view as boilerplate any language that is pre-printed on a standard form.

bona fide purchaser: a person who is interesting in buying the asset or item in question in a good faith, arms' length transaction

bond: a long term debt security issued by a government or a corporation

book value: the worth of an asset or an entity as recorded in the financial statements. The book value of an asset would be its cost less depreciation or amortization; the book value of an entity would equal total assets less total liabilities.

breach: a failure to perform a contractual obligation

bring-down: 1) in drafting, the process of confirming that representations and warranties made at the time an agreement is signed are still accurate at closing; 2) in real estate, the process of confirming whether changes in title have occurred between the time of the original title search and closing

bulk transfer: the conveyance of a major portion of the equipment, inventory, or other assets of an entity made outside the normal course of business

business judgment rule: a principle protecting officers and directors from liability for decisions made in good faith with due diligence

buy sell agreement: an agreement among partners, members, or shareholders that restricts the transfer of ownership or requires the transfer of ownership in certain events

bylaws: the private rules governing the internal affairs of an organization, like when and how meetings should be called, the duties of the officers and directors, and where books and records should be maintained

call: an option to buy a specific asset at a set price within a specified period of time

cancelled stock: shares of stock that were issued but have been repurchased and retired

capital stock: the total amount of stock authorized for issue by a corporation, including both common and preferred shares

capitalization: the funds used to operate a business received from its investors

capitalize: for tax purposes, this means the item must be shown in the financial statements as an asset rather than as an expense, even when all of the cost is incurred up front.

capitalized lease: a lease of property that is considered an asset in the entity's financial statements. The lease obligations for a capitalized lease also appear in the financial statements as a liability. The lease payments are amortized and deducted as expenses over time, rather than deducting the entire cost as of the day it was signed.

carveout: in drafting, language inserted to provide an exception. E.g., an employment agreement might require the employee to assign all rights in intellectual property created during the term but provide a carveout for projects started before the employee begins work.

caselaw: the law derived from the analysis and opinions of the courts regarding matters presented to them, as distinguished from statutory law.

cashier's check: a check drawn by a bank on its own funds

cause, good cause: in drafting, a worthy reason to terminate that is usually specified and defined in the contract

certificate of good standing: a certificate issued upon request by the secretary of state confirming that a business entity has paid all fees due and complied with all filing requirements to date

certificate of incorporation: a certificate issued by the secretary of state to form a corporation after articles of incorporation have been filed

change of control provision: in drafting, language that provides a specific remedy, like acceleration of obligations or early termination, if a significant change occurs with respect to the officers or directors responsible for managing the company

charter: used in some states to refer to the certificate of incorporation

chattel: an item of personal property that is movable and not attached to real estate

choice of law: a boilerplate provision that specifies which state or nation's law will be used to interpret the contract if a dispute arises. Choice of law is different than jurisdiction, which is where a dispute will be litigated.

clawback: a provision that requires an earlier payment to be returned in a specified situation

click wrap agreement: a software license that comes into effect when the licensee clicks a button on the computer screen

closely held corporation: a corporation whose stock is held by a relatively few persons and not freely traded

closing: the formal "meeting" where a transaction is finalized and ownership actually passes from the seller to the buyer

c.o.d.: collect upon delivery, meaning no credit is to be extended and payment is due when the goods are delivered

codicil: an amendment to a will

collateral: assets pledged by a debtor to a creditor to ensure a debt is ultimately paid. If the debt is not paid, the creditor can sell the assets to recover the loaned funds. Any asset can be collateral, but most commonly stocks, real property, inventory, equipment, accounts receivable, or any combination of these are used.

comfort letter: 1) a letter issued by an accountant that has reviewed a company's financial records but has not audited them; 2) a letter issued by a person or entity that backs another person or entity's obligations without actually guaranteeing them. E.g., a parent corporation might issue a comfort letter with respect to its subsidiary's obligations.

commitment: a summary of the terms under which a lender has agreed to lend money, usually on a specified date in the near future, when documentation and other conditions have been completed

commodity: a good that is sold without significant differences in quality, meaning that the good is the same no matter who produces it. Commodities include, but are not limited to, natural resources like gold, silver, coal, iron ore, and oil, and agricultural products like sugar, coffee beans, soybeans, rice, corn, and grains. Commodities are bought and sold on commodities exchanges like the Chicago Board of Trade.

common law: the principals of law that developed over time in England as cases were decided, distinguished from statutory law

common stock: the class of shares of a corporation that has voting rights and proportional ownership interests

company: an entity that is formed by incorporating (in the case of a corporation) or organizing (in the case of a limited liability company) under state law

compound interest: a method of calculating interest where the interest charges are added to principal rather than being paid separately, and interest accumulates on the sum of unpaid interest and principal rather than just on principal

condition: a requirement that must be met before a contractual obligation arises

conditions concurrent: requirements that are to be performed by the parties simultaneously

condition precedent: something that must happen before an obligation arises

condition subsequent: something that terminates a contractual obligation if it occurs

conflict of interests: a situation that arises when a person or entity is involved in two or more pursuits that might lead to a compromise or even the perception of a compromise in the rights of one to the advantage of the other. For example, a member of the board of directors might also be the majority shareholder of a major supplier. It is customary to refrain from voting on matters where a conflict of interests could exist.

conflict of laws: a situation where the laws of two or more jurisdictions could be applied under the circumstances. Most states have conflict of laws principals that provide a framework to enable the courts to determine which state's laws should be applied. In drafting, the parties can specify which law controls to prevent conflict of laws issues if a dispute arises.

conformed copy: an exact copy of a contract where the actual signatures have been replaced with the symbol "/s/" followed by the names of the signers typed on the lines because the signatures could not be reproduced. In the past, documents signed with some inks, particularly blue ink, did not photocopy well. The practice of using conformed copies for this purpose may be atavistic in modern times, since current technology is capable of reproducing virtually everything. Conformed copies may be useful, however, when documents are "signed" electronically.

consent: in drafting, permission granted by one party to allow the other party to do something that is either prohibited in the contract or for which consent is specifically required

consequential damages: indirect loss or injury that is not a direct, obvious result but follows from the consequences of the other party's breach or failure to perform. E.g., compensation for lost profits when a defective product causes a plant to shut down for a day

consideration: ultimately, the reason a party is interested in entering into a transaction. The concept of consideration used to involve benefit or detriment but in most states is now based on the concept of a bargained-for exchange having legal value.

consideration recital: a generally superfluous statement that consideration has been exchanged. For the vast majority of contracts, a simple statement that "the parties agree as follows" is preferable evidence of a bargain. A consideration recital may be useful in unilateral contracts.

consignment: an arrangement where a third party undertakes to sell goods owned by someone else

consolidation: 1) the merger of two or more business entities, usually involving a third entity that acquires the equity of both entities; 2) a financial statement that combines the parent company's results with its subsidiaries

consumer price index: a statistic calculated by the Bureau of Labor Statistics for the U.S. Department of Labor that measures the average change in prices over time used in a variety of long term transactions as a means of adjusting dollar values. E.g., in a commercial lease, rent may be adjusted by the CPI each year so the rent the lessor collects is worth the same amount from beginning to end.

contract: an agreement among two or more parties to do or not to do something that is allowed by law

copyright: a form of protection granted by law for original works of authorship, including literary, dramatic, musical, artistic, and other intellectual works where the owner of the copyright is given the exclusive right to use or reproduce the work for a specified period of years. In the U.S., copyrights may be registered with the Library of Congress, but rights are enforceable with or without registration.

corporation: an entity that is formed by incorporating under state law

coupon: the interest rate on a debt security. Some bonds are sold at a deep discount off the face value with zero coupon, meaning that interest is earned by holding the bond until maturity, when the face value is paid. Other bonds are sold at or closer to face value an earn a specified rate of interest until maturity.

course of dealing: the usual manner of doing business between two parties

covenant: a solemn promise to do or not to do something

CPI: Consumer Price Index

creditor: a person or entity to whom money is owed

---

cross default: an event of default in a debt agreement that occurs when the debtor is in default in any other debt agreement

cross reference: in drafting, a reference in one paragraph or section to another paragraph or section

cumulative preferred stock: a class of stock that earns dividends which are due to be paid in full by the company to the holder(s) before any dividends can be paid to common stock holders

cumulative voting: a method of voting authorized in the articles or bylaws for the benefit of minority shareholders that permits a shareholder to apply all votes to a single candidate as opposed to a panel of candidates. For example, in an election for three directors, a shareholder who holds 5,000 shares under regular voting could vote up to 5,000 shares for each director, but under cumulative voting, the shareholder could vote 15,000 shares for a single director.

cure: to correct a breach

damages: money paid as compensation for injury or loss

d/b/a: doing business as, meaning an entity is using a name to do business that is different from its formal name as filed in the public record

debenture: a long term debt security that is unsecured except by the general creditworthiness of the issuer

debt: what is owed

debt security: an obligation to pay that can be bought and sold over the counter, like government bonds, corporate bonds, certificates of deposit, municipal bonds, and preferred stock

debtor: the person or entity that owes money

declaratory judgment: a court decision that explains to the parties what their respective rights and obligations are concerning a specific controversy

deed: a document by which rights in real property are transferred

deed of trust: a document used to grant a security interest in real property

default: the failure to comply with a contractual requirement

de minimis: trivial, insignificant, unimportant

depreciation: a decline in an asset's value due to normal age and usage

derivative suit: a lawsuit brought by shareholders on behalf of a corporation for misuse of corporate assets by officers or directors or both

direct damages: loss that is immediately and foreseeably caused by breach of contract

director: a person elected by the shareholders to advise and monitor management of a corporation

discharge: 1) termination or completion of a contract; 2) in bankruptcy, the release of a debtor from its debts

discount: to sell something below stated or face value; the amount of the difference between sales price and the stated or face value

dissenting shareholder: a shareholder who does not approve of a corporate action that must be submitted to a vote of shareholders according to state law

dissenters' rights: specific rights granted under applicable law to shareholders who do not approve of a corporate action; for example, the right to receive the fair value of shares in lieu of the arrangement offered other shareholders in a merger

dissolution: the termination of a corporation or partnership

distribution: 1) division of corporate or partnership assets among shareholders or partners, respectively; 2) the process of supplying goods for sale to the public; the chain of distribution

distributor: a person or entity that obtains goods from a vendor and makes them available to the public

dividend: a portion of corporate earnings distributed to the shareholders on a pro rata basis, usually paid in cash but sometimes in additional shares of stock

documentary letter of credit: an arrangement where a bank agrees to pay a certain sum of money to a beneficiary when the beneficiary presents certain documents to the bank for payment

donee: the person or entity that receives a donation

---

donor: the person or entity that contributes an item of value

draft: 1) a document used for transferring money when the drawer instructs the drawee to pay money to someone else; 2) in drafting, a preliminary version of a document; 3) to prepare a legal document

drawee: the person or entity, usually a bank, that is directed by the drawer to pay a sum to a third party

drawer: the person or entity that instructs the drawee to pay a sum to a third party

drop-dead date: the date specified in an agreement where one party has the right to terminate the agreement if the other party hasn't performed a specified obligation

due diligence: in drafting, the appropriate level of review of the financial and corporate records of one party, usually performed by lawyers and other representatives of the other party, to determine whether to proceed with a transaction

earn-out: part of a sales price in an acquisition that is paid to the seller after closing if and when certain objectives are met by the acquired entity

easement: the right to limited use of another person's real property

ebitda: earnings before income tax, depreciation, and amortization

EDGAR: electronic document gathering, analysis, and retrieval system of the Securities and Exchange commission, upon which documents required under federal securities laws can be filed and subsequently obtained by the public.

EDI: Electronic data interchange; the process of allowing entities to exchange documents like bids, purchase orders, and invoices, electronically. The word "allowing" may be deceptive in that companies that have implemented EDI systems generally require their business partners to use them.

effective interest rate: the actual rate of interest that is calculated based on the funds received after fees and prepayments have been deducted. It is usually higher than the APR, or annual percentage rate

engagement letter: a letter agreement issued by lawyers and other professionals to clients outlining the terms under which they agree to represent the client's interests

electronic signature: a facsimile symbol of a true signature that is transmitted over the internet to indicate acceptance of terms

electronic funds transfer: a transfer of money completed by computer without the necessity of checks, drafts, or other paper documents

eminent domain: the power of the government to buy private property for public purposes

encumbrance: a security interest or other lien attached to and binding real property; e.g., a mortgage, judgment lien, mechanics or artisan's lien, easement, or accrued and unpaid taxes

equity: in corporate law, an ownership interest in a corporation; the residual value of a business after deducting liabilities

ERISA: In the U.S., the Employee Retirement Income Security Act; ERISA establishes minimum standards for retirement and other benefit plans and is administered by a division of the Department of Labor.

escrow: funds or items placed with a fiduciary in trust until some specified event occurs

estate: 1) all real and personal property that is left by a deceased person; 2) all property and debts of a bankrupt person; 3) a large piece of property; 4) a manner of referring to legal interest in real property

event of default: an act, event, or failure of condition that is deemed to be a failure to perform a contract

excise tax: a tax on the production, use, or consumption of certain commodities, like petroleum

executed contract: a contract that has been performed. This phrase is so commonly misused to describe a contract that has been signed that few lawyers are aware of the distinction, which most likely arises because at the point "closing" documents are signed, the transaction often has in fact been performed. This would not be the case when "opening" documents are signed, because opening documents are executory contracts. (See Section 3.3.)

---

executor, executrix: the person appointed in a will to carry out instructions after death and distribute the testator or testatrix's estate. Executor is masculine; executrix is feminine.

executory contract: a contract that has not been performed. A contract can be executed by one party and executory by the other.

exhibit: in drafting, an attachment to a contract that is usually a separate legal document directly related to the current transaction. In order to be considered part of the original document, exhibits must be "incorporated by reference," either individually in the text where the exhibit is mentioned, or in a blanket statement in the boilerplate "entire agreement" provision that all exhibits are considered part of the agreement of the parties. Although the words are sometimes used interchangeably, there are minor distinctions between exhibit, appendix, attachment, and schedule. (See those definitions.)

express contract: an intentional agreement between two or more parties to do or not to do something allowed by law. An express contract may be oral or written. The key distinction between an express contract and an implied contract is that in an express contract it is clear that the parties intended to form an agreement of some sort, even though some details may have been left out.

express warranty: an explicit promise about the quality of goods, either spoken or observable. An express warranty can be made by description or without words with a model or sample.

face value: the stated value printed on a debt instrument, like a bond, legal tender, or a promissory note

factoring: the practice of buying or selling accounts receivable for a discount off the face value. The buyer benefits because it ultimately receives the face value of the receivable. The seller benefits because it obtains a lump sum of funds immediately rather than over time as the accounts receivable are paid.

fair market value: an estimate of the value of property or assets based on what a willing, knowledgeable buyer would be willing to pay in an arm's length transaction

FASB; Financial Accounting Standards Board: an organization that develops standards for financial reporting

fee simple, fee simple absolute: an estate in land in which the owner holds unqualified rights in real property; the highest degree of ownership of real proeprty

fiduciary: a person who stands in a special relationship of trust to another person or entity, usually with respect to managing money or property

fiduciary duty: an obligation of highest loyalty and good faith of a person who stands in a relationship of trust to another person or entity

financing statement: a document filed in the public records pursuant to the UCC to perfect a security interest

firm offer: under the UCC, an offer made by a "merchant" that cannot be withdrawn for a specified period

fixture: an item that has been permanently attached to real property that cannot easily be removed

force majeure: an unforeseeable and unavoidable event that prevents a party from being able to perform its obligations under an agreement

F.O.B.; free on board: a designation indicating when title and risk of loss pass from the seller to the buyer. "F.O.B. [destination]" means the seller has title and the risk of loss until the goods arrive at their destination. "F.O.B. [seller's location]" means the buyer has title and the risk of loss from the point of the seller's place of business. Sometimes the words "destination," "seller's location," or "buyer's location" are actually used but more often the names of the cities where the parties are located are used instead. e.g., "F.O.B. Atlanta" means that title and risk of loss pass from seller to buyer in Atlanta.

forum selection clause: similar to and often used in conjunction with a choice of law provision, this clause references the parties' agreement as to the place or specific court where disputes will be resolved

franchise: a business arrangement in which the owner of some form of intellectual property (e.g., trademark, trade name, service mark, patent, copyright) or particular business process allows another to use the property or process, usually in connection with retail outlets owned by independent operators

franchisee: the person or entity granted rights in a franchise

franchisor: the person or entity that owns and grants rights in a franchise

fraud: the intentional misrepresentation of a material fact made knowingly and with the intent to deceive that is justifiably relied upon by and causes injury to another

fraud in the execution: fraud committed in the performance of a contractual obligation

fraud in the inducement: fraud committed to persuade another to enter into a contract

fraudulent conveyance: a transfer of property intended to cheat a creditor

free on board: see F.O.B.

full warranty: a warranty that completely covers a defective product or service by repair, replacement, or refund. A "full warranty" is distinguished from a "limited warranty." A warranty that does not specifically use the words "limited" or "as is" is generally construed to be a full warranty.

fully paid and nonassessable: stock that has been duly authorized and issued according to state law and is immune from issuer demands for further payment when purchased according to the provisions of an applicable purchase agreement or other governing document

fungible goods: goods of a nature that each unit is the same as every other in all significant ways; goods having virtually identical characteristics that can be obtained from many different sources

GAAP; generally accepted accounting principles: accounting standards promulgated by FASB that ensure consistency and accuracy in financial reporting

general partner: a person or entity that is responsible for managing the affairs of a partnership and has unlimited legal responsibility for its debts and liabilities

general partnership: an association formed by the agreement of two or more people or entities who are its owners and are personally responsible for its debts and liabilities

gift: a voluntary conveyance of property or rights without consideration

golden parachute: a provision in an employment contract or severance agreement that requires payment of a specified or calculable sum to a key executive if a change of control occurs

good faith: the status obtained by acting honestly and fairly in business dealings

good faith purchaser: a person or entity that buys without knowledge of any circumstances that would cause a reasonable person to question the seller's capacity or authority to sell

good reason: in drafting, a set of circumstances that the parties agree in advance are grounds to terminate a contract without losing certain benefits. E.g., an employment agreement might specify that an employee may keep stock if the employee resigns because the employer's business office is moved to another state. "Good reason" to quit is usually the flip side of the employer's right to terminate "for cause."

goodwill: a fictitious asset listed on the balance sheet to reflect the difference between the market value of a business and the book value of its assets less liabilities

grace period: the span of time after the date an obligation is technically due during which the lender or obligee will excuse late performance

grant: to convey specific rights to another person or entity

grantee: the person or entity that receives rights from another

grantor: the person or entity that grants rights to another

gross negligence: egregious failure to exercise due care; the lack of even slight care. Gross negligence is worse than negligence.

guarantee, guaranty: 1) an agreement in which one person or entity assumes the responsibility for paying or performing the obligations of another; 2) to assume responsibility for paying or performing the obligations of another

guarantor: the person or entity that assumes responsibility for paying or performing the obligations of another

guaranty of collection: an agreement where the guarantor promises to pay but only after the creditor has attempted to collect the amount due from the borrower

guaranty of payment: an agreement where the guarantor's responsibility to pay comes into effect immediately after the debtor fails to make a payment when due

guardian: an individual appointed to act on behalf of another person who lacks capacity; usually, a minor or an adult with impaired mental capacity

hazardous waste: a substance that could be dangerous to humans or to the environment

heir: a person who does inherit under a will or who is entitled by law to inherit the estate of another

HIPAA: the Health Insurance Portability and Accountability Act enacted in 1996 to protect patients from unauthorized disclosure of personal health information

holding company: a company that owns all or substantially all of the stock of other companies; most often, the parent corporation of multiple related subsidiary businesses

holographic will: a will that is handwritten by the testator or testatrix, valid in some states but not all

hypothecate: to pledge stock or other property as collateral without transferring title

illusory promise: in contracts, something that appears to be a promise but does not actually require the promissory to act. E.g., a promise to buy if the buyer needs something in the future is illusory and is insufficient consideration for a contract.

implied contract: an agreement that is understood by the conduct of the parties rather than by formed by oral or written promises

implied warranty: a warranty that arises as a matter of law rather than expression of the seller

implied warranty of fitness for particular purpose: a warranty that arises as a matter of law when the seller knows of buyer's particular purpose and buyer relies upon the seller's advice that the product is suitable for that particular purpose

implied warranty of merchantability: a warranty that arises as a matter of law that the goods are of average quality and fit for ordinary usage

incorporate: to form a corporation according to state law

incorporated by reference: information outside the four corners of a legal document that is made a part of the document (incorporated into it) by specifically referencing and adopting it. E.g., "Exhibit A is incorporated by this reference."

indemnification: an agreement to protect another person or entity against claims filed by third parties, usually used in situations where the indemnifying party has greater ability to prevent the third party claims. E.g., an acquired company may provide indemnification to the survivor with respect to claims for unpaid taxes.

indemnify: to protect another person or entity against third party claims

indenture: a contract between the issuer and the holder(s) stating the terms under which bonds or debentures are issued

independent contractor: a person or entity that provides services for a principal without direct supervision but is not employed by or eligible to participate in benefit plans of the principal

indirect damages: loss that is not obviously foreseeable as a result of defective goods or breach of contract but nevertheless caused by it

infringement: violation of the legal rights belonging to another person or entity, most often used in the context of intellectual property or constitutional rights

inheritance: property that is inherited by will or through the laws of descent and distribution

innocent misrepresentation: mistake regarding facts that is made without the intent to deceive

inside information: material information about a publicly traded corporation's business that is known by the officers, directors, key executives, and representatives but is generally not known by the public

insider: a person having material information about a publicly traded corporation's business that is not generally known by the public

intangible: incapable of being seen or touched or precisely identified

intellectual property: intangible personal property that involves some degree of creativity, namely ideas, inventions, designs, literary works, musical compositions, and art. In drafting, "intellectual property" generally refers collectively to patents, trademarks, service marks, trade names, trade secrets, logos, and copyrights.

inter vivos: during life; inter vivos gifts are gifts made during life as opposed to upon death via will

interest: 1) a charge incurred for borrowing money, usually expressed as a percentage; 2) something that gives relevance, importance, or concern. E.g., how well a company performs is relevant and important to a person who has an ownership interest. See conflict of interests.

interested director: a director who stands to receive an outside benefit in a transaction. See conflict of interests.

intestate: deceased without a will

inventory: a detailed list of all goods and materials held by an entity for use in its day to day operations

investor: a person or entity that contributes funds or assets to a business with the expectation of earning future gains

involuntary bankruptcy: a proceeding that is filed by creditors primarily for their benefit for dissolution of an entity or a restructuring of its debts

irrevocable letter of credit: a document issued by a bank that guarantees payment of a customer's debt and cannot be cancelled or amended without permission of the entity receiving the payment

issued shares: the number of authorized shares of stock that have actually been distributed to shareholders

joint and several liability: an arrangement where two or more parties agree to be legally responsible for an obligation and full responsibility for the total amount of the obligation may be enforced against all or any one of them

joint tenancy with right of survivorship: an ownership arrangement where an undivided interest in property is owned by two or more people, whose ownership interest is automatically transferred to the other tenant(s) upon death rather than becoming part of the deceased's estate

joint venture: an association of two or more entities formed to pursue a common business objective

laissez-faire: the concept that government should not interfere in commerce but allow natural market forces to operate; the French phrase translates roughly as "leave it alone"

landlord: the person or entity (not necessarily the owner) from whom a tenant leases property

LBO: leveraged buy-out

lease: 1) an agreement to use property for a specified period of time, usually for rent, without receiving ownership; 2) to obtain the right to use property; 3) to grant the right to use property

legal description: a formal description of the boundaries real property measured by metes and bounds or by reference to a recorded plat used in conveying property or a security interest in it

legend: language added usually on the back of a debt or equity instrument warning potential buyers of restrictions on transfer that may be in affect

lessee: the person who receives a lease

lessor: the person who grants a lease

letter of credit: a document issued by a financial institution authorizing a third party to draw a stated amount of money from the institution; used to facilitate commerce, especially international commerce, by substituting the stronger credit of the bank for the credit of the customer

letter of intent: a letter that summarizes the key business terms of a proposed transaction; this preliminary document may be drafted by lawyers but is sometimes drawn up by the parties themselves

---

before due diligence and more formal legal documents are prepared

leveraged buy-out: a method of acquiring a corporation using borrowed funds where the stock or assets acquired are used as collateral to secure financing

LIBOR: London Interbank Offered Rate: the average interest rate calculated by Thomson Reuters and published by the British Banker's Association at which a member of the BBA can borrow funds from another member

license: 1) the right to use property owned by another for a fee; 2) to obtain or give permission to use property owned by another; 3) the agreement to permit use of property owned by another

lien: an encumbrance filed against property in the public records to force payment of a debt

life estate: the right to use and possess property during the recipient's life that does not include the right to transfer the property without consent of the designated owner of the remainder interest

limited: a word used to put the public on notice that the owner's potential liability is capped

limited liability company: an entity where the owners' potential liability is capped, which is created under state law by filing articles of organization with the secretary of state and which may elect under I.R.S. regulations to be treated as a company or as a partnership for tax purposes

limited liability partnership: a partnership where a partner is not liable for the acts of another partner

limited partner: a partner who does not play an active role in managing the affairs of a limited partnership and whose liability is limited

limited partnership: a partnership comprised of one or more general partners having unlimited liability who manage the business and operations and one or more limited partners who contribute capital but do not manage the business and whose liability is limited to the amount of their contribution

limited warranty: a warranty that is explicitly restricted in terms of coverage or duration

line of credit: a lending arrangement where a borrower can draw funds from time to time during the term of the loan up to the specified maximum amount established by the creditor. The advantage of a line of credit is that the borrower accesses the line of credit as funds are needed but only pays interest on the amount actually borrowed.

liquid assets: cash and assets that can be quickly converted to cash, like publicly traded stocks and money market accounts

liquidated damages: an estimate of loss that will be incurred if a contract is terminated prematurely

liquidation: the process of converting all assets to cash in order to pay creditors in bankruptcy or to wind up the affairs of a business or other entity

living will: a will made according to applicable state law to enable a person to express his or her wishes regarding future medical care and treatment when death is certain

L.S.: locus sigilli, a Latin designation roughly translated as "the place of the seal" that may be used instead of a seal in some jurisdictions where the concept of seal is still relevant

maker: the person or entity that signs a written promise to pay

manager: in limited liability companies, the person responsible for overseeing the affairs of the business who may or may not be a member

margin: 1) the difference between the cost of an asset and its selling price; 2) profit expressed as a percentage, e.g., gross margin; profit margin; 3) an arrangement or account where borrowed money is used to purchase securities or other assets

market maker: a dealer that derives its income by buying and selling a particular stock, bond or commodity on a regular and continuous basis

market value: 1) the price at which buyers and sellers trade an asset or stock in an open marketplace; 2) the current trading price of publicly traded stocks and bonds

marketable title: ownership interest in property that is free from claims of outside parties or any form of encumbrance except those to be paid off at closing

---

material adverse change: an event or circumstance that negatively affects the value or quality of a business, an asset, or an investment. The term is used most often in financial statements to explain a change in valuation, in commercial loans to describe an event that gives the creditor a right to accelerate a debt, or in merger documents to describe a change that gives the other party a right to rescind the transaction.

material mistake: a significant but unintentional error that affects the costs or benefit expected in a transaction

materialmen's lien: a lien filed against real property by a supplier of construction materials used on the property to force payment of unpaid sums

maturity; maturity date: the date a debt becomes due

mediation: an alternative method of dispute resolution by which the parties attempt to resolve their dispute with the help of an independent mediator

member: 1) a person or entity holding a full voting and ownership interest in a limited liability company; 2) a person who joins a nonprofit membership corporation

merchant: under the UCC, a person or entity that is knowledgeable of and deals in a particular type of goods

merchantable: of average quality and suitable for ordinary use

merger: the process of combining two or more entities under which the surviving entity acquires all of the stock of the other(s)

merger clause: a boilerplate provision stipulating that the document is complete as written and that any discussions or documents that preceded the written agreement are specifically excluded; also called entire agreement or integration clause

metes and bounds: a method of measuring the boundaries of real property; each mete is the length of a straight run between two points, so a property that is exactly square would have four metes but an odd shaped property would have many more; and each bound is a landmark or other feature that defines a edge of the property, like a public road that forms a boundary.

milestones: in drafting, specific tasks that must be performed during the term of a contract, usually separately and in chronological order

minimum contacts: the smallest action or circumstances that allows the courts in one jurisdiction to require a person or entity located in another jurisdiction to submit to their authority

minor: a person who has not yet reached legal age according to applicable law

minority interest: 1) an ownership interest in a company or partnership that is less than 50%; 2) a specific disclosure on the balance sheet required by GAAP that reflects the proportion of a subsidiary that is owned by other shareholders

minute book: a binder containing organizational records, key corporate documents, and minutes of meetings or written consents of shareholders and directors

minutes: a written record of what action was taken at a meeting

misappropriation: the wrongful taking of property for dishonest purposes

misrepresentation: a false statement of fact

model: an item produced by the seller to demonstrate to the buyer the characteristics of goods or property to be sold; a model can be the basis of an express warranty

Model Business Corporation Act (MBCA): a set of laws prepared by a committee of the Business Law Section of the American Bar Association to establish a "uniform" system of business corporation codes that can be adopted by state legislatures (modifications enacted by each state's legislature destroy the uniformity but the general framework is consistent from state to state in the 24 or so states that have adopted it)

mortgage: a long term but not permanent, written lien on real property as collateral for a loan

most favored nation clause: a provision derived from international law now sometimes used in commercial contracts to stipulate that if another customer gets a better rate or price, the contracting party will receive that rate or price; designed to ensure that the contracting party is treated as well as subsequent customers

natural person: a human being. If the word "Person" with a capital P is used in legal documents, it usually includes natural persons and entities but this should always be specified in the defined terms.

negligence: the absence of the level of care a reasonable person would apply under similar circumstances

negotiable: capable of being legally transferred from one person or entity to another; under common law an instrument is negotiable when it is: 1) in writing; 2) signed by the maker; 3) an unconditional promise to pay; 4) a sum certain; 5) payable either upon presentation or on a specific date; and 6) payable to order or to bearer.

negotiable instrument: a special type of contract for the payment of money that is unconditional and can be transferred from one person or entity to another

negotiation: 1) the process of discussing the terms of a transaction in cooperation with another party to resolve differences and achieve a compromise that is beneficial to both parties; 2) the process of transferring a negotiable instrument

net 10; net 30: accounting terms specifying when payment is due for goods; net 10 means payment is due on or before the 10th day; net 30 means payment is due on or before the 30th day. Similarly, **"2/10, net 30"** means a two percent discount is offered when payment is made on or before the 10th day but payment in full is due no later than the 30th day

net income: earnings calculated by subtracting costs from revenues

net worth: an accounting term meaning the book value of a company calculated by subtracting total liabilities from total assets

non-accredited investor: according to Regulation D of the Securities and Exchange Commission, an investor who has a net worth of less than $1 million (including spouse) and who earned less than $200,000 annually (or $300,000 with spouse) in the last two years.

noncumulative dividends: dividends on preferred stock that are only paid if and when declared by the board of directors; if a noncumulative dividend is missed it is not an obligation to be paid later, as is the case with cumulative dividends

noncumulative preferred stock: a class of stock for which dividends do not accumulate if they are not declared by the board of directors

nonprofit corporation: an organization that does business for public good and does not distribute earnings to owners or shareholders

no par stock: stock that is issued without specifying a par value in the company's articles of incorporation and on the share certificate.

note: informal for "promissory note": an unconditional, written promise to pay a sum of money in the future that usually includes key terms like rate of interest and the date(s) payment is to be made

notice: in drafting, a formal announcement given by one party to the other pursuant to a contractual obligation, like notice of defective goods, notice of a bona fide purchaser for value, or notice of termination

novation: 1) the substitution of a new obligation for a pre-existing obligation; 2) the substitution of a new party for a previous party to an agreement. A novation differs from an assignment because under common law an assignment transfers only rights in a contract while a novation is actually a new contract which transfers rights and duties of one existing party to an outside party.

obligee: an awkward term referring to the person or entity who is entitled to receive performance of an obligation (creditor or promisee are better alternatives)

obligor: an awkward term referring to the person or entity who is required to perform (debtor or promissor are better alternatives)

offer: a proposal to transact business intended to create a contract if accepted by the offeree

offeree: the person or entity receiving an offer

offeror: the person or entity making an offer

officer: in corporate law, a person who is appointed by the board of directors to manage the day to day operations of a business and is authorized to sign legal documents on behalf of a corporation. The president, vice president, treasurer, secretary, and any assistants of the foregoing are officers.

---

operating agreement: a contract between partners or members of a limited liability company that describes how the partnership or company is to be managed, what the rights and duties of the parties are, and whether any restrictions on transferability of interests exist. An operating agreement for a partnership or LLC contains essentially the same type of provisions found in a corporation's bylaws and shareholders' agreement.

opinion of counsel: a letter written by a lawyer upon request of a third party that expresses the lawyer's professional judgment on legal issues concerning a client, a particular transaction, or both that the third party has determined to be important in connection with the transaction. In most forms of representation, a lawyer is responsible to the client for errors and omissions, but when an opinion of counsel is issued, the lawyer's responsibility for errors and omissions extends to the third party as well.

option agreement: an agreement between two or more parties that gives a party the right to buy or sell a specified item at an agreed upon price (the "strike price") at a specified time in the future

organizational meeting: the first meeting held by the shareholders of a corporation or the members of a limited liability company to adopt the corporate documents, approve the issuance of stock or membership interests, appoint the board of directors, and approve any other actions taken by the organizers prior to incorporation or organization. In most jurisdictions, the functions to be performed at an organizational meeting may be performed by written consent.

output contract: an agreement where a buyer agrees to buy all of a particular type of goods produced by a seller

outside director: a member of the board of directors who is not an employee of the company or affiliated with it in any way

outstanding shares: the number of shares currently held by shareholders of a corporation

over the counter: stocks and bonds traded directly between two people or entities, one of which is usually a "market maker," rather than sold on an exchange like the New York Stock Exchange or the Chicago Board of Trade

paid-in capital: an accounting term meaning the total amount paid to a corporation for its stock in excess of the par value of the outstanding shares

par value: the stated value of a share of stock authorized in the articles of incorporation and usually printed on the face of a certificate; this is the minimum amount a company can accept for a share of its own stock but par value doesn't represent market value and a share is usually sold for much more than the par value

participating bonds: a bond that pays dividends based on a company's profits in addition to the stated rate of interest

participating preferred: a specific class of stock that receives additional dividends over the stated rate based on earnings

participation loan: an arrangement where a number of banks cooperate to provide a loan to a single borrower that would be too big for any one bank to finance independently

partner: a member of a partnership

partnership: an enterprise formed by two or more people or entities for the purpose of pursuing some activity of common interest

payment in kind: compensation made in goods and services rather than cash

per annum: per year

perfection: the legal steps required to complete a secured party's priority interest in collateral

performance provisions: the portion of a contract that describes the promises each party has made to the other, for example, who is obligated to do what and when, how payment is to be made, and what happens if either party fails to carry out its obligations. Performance provisions usually vary more widely than boilerplate from one transaction to the next and are more heavily negotiated.

personal property: any tangible or intangible asset other than land or assets built or growing on land

personal representative: a person who manages the affairs of another person; most often refers to an executor or executrix but the term also has broader applications

pierce the corporate veil: the concept of attaching personal assets of a shareholder to satisfy corporate debts due to the lack of formality and separation between the shareholder's corporate and personal affairs

pledge: a transfer of assets or rights in them to a creditor as security for repayment of a debt or obligation; to transfer assets or rights in them to a creditor as security for repayment of a debt

poison pill: a provision designed to discourage a hostile takeover usually by allowing shareholders to acquire a large number of new shares making it harder for an outside party to gain voting control

postdate: to date a document as of a later date than when it is signed

power of attorney: 1) the authority to act on behalf of another; 2) a legal document that gives one person the authority to act on behalf of another

preemptive right: a right established in the articles of incorporation which grants existing shareholders the first opportunity to buy a new issue of stock in order to avoid dilution of their interests

preferential transfer: a payment of money or conveyance of property made within a certain period of time (usually 90 days) before bankruptcy is filed that can be recovered by the trustee in bankruptcy to settle claims of other creditors

preferred stock: a class of stock created in the articles of incorporation that has priority over common stock in terms of payment of dividends and distributions upon dissolution

prenuptial agreement: an agreement made by couples before marriage that describes their intentions regarding the distribution of marital assets in the event of a divorce

presentment: the act of physically delivering a negotiable instrument to collect payment of the principal

prime rate: the published rate of interest as of a given date that a bank charges its best clients; "prime + 2" means the rate of interest is the published prime rate plus two percent

principal: 1) a person or entity that an agent acts for; 2) the sum of money owed as a debt upon which interest is accrued

private offering: an offering of debt or securities to a limited number of investors under exemptions to registration requirements of the Securities and Exchange Commission and state regulatory authorities

private placement memorandum: a legal document that describes a company's assets, operations, business plan, management team, and the characteristics of the specific securities offered to a limited number of investors

privity: standing to sue to enforce contractual rights; usually only parties to a transaction have privity

professional corporation: a special type of corporation permitted in some jurisdictions for licensed professionals like lawyers and doctors who still have professional liability but seek to limit other kinds of liability and to obtain certain other corporate tax benefits

pro forma: a term used in financial reporting to designate financial statements that are based on historical data that has been reconfigured to incorporate certain assumptions or actions; often used in mergers to project what the financial data would have been if the companies had been merged in the prior year

promissory note: an unconditional, written promise to pay a certain sum in the future that usually includes key terms like rate of interest and the date(s) payment is to be made

property: an abstract term meaning the collection of rights usually associated with owning a tangible or intangible thing that has value

prospectus: a formal written offer to sell securities which contains the facts and financial information an investor needs to make an informed decision

proviso: in drafting, a phrase that begins with the words "provided, that" or "provided, however" usually used to alter the preceding language

publicly held corporation: a corporation that has obtained permission from the Securities and Exchange Commission or other appropriate authority to offer its stock for sale to the general public; a corporation whose shares are freely traded in the open market

puffing: making general statements about the quality of goods or assets, which statements are not intended or sufficient to create an express warranty; "this car gets great mileage" is puffing; "this car gets 30 miles per gallon" is an express warranty

purchase money security interest: a security interest granted under the UCC to the seller or creditor who financed the purchase of the property that is the collateral

put; put option: the right to sell a specific asset at a specific price in the future

qualify to do business: to obtain authorization to conduct business in a state other than the state where a corporation or limited liability company is formed

quasi contract: a concept applied to prevent unjust enrichment in situations where the parties did not create a contract but the courts determine that an obligation is owed under the circumstances

quiet enjoyment: the right to undisturbed use of a property

quitclaim deed: a document used to convey property where the grantor simply turns over existing rights without making any warranty as to clear title

quorum: the number of members or shareholders specified in the organizational documents required to be present in order to conduct business

REIT; real estate investment trust: a tax designation for an entity that owns and manages a pool of commercial properties

real property: the collection of rights associated with land and structures permanently attached to it

reasonable: in law, what a normal person would consider sensible under the circumstances

recital of consideration: a statement in a contract that consideration has been exchanged

red herring prospectus: a preliminary prospectus filed with the Securities and Exchange Commission as part of a registration statement that has not yet become effective

redeem: to repurchase bonds or securities bonds or securities from the holders by the issuer; an issuer "redeems" when it repurchases; a holder "redeems" when it turns in the instrument to be redeemed

redemption right: the right of a company to buy back a certain percentage or class of outstanding shares

registered agent: the person or agent listed in the records of the secretary of state who is authorized by a corporation or limited liability company to receive legal notices on its behalf and to accept service of process when it is sued

registration rights: the contractual rights of holders of restricted shares to require the issuer to register the shares under applicable securities laws

registration statement: a document filed with the Securities and Exchange Commission and state regulatory agencies to obtain authorization to offer securities to the general public or a particular sector of investors like employees

remainder: in estate planning, the property or interests that are left over after an initial bequest is distributed

rent: the payments made under a lease by a lessee to a lessor

reorganization: in bankruptcy, the restructuring of an entity's debt obligations and possibly its business affairs

repossess: in lending, to take full ownership of collateral after the debtor has defaulted

representation: in drafting, a statement of fact as of a certain point in time that can be relied upon by the other party

repudiation: in contracts, a party's words or actions that indicate the party is unwilling or unable to perform future obligations

requirements contract: an agreement where a buyer agrees to purchase all of a particular item used in its business from the seller

rescission: in contracts, withdrawal of a contract with the intent of returning the parties to the position they were in before the contract was formed

restrictive covenant: 1) in contracts, a solemn promise or obligation not to do something that alters rights the promissor would otherwise have, often used in the context of preventing competition or protecting intellectual property; 2) in real estate, an enforceable obligation not to do something with or on a real property

retained earnings: the portion of net income that is not paid out to the shareholders as dividends but kept by the corporation to be used in its business operations and future growth

revolving line of credit: a lending arrangement where a borrower can draw funds from time to time during the term of the loan up to the specified maximum amount established by the creditor and amounts that have been borrowed and repaid can be borrowed again

rights agreement: see "poison pill"

right of first refusal: this provision requires that before a party to a contract can consummate a transaction with an outsider it must first give the other party the chance to do the transaction upon the same terms as the outsider; usually used in agreements that contain some restriction on transferability of a property interest

risk of loss: in contracts, the potential expense incurred when goods or assets are damaged, destroyed, or lost; most commonly used in the context of determining when the risk of loss passes from seller to buyer for goods in transit

rule against perpetuities: a complicated common law principal requiring that a property interest must vest within a span of time equal to a life in being plus 21 years, or within 21 years after the death of a person who was living at the time the interest was created, intended to prevent owners from controlling property for many generations after death.

S corporation; Sub-S Corporation: a corporation formed according to applicable state law that elects to be taxed as a partnership according to the requirements of Sub-chapter S of the Internal Revenue Code.

schedule: in drafting, an attachment to a contract that provides detailed supplemental information but is not a separate legal document. A schedule may contain a list of items, description of services, milestones, prices, calculations, or similar information.

seal: traditionally, an emblem applied to a contract in some formal manner that proved authority and intention to enter into the transaction; in modern times a seal usually has little, if any, significance to the signer and is often word processed on the page, but a seal still has legal significance in some jurisdictions especially with respect to the statute of limitations

seal recital: a declaration that appears immediately before the signatures that a document is signed under seal

secured creditor: a lender that at the time of making a loan takes an assignment of rights in assets that can be sold to repay the debt if the debtor defaults

secured debt: an obligation that is backed by assets assigned to the creditor that can be sold if the debtor defaults

secured transaction: a loan or obligation for which the debtor assigns to the creditor rights in assets that can be sold to repay the debt if the debtor defaults

securities: stocks, bonds, debentures, and similar investments evidencing ownership or debt of the issuer

security agreement: a written contract by which a debtor can assign rights in collateral to a creditor

service mark: a distinctive symbol, image, icon, word or phrase used by an entity to identify its services and distinguish those services from competitors

set-off: a way to match an obligation that is owed by one party against an obligation owed by the other party so that both are reduced or satisfied; some contracts and loan documents specifically prohibit set-off

severable; severability: able to be removed from a contract without affecting the remaining provisions; a severability clause is often included in the boilerplate to request that if one or more provisions are determined to be unenforceable, those provisions should be "severed" so the rest of the contract remains intact

share: one unit of ownership interest in a corporation; see "stock."

share subscription agreement: an investor's commitment to purchase a specific number of shares either upon formation of a corporation or from time to time when the corporation issues new shares

---

shareholder: a person or entity that owns stock in a corporation; a stockholder

shareholder of record: a person or entity whose name appears on the corporation's stock transfer records as of a specific date; the shareholders of record are constantly changing when shares are publicly traded but remain fairly constant in a closely held corporation

shareholders' agreement: a contract among the owners of a relatively closely held corporation regarding management of the corporation, internal restrictions on transferability of shares, rights and duties of shareholders, and similar matters

shrinkwrap license: the terms and conditions of use that licensees are deemed to have accepted when they break the seal on a package containing a copy of software; because the terms and conditions can only be read after the package is opened, the validity of shrinkwrap licenses is still uncertain in some jurisdictions

signed under seal: a contract that contains a seal recital and a seal or the word "seal" after one or more of the signatures; in some jurisdictions a contract can be signed under seal by one party but not the other

sole proprietorship: a business entity owned and managed by one person

special stipulations: in drafting, additional terms and conditions that are added to a contract in an attachment; to be binding, the special stipulations should either be signed by both parties or the phrase "special stipulations attached" should be inserted above the signatures of the original document

specific performance: in contracts, an equitable remedy for breach requiring the breaching party to carry out its obligations as originally agreed

staggered board: an arrangement intended to provide internal stability and discourage hostile takeovers where board members are grouped into classes and only one class comes up for re-election each year instead of electing the entire board each year; usually there are three classes and members are elected for three year terms so only a third of the board is elected in any given year

standby letter of credit: a guarantee of payment issued on behalf of a client by a financial institution authorizing a third party to draw a stated amount of money from the institution as a last resort if the client defaults;

stated capital: an accounting term meaning the par value of shares multiplied by the number of shares outstanding; see paid-in capital

Statement of Changes in Financial Position: a financial statement that focuses on cash and changes in cash that reveals how a company acquired money and how it was spent

Statement of Income; Income Statement; Profit and Loss Statement; P&L: a financial statement that measures revenues, expenses, and earnings or losses from operations over a stated period of time

Statement of Retained Earnings; Statement of Net Worth: a financial statement that explains changes in earnings retained by the company over a stated period of time due to items like profits or losses, dividends paid, and other charges to retained earnings

statute of frauds: a common law principle that defines what types of contracts have to be in writing to be enforced by the courts

statute of limitations: statutory guidelines enacted by legislatures that establish time limits for filing various types of lawsuits

stock: in corporate law, 1) an ownership interest in a corporation comprised of the sum of units owned; 2) the aggregate of a class of ownership interests in a corporation: e.g., common stock; preferred stock. The words "share" and "stock" are commonly used interchangeably but a technical distinction exists: a "share" is a single unit but "stock" is composite.

stockholders' agreement: a contract among the owners of a relatively closely held corporation regarding management of the corporation, internal restrictions on transferability of shares, rights and duties of stockholders, and similar matters

stock option: the right granted by a corporation to buy a specific number of its shares at a specific price within a stated period of time in the future

sublease: 1) a document that assigns a lessee's rights and obligations in a lease to a third party; 2) to assign rights and obligations in a lease to a third party

subordination agreement: an agreement by a secured creditor having a priority interest in collateral to accept a secondary interest so another creditor can be fully secured with the same collateral; useful in these situations: 1) when the outstanding balance due to the original creditor is small compared to the current value of the collateral; 2) when the debtor desires to refinance a first mortgage and there is a second mortgage which would otherwise then have priority; and 3) in restructurings where the debtor is at risk of becoming insolvent, resulting in higher risk to the creditor, if additional financing cannot be obtained

subrogation: the substitution of one creditor in the place of another

subscribe: to promise to buy a specified number of shares at a specified price

subsidiary corporation: a corporation that is at least 50% owned by another corporation called the "parent"

successor liability: a risk or claim that may arise against an assignee due to the acts of the previous owner

surety: a person or entity that has contracted to be responsible for the debts or obligations if another person or entity defaults

surviving corporation: the corporation that acquires the assets of another entity and remains intact after a merger

survivorship, right of: an entitlement attached to an undivided interest in property owned by two or more people so that upon death of one owner, the ownership interest is automatically transferred to the other owner(s) rather than becoming part of the deceased's estate

syndicate: a group of investment banks that jointly underwrite an offering of securities for another entity

syndicated loan: a loan made by multiple lenders that each provide a proportion of the borrowed funds

takeover: to obtain control of an entity, not necessarily as a mutual decision; e.g., a hostile takeover

tenancy: the collection of rights conveyed to a tenant in real property

tenancy at sufferance: wrongful occupation of a leased property by a tenant whose lease has terminated

tenancy at will: authorized possession of real property without a fixed term

tenancy by the entirety: ownership of real property by a husband and wife which includes rights of survivorship

tenancy in common: ownership of real property by two or more people who each own an undivided interest real property that becomes part of his or her estate and can be passed to heirs

tenant: a person or entity that owns any kind of rights in real property; a "tenant" under a lease owns the right to use the property for a period of time; a "joint tenant in common" denotes ownership of the property

tender offer: an offer to buy shares of a corporation at a fixed price usually higher than current market price, typically in connection with a takeover

tender of performance: an offer to carry out obligations which must be made before a party can seek judicial enforcement of the contract the other party has breached

termination statement: a document filed in the public records according to the UCC to release a security interest in collateral

term sheet: a summary listing the key business terms of a proposed transaction

testator: a male person who makes a will

testatrix: a female person who makes a will

third party: in drafting, a term used to refer to a person or entity that is not a party in the original agreement or transaction

third party beneficiary: a person or entity that is not a party but for whose benefit a promise is made in a contract

title: 1) the collection of all rights that constitute ownership of a property which is superior to all other claims; 2) a document for transferring ownership rights

title insurance: a policy of insurance that is used to underwrite the risk of any undisclosed claims against real property existing in the chain of title at the time of conveyance; for example, if someone in the chain of title signed a deed but did not actually own the property at the time, title insurance proceeds could be used to correct the problem

trademark: a distinctive symbol, image, icon, word or phrase used by an entity to identify its products and distinguish those products from competitors

trade name: the name of a business or one of its products that is commercially recognized

trade secret: business information protected by statute in most jurisdictions, including a formula, pattern, compilation, program, device, method, technique, or process that is valuable because of not being generally known to the public or competitors and is subject to efforts that are reasonable under circumstances to maintain its secrecy

treasury stock: shares that have been issued to shareholders and subsequently required by the corporation

trust: 1) a document that authorizes a trustee to hold and manage property on behalf of another person or entity; 2) possession of property held for the benefit of another; 3) an account established to hold and manage property held for the benefit of another

trustee: the person or entity that manages a trust on behalf of a beneficiary

unaccredited investor: see "non-accredited investor"

unconscionable: unscrupulous dealings by someone in a superior bargaining position

under water: jargon that describes the situation when the strike price under an option agreement is higher than the asset is currently trading

underwriter: a person or entity that assumes financial risks on behalf of another person or entity either for a fee (as in the case of insurance) or for a stake in a transaction (as in the case of a securities offering)

undisclosed principal: a person or entity that uses an agent to conduct negotiations and enter into transactions with a third party that usually is not aware of the agency and does not know the identity of the principal

UCC, Uniform Commercial Code: a set of laws drafted by a team of lawyers and judges that establishes a "uniform" commercial code that can be adopted by state legislatures (modifications enacted by each state's legislature destroy the uniformity but the general framework is consistent from state to state and all 50 states have adopted it)

unilateral contract: an agreement in which only one party makes a promise in exchange for an act that the other party cannot be forced to perform; if the other party performs then the original party is obligated to fulfill the promise; e.g., a reward offered for return of lost items

unsecured bonds: bonds that are backed by the issuer's promise to pay and general credit worthiness rather than by any particular assets

unsecured creditor: a lender that lends money without taking collateral

usury: the practice of charging exorbitant interest rates

vendee: outdated term for a buyer

vendor: a seller of goods; in technology-based contracts, the person or entity that provides products and services that are licensed, not bought

vest; vested: to settle without contingency; to mature, as in the case of an employee's ownership interest in stock that vests after five years of service

void: 1) null, having no effect; 2) to invalidate, annul, or cancel

voidable: in contracts, an agreement that is enforceable as to one party but not the other; the agreement will be performed unless the party having legal grounds to do so (like a minor) cancels it

voting agreement: a plan among two or more shareholders to vote their shares as a block

---

voting trust: an arrangement among two or more shareholders to contribute their voting rights to a trustee who will vote on their behalf

waive: to relinquish or give up a right voluntarily

waiver: a written document in which rights are waived

warranty: an assurance by a seller about the quality or character of goods and services

warranty against infringement: assurance given by a seller or licensor that a product or service will not violate the intellectual property rights of any third party

warranty deed: a legal document used to convey and warrant title to real property

warranty of title: a warranty implied in law that the seller of goods has the legal right to sell them

will: a testator's or testatrix's written declaration of how he or she would like his or her property distributed upon death

winding up: the process of terminating a corporation or partnership that involves liquidating assets, paying off liabilities, and distributing proceeds to owners in proportion to their interests

work made for hire: a buzz phrase from copyright law that must be included verbatim in a contract to assign rights effectively in the work of an independent contractor (as opposed to an employee)

working capital: an accounting term for current assets minus current liabilities; used to reflect the funds available to operate a business in the immediate future

workout: a process undertaken without resorting to bankruptcy in which a debtor negotiates with existing creditors to restructure debt

written consent: a document signed by shareholders or directors of a corporation to take action without holding a meeting

zero coupon bond: a bond that is bought or issued at a discount off the face value and does not accrue interest; the investor's profit is the difference between the discounted price and the face value, which is paid at maturity

zoning: the regulations governing the use of particular tracts of real property, including what type of structures can be built in specific locations; zoning policies are used to enhance aesthetic appeal and promote safety; major zoning categories include single-family residential, multi-family residential, commercial, and industrial

Index

About the Author

Lenné Eidson Espenschied has practiced corporate and intellectual property law for 25 years, representing technology-based businesses in a wide variety of transactions. She is an adjunct professor at the University of Georgia School of Law where she teaches a course on advanced legal drafting. Ms. Espenschied is President of Legalease Seminars, Inc., an Atlanta-based company that provides continuing legal education.

Teaching aides for this book including teaching notes, sample documents, drafting assignments, and grading rubrics are available to law school faculty at www.draftingpowerfulprose.com.